D1445286

THE BASICS OF SPEECH

SECOND EDITION

THE BASICS OF SPEECH

learning to be a competent communicator

Kathleen M. Galvin
School of Speech
Northwestern University

Pamela J. Cooper
School of Speech
Northwestern University

Jeanie McKinney Gordon
Baker Middle School
Corpus Christi, Texas

National Textbook Company
a division of *NTC Publishing Group* • Lincolnwood, Illinois USA

To our children:
Matthew, Katie, and Kara
Jenifer and Jamie
Natalie, Thomas, and Bill

Cover photo: Jack Demuth

Published by National Textbook Company, a division of NTC Publishing Group.
©1994, 1988 by NTC Publishing Group, 4255 West Touhy Avenue, Lincolnwood
(Chicago), Illinois 60646-1975 U.S.A.
Manufactured in the United States of America.
Library of Congress Catalog Card Number: 92-80477

3 4 5 6 7 8 9 AG 9 8 7 6 5 4 3 2

Acknowledgments

The authors and publisher are grateful to the following people for their helpful suggestions, encouragement, and support during the development of the first and second editions of *The Basics of Speech*.

Louise Abernathy
J. P. Bonnette Junior High School, Deer Park, Texas

Melissa L. Beall
University of Northern Iowa, Cedar Falls

Don Boileau
George Mason University, Fairfax, Virginia

Sandra Lind
West Springfield High School, Fairfax County Public Schools, Springfield, Virginia

Connie Newcomb
Bremen Senior High School, Bremen, Indiana

Rosalie Lesser
Luther Jackson Intermediate School, Falls Church, Virginia

Ouida Garner
Bailey Junior High School, Arlington, Texas

Maureen Gilbert
Jane Lathrop Stanford Middle School, Palo Alto, California

Bob Stockton
Western High School, Anaheim, California

Karen Tuffnell
Polaris High School, Anaheim, California

Ann Layton
Forest High Central High School, Grand Rapids, Michigan

Merle Ullery
North Miami Beach Senior High School, Miami, Florida

Many other people helped with this book. Special thanks to Bernadette Burke; Frances Pearcy; the students at Baker Middle School in Corpus Christi, Texas; Ola Underhill; Ginger Allen; Doris Antonetz; and the staff at National Textbook Company.

—K.G., P.C., J.G.

CONTENTS

PART ONE
THE BASICS OF COMMUNICATION

Chapter 1 The Communication Process   2

Oral Communication   3
Your Experience with Communication   7
Communication in Your Life   9
Types of Communication   14
Summary   17
Chapter Review   18

Chapter 2 Elements of Communication   20

Verbal Messages   21
Nonverbal Messages   24
Perceptions   30
Channel   33
Feedback   34
Context   36
Summary   37
Chapter Review   38

Chapter 3 The Work of Speaking and Listening   40

Vocal Production   41
The Listening Process   47
Types of Listening   49
Barriers to Listening   55
Guidelines for Good Listening   61
Summary   67
Chapter Review   68

TO THE STUDENT

This book addresses a very important life skill—communication. Ever since birth you have been making contact with other people—your parents, friends, teachers, relatives, and the people in your community. Some of these contacts have been easy; others have been difficult. Your ability to communicate effectively touches every part of your life. Although you already have many communication skills, you can always become a more competent communicator.

In this book you will encounter many different ways of thinking about your communication skills. We hope you will understand the communication process and will learn to appreciate your communication strengths. We also hope you will develop greater strengths during the course. We believe a competent communicator makes choices. He or she (1) analyzes a situation, (2) chooses a way to deal with it, (3) acts on that choice, and (4) evaluates the results. Therefore a competent communicator is able to cope well in many situations. In addition, a competent communicator takes personal responsibility for the choices he or she makes.

The Basics of Speech has special features to guide you through understanding the communication process and improving your communication skills. Each chapter opens with a list of Objectives and Key Words. Within the text, you will discover Journal Entries and the Interact, Apply, and Observe features. The Chapter Reviews contain Think About It, Try It Out, Put It in Writing, and Speak About It.

Checklists, charts, evaluation forms, sample scripts, speeches, student comments, and many literature selections are found throughout the text. The wide variety of materials will stimulate your interest and involve you in an enjoyable and rewarding learning experience.

CHAPTER OBJECTIVES

Good speakers and listeners need "road maps" or some way of knowing where they are going. The objectives give you a road map for the chapter and tell you what you should be able to do when you have completed the chapter.

KEY WORDS

A competent communicator has a large vocabulary and uses words correctly. In order to communicate about communication you need to develop a proper vocabulary. The Key Words that appear at the beginning of each chapter are the most important vocabulary words in the text.

JOURNAL ENTRIES

Often, when a friend describes an experience or feeling, you may think, "I've felt that way" or "Something like that happened to me." Throughout the book you will find Journal Entries written by teenagers about the topics in the book. You may find that the Journal Entries help you understand someone else better. We are grateful to the teenagers who shared their entries with us.

OBSERVE

Seeing and hearing are important parts of understanding communication. The assignments in the Observe boxes are designed to help you really see and hear what is going on around you so you can respond in the best way. By doing these assignments, you should become a more careful observer of others' communication.

INTERACT

Reading and observing will tell you a great deal about communication. But talking about communication situations or trying out communication strategies can teach you a great deal as well. The Interact boxes contain directions to get you involved with other people in the class. You may be asked to share your ideas or to try out a specific communication skill.

APPLY

Within the text you will find sections set off that require you to respond actively to the text. Sometimes you are asked to complete a checklist, analyze an example, or find solutions to a problem. These sections are designed to help you apply the ideas you are learning.

THINK ABOUT IT

Before you can apply what you have learned, you need to understand the content. Questions and statements at the end of the chapter ask you to review what you have learned. If you can answer these questions correctly, you are well on your way to understanding communication principles.

TRY IT OUT

When people work together to solve a problem or to create something, they learn a lot in the process. The activity suggestions at the end of each chapter contain ideas for applying what you have learned.

PUT IT IN WRITING

Sometimes a good way to make sense of what you see, hear, or think is to write it down. Writing may help you clarify your experience. It may help you see how ideas go together. The Put It in Writing sections ask you to record ideas in a journal, analyze an event you observe, or describe what might happen in the future.

SPEAK ABOUT IT

The only way to develop your ability to speak in front of others is to practice your public speaking. The Speak About It activities will give you many opportunities to deliver short speeches to your class or to small groups.

GLOSSARY

All the Key Words found in this text plus many other important vocabulary words are defined in the Glossary. You will find it is a handy reference tool when you need to review word meanings.

PART

1

THE BASICS OF COMMUNICATION

CHAPTERS

The Communication Process

Elements of Communication

The Work of Speaking and Listening

The Competent Communicator

CHAPTER

1

THE COMMUNICATION PROCESS

After completing this chapter, you should be able to

- define *communication* as a process.
- describe how communication skills influence family life, friendships, school, work, and citizenship.
- describe the four types of oral communication.

KEY WORDS

communication

group communication

interpersonal communication

interpretive communication

meaning

message

public communication

2

Communication
Verbal/nonverbal
Trying to connect
Watching, laughing, questioning, talking
Work

Communication
Speaking and listening
Making thoughts clear
Sharing feelings and questions
Contact

Communication
Scared, shaking
Standing up alone
Feeling my heart explode
Speaking

Communication
I say
Nothing but
People from all places
Understand

Communication
It is not
How it goes in
But how people take it
Out

Suppose you were asked, "What does the word *communication* mean to you?" How would you answer? You might respond by telling how you talk with friends or family members, how you speak in front of an audience, or how you function in a group. Even before studying the subject you can explain what *communication* means to you now. The above poems represent five students' interpretations of the word *communication*.

ORAL COMMUNICATION

What is communication really? **Communication** is the process of sending and receiving messages in order to share meanings. The communication process involves two or more persons attempting to share their ideas, feelings, and attitudes. In almost all communication situations, speakers and listeners interact with each other over a period of time, trying to understand what the other persons mean.

Communication also involves sending messages using written language. This book does not emphasize written communication. Rather it explores oral communication, which involves speaking and listening.

A PROCESS

Communication is a process because it moves forward from a beginning point. Imagine the start of the communication process as being the first moment two people meet. The next minutes or hours continue the process. If these people come together again over weeks or years, the process continues.

For example, every conversation you have with a good friend reflects what you already know about that person. You know what kind of jokes your friend likes, what topics to avoid, how to read your friend's moods. The communication process began the first time you and your friend met and continues throughout your relationship.

VERBAL AND NONVERBAL MESSAGES

A *message* is the way meaning is conveyed. Messages are at the center of the communication process. Without a message, there can be no communication. A message may be verbal or nonverbal. Verbal messages are spoken messages. They rely on words to carry the meaning. Nonverbal messages are those expressed without words. They rely on the use of facial expressions and body movements.

Think about the verbal and nonverbal messages that you sent and received today. Do you know how much you communicated verbally through your words? How much was communicated nonverbally through your facial expressions or body movements? You probably haven't thought about these two areas separately, because they usually work together.

Speakers and listeners share the responsibility for being good communicators. Communication works like a skilled tennis match. Both communicators are involved continuously in the process, just as both tennis players are involved constantly in the game. Once a good player hits the ball, he or she gets into position to deal with the return shot. In communication, you send and receive messages simultaneously. This process may be pictured in the following:

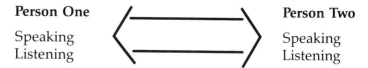

Person One   **Person Two**

Speaking   Speaking
Listening   Listening

Think about your own communication with others. Suppose you and your brother are discussing plans for Friday night. Even as you are speaking, he is frowning, smiling, looking puzzled, or muttering "Yeah, yeah...." He might interrupt you or ask you a question. After you stop talking, he might tell you that he wants to use your bicycle while you smile, groan, or look annoyed. You and your brother are equally involved and are constantly sharing. It is important to realize that the listener is working just as hard as the speaker.

MEANINGS

Common meanings for words, gestures, and facial expressions make it possible to communicate. *Meaning* is the interpretation you place on verbal and nonverbal messages. If you and another person do not have the same meanings for words such as *funny, pretty, help,* or *soda,* you will have difficulty communicating. If you have different meanings for concept words such as *justice, friendship, liberal,* or *responsibility,* your communication will have even greater difficulties. If you do not have similar meanings for nonverbal messages such as thumbs down or a raised eyebrow, there will be confusion about the meaning of the messages.

Finding the Meaning

Finding the meaning of a message requires more than understanding the individual words in the message. It also requires interpreting the message. For example, when Martina says a class is "hard," she means there is a lot of homework. When Philip says a class is "hard," he means he finds the teacher's vocabulary unfamiliar and therefore difficult.

In the following journal entry, a student describes a typical communication problem.

JOURNAL ENTRY

After winning the first meet at 10:00 A.M., I was told the track meet final for the school tournament was at 2:00. The meet was actually two hours later, and I had to forfeit because I had left for lunch.

Communication can also break down when common words that sound alike but have different meanings are mistaken for one another. For example, one student listened very carefully as her teacher discussed the next day's exam. The teacher said, "Know percentages." The student thought, "Thank goodness, no percentages." Needless to say, the student's grade suffered from this confusion over the meaning of *know/no!*

THREE MAIN IDEAS

The definition of communication includes three main ideas to remember.

- Speaking and listening happen at the same time.
- Speakers and listeners must be aware of both verbal and nonverbal messages.
- Effective communication occurs when the speakers and listeners share common meanings.

OBSERVE

Observe two classmates having a typical conversation in the cafeteria. Pay careful attention to the behavior of each person when he or she is *not* speaking. Record the ways each person stays active in the conversation while listening.

YOUR EXPERIENCE WITH COMMUNICATION

You have been communicating with other people almost all your life. You have discussed plans, shared secrets, asked questions, given directions, and listened to problems. You have told stories, delivered oral book reports, acted in skits, and listened to the nightly news.

Most people find that they are better in some communication situations than in others. They might argue well but get uncomfortable listening to others talk about their feelings. They may be great at conversation but poor at speaking before a group. Everyone has strengths in communication and areas of needed growth. And with work everyone can overcome fears or difficulties in communication.

Although you have had experience in the area of communication, it is unlikely that every interaction with another person was perfect. You may have come away from a discussion, argument, or conversation thinking, "Why couldn't we both understand each other?" or "Why don't I feel really good about how we talked to each other?"

Most likely you have had some difficulties talking to a parent or a friend. You may have felt unsure of yourself during a speech or performance. You may even have avoided talking to certain people.

Apply

The following questions refer to situations with which people often have problems. See if you have ever found yourself in a similar situation. Do you ever have trouble

COMMUNICATION CHECKLIST

Use this checklist to begin a study of your own communication strengths and weaknesses. Which statements *never* apply to you? Which statements *sometimes* or *frequently* apply? Which statements *always* apply?

1. When I'm introduced to people, I immediately forget their names.
2. I stumble over my words when I give an oral book report.
3. I say what's on my mind when working in a group.
4. I tune out during a newscast.
5. I have trouble telling a friend that I'm upset or angry with him or her.
6. I have trouble carrying on a conversation with a person I just met.
7. I get uncomfortable when my friend expresses sadness or anger.
8. I find myself thinking about what I'm going to say instead of listening to other people.
9. I am afraid to join class discussion because I might say something silly.
10. I avoid making eye contact with people when I talk with them.

- telling a teacher that you do not understand the problem she just explained?
- talking to a friend about the problems you are having with your boyfriend or girlfriend?
- asking a stranger for directions if you are lost?
- convincing your parents to let you go out with friends even though you haven't finished your chores?
- explaining to your instructor or coach why you have to miss practice?
- expressing your opinion on a current topic?
- reading a poem aloud in class?
- understanding what a friend's facial expressions mean?
- telling a joke to a group?
- expressing feelings of anger, hurt, concern, or love?

- disagreeing with someone you like?
- looking people in the eye when you talk to them?

Good communication skills can help people to deal with situations like these. A goal of this book is to help you develop strong communication skills.

INTERACT

With a partner take turns describing a person who is the best communicator you know. Be specific in telling how the person acts and what situations he or she handles well.

COMMUNICATION IN YOUR LIFE

Communication affects every area of your life, now and in the future. Think of the various kinds of communication that took place today. Did your mother or father pat you on the back or smile good-bye? Did you talk to the bus driver, your friends, an acquaintance, or a stranger? What did the school crossing guard communicate to you by holding up her hand? How did you interpret a friend smiling? a teacher standing up, pushing a chair in, and opening a book? the principal's booming voice over the public address system?

Every day you spend hours communicating. You may request help from a salesperson in a store. You may give directions to a visitor in your community. You may listen to your favorite music or to conversations among classmates. In addition to general, everyday situations, there are five areas of your life that require highly developed communication skills. These are the areas of family, friendship, school, work, and citizenship. In order to be a caring family member, a good friend, a good student, an efficient worker, and an involved citizen, you will need to develop and use specific communication skills.

FAMILY

A person's ability to speak and listen carefully has a great effect on life at home. Counselors report that some of the greatest difficulties in family life come from poor listening habits. A husband thinks he knows what his wife feels, so he doesn't listen to what she actually says. A teenager thinks she knows what her parents will say and does not listen to them. Much of the arguing, blaming, and fighting in homes could be reduced if family members worked to communicate more clearly.

INTERACT

With a partner take turns recalling a past experience when you and a family member or friend assumed what the other was thinking and caused a misunderstanding. Discuss how the problem could have been avoided.

Some of the best moments in family life occur when people feel connected to each other. This may happen when you and your mother or father have a good talk about something that is worrying you. Or, it could be when you are reading a story to your little sister or brother. It often happens when a family tries to show caring directly. Statements such as "I missed you," "You are special," or "I'm proud of you" make people feel connected. Actions such as a hug or a pat on the shoulder have the same effect. Good communication gives family members a feeling of belonging.

FRIENDSHIP

Some of the most important people in your life are your friends. Good friends laugh with you, support you, listen to you, and tell you honestly what they think and feel. People often take friends for granted until a friend moves away or becomes a better friend to someone else.

Most strong friendships are built on clear communication, the one-to-one sharing between friends. As you will see later (Chapter 6), the qualities of good friendship are tied to communication skills. They include: keeping secrets, loyalty,

warmth, supportiveness, honesty, and a sense of humor. If you think about your good friends you will probably conclude that these are people you can talk with easily. Most of the time you may talk about sports or school or other people, but sometimes you can share a worry or problem. Communication in friendships is a two way process—to keep a good friend you have to be a good friend.

JOURNAL ENTRY

My best friend heard from someone that I was talking about her behind her back when, in fact, I wasn't. We had a terrible fight, but when we talked it out we were friends again. If we weren't able to talk it out, our friendship would have been over.

SCHOOL

Your speaking and listening skills affect your school life in many ways. Often you are expected to give oral reports or explain your ideas to the class. You may be asked to give speeches or introduce speakers. You may have to lead a group project during class or organize group work for school charity drives or after-school events. In these situations, you need to feel comfortable speaking to a group of people. If you are not willing to ask and answer questions or share your ideas, you may feel like an outsider in class.

As a student you will spend between 53 and 90 percent of your class time listening, mostly to the teacher, but also to other students. Even on breaks from classes, you spend time listening to your friends. You might be surprised at how many hours a year you spend listening in school.

WORK

The jobs you have after school or over the summer require good communication skills. If you baby-sit, you need to communicate with the parents, the children, and, in an emergency, doctors or the police. If you do yard work, you must talk with your neighbors. A paper route requires dealing with customers. Employers were recently asked to rate the importance of communication skills for new workers. The skill receiving the highest rating was a listening skill—understanding directions.

Apply

Communication is part of almost every job. From the following list of career opportunities, try to select one in which communication skills would *not* be a basic job requirement. Explain your choice.

postal worker	salesperson	insurance agent
flight attendant	teacher	farmer
accountant	welder	actor
travel agent	driving instructor	reporter
truck driver	lawyer	child care worker
store manager	machine operator	aerobics instructor
gas station attendant	resort manager	computer operator

Almost every area of life requires some type of communication skill. Some listening experts estimate that 75 percent of a person's daily communication involves listening and speaking. We listen more than we speak, we speak more than we read, and we read more than we write. Some people say that we write a book a year, read a book a month, speak a book a week, listen a book a day. Oral communication certainly affects every area of a person's life.

INTERACT

In a small group, discuss the kinds of communication situations in which a person such as a principal, cafeteria worker, secretary, teacher, or maintenance worker takes part. Does this person have to greet others, give directions, solve problems, give advice, or discipline others? Does this person listen or speak more frequently? What communication skills does this person need?

CITIZENSHIP

Citizens are called upon to listen and speak as they serve their community, state, and nation. Citizens must make intelligent decisions in voting for local, state, and national candidates. Before making these decisions, they need to listen to speeches, debates, and political advertisements by the candidates. Responsible citizens use this information to help them decide for whom to vote. Responsible citizens must also be able to analyze the ways politicians communicate. Some active citizens serve as candidates. Others become campaign workers who try to persuade voters to vote for a certain candidate or in support of a particular issue. Still others get involved on library boards, environmental control boards, scout troops, or parade committees.

A democratic government depends on its citizens' right of freedom of speech. As a participating citizen living in a country with a government "of the people, by the people, for the people," you must be prepared to practice this right. Responsible citizens have many opportunities to use their communication skills.

Communication is a critical life skill. You can use your communication skills to learn more about yourself and others, to

sort out ideas and values, and to share ideas and feelings. To be most effective you need to exercise your ability to be fair and ethical, or honest, as you deal with others. Well-developed communication skills enable you to make decisions, work in groups, create imaginative situations, and analyze arguments. Communication is the means by which you reach out to the rest of the world, and by which the world reaches out to you.

TYPES OF COMMUNICATION

There are several different types of oral communication, or speaking and listening. These include:

1. Interpersonal communication
2. Group communication
3. Public communication
4. Interpretive communication

After completing the text, you should be able to understand how people communicate in each of these situations, and how you can improve your communication in each area.

INTERPERSONAL COMMUNICATION

When you talk to a classmate on the telephone, meet someone at a party, or discuss your worries with your best friend, you are taking part in **interpersonal communication.** The word *interpersonal* means "between people." Much of your day is spent talking one-to-one with another person. Although you may not be aware of it, you follow certain rules when you talk with another person. A study of interpersonal communication will help you understand more about the communication process that occurs when individuals talk to each other.

GROUP COMMUNICATION

When you meet in a committee such as the student council, work on a class assignment in a small group, or plan a youth group event with your friends, **group communication** is occurring. Throughout your life you will have to work in groups in order to solve problems or plan events. Group discussion works best when members follow certain rules or patterns and when leaders are prepared to help the members communicate well. A study of group communication will help you to become the best group member and leader you can be.

PUBLIC COMMUNICATION

When you present an oral book report, make class announcements, or give a talk at a religious service, you are involved in **public communication.** Speaking in public requires you to be informed and organized. You must be able to connect with your audience. You may have to give different kinds of speeches, such as a speech to inform or to persuade. You may even have to debate with another person. A study of public communication will help you learn how to prepare a speech, practice your public speaking skills, and develop your analytic listening skills.

INTERPRETIVE COMMUNICATION

When you read a story aloud to a child, recite a poem to the class, or quote a passage by a famous person, you are involved in **interpretive communication.** Interpretive communication involves bringing literature to life for your audience. You must understand the written material very well and know how to

present it interestingly for the listeners. You may even write some of the material yourself, such as an oral history of a grandparent's life. A study of interpretive communication will help you learn how to prepare to interpret written material and to practice your interpretation skills.

OBSERVE

Observe people communicating in two of the four areas of communication. You might observe two friends talking, your family planning a trip, a pastor or rabbi giving a sermon to a congregation, a teacher listening to a class, or a talk-show host talking to a TV audience. How does the communication process keep both speaker and listener involved? Give examples of the verbal and nonverbal ways both parties send and receive messages.

SUMMARY

This chapter introduces the study of communication. Communication is a process of sharing meanings. It affects every aspect of daily life. It relates to your life as a family member, a friend, a student, a worker, and a citizen. This textbook discusses four major types of communication. They are (1) interpersonal communication, (2) group communication, (3) public communication, and (4) interpretive communication.

CHAPTER REVIEW

THINK ABOUT IT

1. Why is communication considered a process?
2. Why are common meanings important in communication?
3. In what ways can good communication skills help you in your after-school job, in your family, in your community, and at school?
4. Describe the four types of communication and provide an example of each.

TRY IT OUT

1. In a small group, brainstorm a list of guidelines for good family communication. Compare your list with those of other groups.
2. In small groups, create some role-play situations in which persons have problems communicating. Ask a few members of the group to act out the role-play for the class. Discuss these characters after the role-play and explain how they could have communicated better. Example situations: a spoiled child at a supermarket; a snob refusing to dance with an unpopular person; a bully pushing a shy person around; a tough gang of boys picking on some intellectuals; a popular group of girls ignoring an unpopular girl; an intellectual group putting down other students.
3. Provide your meanings for the following words or create your own list.

happiness	war	education
honesty	stepmother	brother
rich	breakfast	

Share your definitions with your classmates and discuss the similarities and differences in your meanings. Also discuss what happens to communication if your meanings are not the same as those of the persons with whom you communicate.

PUT IT IN WRITING

1. Begin a communication journal and keep it during the entire course. In your journal, enter the assignments that will be made at the ends of other chapters. You can also write in your communication journal about communication events you observe. You may wish to include cartoons, poetry, quotes, and pictures or drawings that relate to the topic of communication. Describe in your journal why you liked the cartoons, poems, or other items you chose. Try to use key words when writing in your journal.
2. Using the word *communication* as your topic, write a poem similar to the ones at the beginning of this chapter. Share your poem with your classmates.
3. Describe a situation in which you had to make a choice about how to treat another person. Select a situation that involved thinking about your values. Describe the way you analyzed the situation and the choices you made. Examples may include standing up for a friend, explaining a mistake, or revealing your feelings.

SPEAK ABOUT IT

1. Choose any of the professions listed on page 12. Talk to a person in one of these professions. In a short presentation, explain to the class how the person uses communication in her or his profession.
2. Choose an abstract word, such as *freedom, justice, friendship,* or *sadness.* In a one-minute speech, define the word for your classmates. Use at least one example to clarify your meaning.
3. With a classmate, make a collage of pictures from magazines and newspapers that illustrate the ways people use communication. Make a list of all the different ways in which communication is used. Share your collage with the class.

ELEMENTS OF COMMUNICATION

KEY WORDS

channel

connotative meaning

context

denotative meaning

feedback

noise

nonverbal messages

perception

slang

verbal messages

After completing this chapter, you should be able to

- define the elements of communication.
- explain the categories of nonverbal communication.
- describe the connection between verbal and nonverbal communication.
- describe how noise in the channel affects communication.
- describe how feedback works in the communication process.
- observe a communication event and label the parts of the communication process.

How often have you thought you explained something well only to discover your friend did not understand? What silly conversational mistakes have caused some serious misunderstandings in your life? Can you identify exactly why the problems happened? Even simple misunderstandings cause embarrassment, as you can see from the following journal entry:

JOURNAL ENTRY

I went to my friend's house for the weekend to help paint her room. My mom was helping me pack. I told her I needed my black and yellow sweats. When I unpacked I had my good black sweater and my good yellow sweater. Was I embarrassed! I looked like a fool painting in my good clothes.

As you know, communication is the process of sending and receiving messages in order to share meanings. All communication involves certain essential elements. If someone were to ask you, "What is needed in order for communication to occur?" your answer ought to include the following essential elements of communication: (1) verbal messages, (2) nonverbal messages, (3) perception, (4) channel, (5) feedback, and (6) context. The better you understand these elements, the more effectively you can communicate. In this chapter you will look at each element separately and then see how they work together.

VERBAL MESSAGES

Verbal messages are the spoken words you use when communicating. Verbal communication involves both the choice of words (*hungry, starved, famished*) and the order of the words in a sentence. For example, you can say, "Can you tell me how to get to the movie house?" or "The film theater—where do I find it?" Or you might even say, "Hogy tudok eljutni a moziba?" (Hungarian). All these verbal messages contain the same idea, but none would work equally well at all times.

Most children begin to use words by the time they are twelve months old, but there is no age by which people's use of words is "perfect." Words do not have the same meaning to everyone. Also, words change their meanings over time. Communicators need to know how to select the most exact words to get their messages across accurately.

DIFFERENCES IN MEANING

Different people may have difficulty understanding the same message even when all the words are English. Although words are an important part of communication, they do have certain limitations.

Apply

Look at the following statements and predict what problems someone might have in understanding their meanings.

"Don't have a cow, man."
"Quit acting like a wannabe."
"Take the scoop up and attach it to the batten."

You probably understood the first items. But it is unlikely you understood the third unless you have worked backstage in a theater.

Not all words mean the same thing to all people. In fact, no word means the same thing to everyone! Even a simple word like *right* has different meanings in different situations. It can mean *correct*, as in "I have the right answer." It can be a direction, as in "Take a right turn." It can also mean *privilege*, as in "I have a right to know."

INTERACT

With a small group of classmates, list the possible meanings of the following words and phrases.

expensive	party	See you later.
tall	hot	What a day!
free	What are you doing	She is cool.
bad	Friday night?	That's a really interesting video.

Although you can go to the dictionary for the definition of any word, the definition you will find consists of other words or phrases that stand for the word you are looking up. However, because people experience words in personal ways, they may have different emotional responses to them. The definition found in the dictionary is called **denotative meaning.** An emotional or personal response to a word is called **connotative meaning.** All words have a common denotative meaning, but they may have a different connotative meaning for each person.

For example, the denotative meaning of the word *marigold* refers to a type of plant with yellow or orange flowers. Someone may have a positive connotative meaning for marigolds because they remind the person of happy times in grandmother's flower garden.

CHANGES IN WORDS

Language is in a state of constant change. Old words change in meaning or disappear from use altogether, and new words are constantly added. For example, the word *score* used to mean "twenty." Today, it is seldom given this meaning. When used in "a musical score" and the "score of the game," its meanings are entirely different. Words such as *robotics, dual disk drive, digital,* and *laser* are part of your everyday vocabulary, but your

great-grandparents wouldn't know their meanings because the words stand for new technical inventions. As children even your parents did not know these words.

Slang is informal language that is unique to a particular group. Slang words are the words that change most often. They are used in informal conversations, often between persons within a certain age group. They fall out of favor very fast and are often understood only by a small number of people. The word *awesome* is such a word. Chances are that *awesome* will sound as strange to your children (or even to your younger brothers or sisters) as *keen* does to you.

As a communicator you need to be aware of the different meanings of words and how words change over time. The more carefully you choose your words the more easily a listener can understand your message.

INTERACT

Interview someone over the age of fifty. Ask the person to list ten words in use today that he or she did not know as a young person. Combine your lists with three or four other classmates', and share the list with the class.

NONVERBAL MESSAGES

Nonverbal messages are messages expressed without words. Your appearance, facial expression, eye contact, posture, gestures, voice, and factors such as space, time, and place affect how your words are understood. Though you probably don't think about it often, you depend heavily on the wordless part of communication.

Exactly what fits under the label *nonverbal communication?* The next part of the chapter will help you understand the many ways you communicate nonverbal messages.

APPEARANCE

If you needed to ask someone for directions, who would you ask first: an old man in dirty clothes, a cute teenage boy or girl, a woman with an infant, or a woman in a sari? Clothes, body size, hairstyle, makeup, and decorations such as jewelry or slogan buttons all send messages about how a person sees herself or himself. You probably make quick first judgments about others based on appearance. So it stands to reason that others make first judgments about you based on your appearance. If you are shopping and need to know the time, your decision of whom to ask will be influenced by other shoppers' appearances. When a new student is added to your class, you form a first impression based on that person's appearance.

FACIAL EXPRESSION AND EYE CONTACT

Smiles or frowns tell others a great deal about how a person is feeling. A person's face often reveals rather quickly that a person is angry, happy, frustrated, or nervous. What is the look

that tells you not to bother your parent? How can you tell whether a friend is tired or simply relaxed? Most people believe the eyes are the most expressive part of the body. Eyes show feelings that might be hidden otherwise. You can learn a great deal from a person's willingness to look at you. You can often read feelings such as anger, surprise, or delight by watching someone's eyes. According to an old expression, "The eyes are the windows of the soul."

OBSERVE

Observe several people in various situations. Try to guess their moods by observing their nonverbal cues. For example, you might notice the cafeteria workers smiling or frowning or rushing you through the line, your teacher standing behind you with arms folded, or your best friend giving you a knowing look. Record your observations in your journal or share them with the class.

POSTURE

Posture refers to your body's position as you sit, stand, or walk. The way you sit or stand communicates a great deal about your mood or feelings. If you are slouching, you create a very different image than if you are standing or sitting up straight. A person's posture often tells whether it is all right to start a conversation or make a request. If your mother is sitting slumped at the table with her head in her hands, then it's probably not the best moment to tell her that you need new shoes for gym class.

Posture can also send other messages. Models are taught to "walk tall" or "stand tall" to make a good impression. Persons interviewing for jobs are taught to stand and sit up straight because they will seem more confident. Interviewers usually notice people's posture while they talk with them about their other qualifications.

GESTURES

The way people move their arms, hands, and fingers plays a part in communication. Most good speakers use gestures to help make a point. The way gestures are used may also tell others something about a speaker's enthusiasm. Some people tend to talk with their hands constantly moving. You may have heard someone say, "If I tied your hands behind your back, you couldn't talk."

Besides the larger gestures, people use hand signals to communicate. Think of the different meanings of the peace sign, the OK sign, or crossed fingers. Can you think of other gestures that are used to send messages?

VOICE

A person's voice, that is, not *what* is said but *how* it is said, conveys important messages. Voice includes

1. Pitch—how high or low the voice is
2. Rate—how quickly or slowly something is said
3. Vocal quality—the tone or sound of a voice
4. Volume—the loudness or softness of a voice

Some voices can put the listener to sleep; others will make the listener pay attention.

Pitch, rate, quality, and volume are four elements of your voice that you can change for different effects when you communicate. If you always talk slowly, in a low-pitched, quiet, mellow voice, you probably will put your listeners to sleep. On the other hand, a rapid, high-pitched, loud, squeaky voice can be annoying. Either vocal pattern can be effective for a short time. But to hold people's attention and to emphasize points in varying ways, you will have to change your voice. These changes make your voice interesting and help make your meaning clear.

OBSERVE

Observe at least two famous people with voices that appeal to you. You could choose a television personality, a favorite disc jockey, your minister or rabbi, or a friend. Listen to the pitch, rate, quality, and volume with which they speak. What did you observe? Share your observations in class.

SPACE, TIME, AND PLACE

The environmental factors of space, time, and place affect communication. How close you stand or sit to someone says a lot about your relationship to that person. Friends often sit close together, while strangers keep a certain distance between them. In places such as crowded elevators or hallways, a group may be forced to bunch together, but if you watch people walking together on the street, you can often tell something about their relationship by noting the distances between them. In an uncrowded bus, strangers sit apart, while friends sit together. These differences in space send messages about the relationship.

Time also affects communication. If you are rushed, you will speak more rapidly than if you are relaxed. You may sound very different on the phone at 7:00 A.M. than at 7:00 P.M. Are you a morning person or a night person? How does this affect your communication? Time itself also sends messages. The amount of time you spend with someone may tell that person and other people that you are friends.

You probably notice the ways in which surroundings affect communication. If you are talking with a close friend, you may talk about different things in your kitchen than in the privacy of your room. If you are sitting in the principal's office, you may control your volume or choose words more carefully than you would at basketball practice. The different settings shape the way you communicate.

FEELINGS

You depend heavily on nonverbal messages to understand feelings and attitudes. When you exchange information, the words may be of great importance; for example, "The track meet will be Saturday morning at the school field." When you share feelings, the nonverbal part of the message becomes most important; for example, "When Susan said, 'No, I can't go,' she didn't need to say any more. Her eyes told me she was sad."

INTERACT

Form a small group of four or five people. Take turns expressing the following feelings using only nonverbal messages: happy, tired, frustrated, hurt, angry, silly, surprised, jealous. See how many feelings the class can guess correctly.

Good communicators learn to read nonverbal cues rather than rely only on the verbal message, because almost 90 percent of a person's feelings are communicated nonverbally. Sometimes it is true that "actions speak louder than words."

Apply

You may have found yourself in either of the following situations:

Someone says, "Well, I've got to go," and continues to talk to you on the phone.

Someone says, "I like you a lot," but ignores you in the hallway when there are other people around.

How do you react when this happens to you? These people's actions communicated their feelings more clearly than their words. Even when words are spoken, the nonverbal message speaks louder than the verbal one.

Verbal and nonverbal messages are central to the communication process. A good communicator sends and interprets verbal and nonverbal messages. In addition, the communicator understands the vocal production process. Yet messages are only one element of the whole communication process.

PERCEPTIONS

The meaning of a message tends to change as it moves from person to person. For example, what Tony thought was a joke, Aaron considered an insult. This explains many misunderstandings and conflicts that interfere with communication. The meanings change because of the perception process.

DIFFERENCES IN PERCEPTIONS

Every person views the world slightly differently, and therefore no two people interpret the same message in the same way. If you are angry at Laura, you may not see her smile as being friendly. If you just failed math, you may not want to listen to your older sister say, "When *I* had that class, I got an A." If Karen doesn't think Sandy likes her, she may be careful about what she tells her. These little personal moods or prejudices are part of everyone's individuality. For this reason, communication depends on the perception of the people involved in the communication process.

Perception is the process of giving meaning to information you learn through your five senses. Taste, touch, hearing, sight, and smell provide you with information about the

world. When you perceive this information, you are making sense out of it for yourself. This perception process involves two steps:

1. Something affects your senses. (You see, hear, taste, smell, or touch something.)
2. You interpret and explain the sensation to yourself. (You give meaning to what you are seeing, hearing, tasting, smelling, or touching.)

For example, you may hear a friend say loudly, "It's about time you showed up." Seeing his tight mouth and wrinkled forehead, you get the meaning, "He is angry."

Yet not every person gives the same meaning to the same sense information. People may perceive the same sense message differently for many reasons. Three major factors that influence perception are:

1. Physical differences
2. Past experiences
3. The present situation

Physical Differences

Although most people have the use of all their senses, they may have very different abilities. For example, you might be farsighted, but your brother is nearsighted. You may have fine hearing, while your friend's ear infection may have reduced her ability to hear. As you sit in the back of the room, you may be able to see the handwriting on the board and your teacher's serious facial expression. You can hear the homework assignment. Your brother and friend may miss part of the assignment because of their reduced ability to see or hear. Such physical problems may affect a person's ability to take in information through his or her senses.

Past Experiences

Your past experiences add to differences in perception and to your ability to understand what you perceive. Past experiences may range from those that are considered general, to those shared by many people you know, to those that are unique or shared by few people you know. For example, depending on where you grew up, you might order a soft drink using the term *soda, pop,* or *Coke.* If your family is Jewish you know what happens at bar mitzvahs and bas mitzvahs, while other friends need a careful explanation.

Your past experiences will influence how you accept or reject a message. If you enjoy learning about outer space, you may be pleased to learn that the graduation speaker is a former astronaut. If you meet another gymnast at a party, you may talk to each other about kips and scales. Other people may not understand your conversation.

Past experience influences how people talk and how they listen. People with very different backgrounds may have to work hard to communicate well. It may be difficult to imagine how important a bas mitzvah is if you've never been to one. If your friend is a gymnast but you are not, you may get tired of listening to him use words you don't understand.

Present Situation

How you feel mentally and physically also affects communication. If you are upset about an argument with your best friend, you may snap at your parents when they ask you to help in the kitchen. Your desire to make money may lead you to pay close attention to a radio ad for a summer job. If you have a headache or you are daydreaming about a person you like, it may keep you from paying close attention to a conversation.

The cartoon gives an example of the different ways people react to messages while they are communicating.

CHANNEL

People need a way to send and receive their messages. Verbal and nonverbal messages are sent through a channel that uses the human senses. In communication terms, the **channel** is the means by which a message is transmitted. Suppose Susan tells you that she is very nervous about a test coming up tomorrow. You pat her on the shoulder and say, "Don't worry. You always do well in math." You have, even in this brief conversation, communicated through many channels:

Susan hears you speak. (sound)
Susan watches your facial expressions. (sight)
Susan smells your cologne. (smell)

Susan feels you pat her shoulder. (touch)
You watch her facial expressions. (sight)
You hear her speak. (sound)
You pat her shoulder. (touch)

Like a television set or a radio, you have many channels and can switch them at will. If your parents are telling you something you don't want to hear, perhaps you tune out that channel and focus on their facial expressions or think about something else entirely, like the smell of dinner cooking.

People tend to place greater importance on one channel than on another. For example, you may pay more attention to facial expressions or movements you receive through sight. Someone else may pay more attention to words or tone of voice—channels of sound.

NOISE

When a person has trouble understanding a message, there is said to be "noise in the channel." Perhaps the person was daydreaming and therefore didn't listen carefully. Or maybe the TV was on too loud so he or she couldn't hear what was being said. These are examples of noise. **Noise** is anything that interferes with a listener's ability to receive a message. The noise can be outside the listener, such as loud stereo music, a freezing room, or a hard chair. The noise can also be inside the listener. A headache, worry about something, and boredom are examples of noise inside the listener.

Sometimes you can control the noise; at other times you cannot. You can turn down the stereo, but you can't turn up the school's heating unit. You may be able to force yourself to stop daydreaming, but you may start worrying about tomorrow's science test. Noise in the channel can lead to faulty perception and misunderstanding.

FEEDBACK

How do senders and receivers know if they are communicating effectively? To communicate successfully, a person must interpret other people's **feedback,** or responses. When you are communicating, the person you are talking with responds to

you verbally and nonverbally. Feedback consists of the verbal and nonverbal messages that tell speakers how they are being perceived.

POSITIVE AND NEGATIVE FEEDBACK

Feedback may be positive or negative. Positive feedback tells you that you're doing fine. A smile, nod of the head, and laughter at your joke all indicate that you are "getting through" as you intended to. The feedback is negative if you see a frown, a questioning look, or hear a mutter or grumble. These responses help you realize that you need to change your communication. Positive feedback tells you to continue what you are doing. Negative feedback tells you there is a problem and you should make changes.

SELF-FEEDBACK

Feedback also may come from yourself. Self-feedback is the message you give yourself as you pay attention to your own behavior. Although you may not be getting much external feedback, you may say to yourself, "I think I'm talking too much. I'd better be quiet for a while" or "I can feel myself getting too silly. I'd better calm down." Sometimes you may tell yourself to keep going even though the feedback is negative. Perhaps you are saying to yourself, "I'm finally saying what I really want to, so I will keep going this way."

Communication goes smoothly when speakers and listeners pay attention to feedback. You may see some puzzled looks and think, "I'm going too fast, so I'll summarize and slow down." Without feedback speakers and listeners would not be able to adapt to each other.

OBSERVE

Select a communication situation in which one person is an active speaker and the others are listeners. Carefully note the kinds of feedback the listeners give the speaker, such as questions, smiles, and yawns. Describe any ways the speaker shows that he or she is paying attention to the listener feedback.

CONTEXT

Finally all these essential elements of communication come together within a context. A **context** is the setting and people that surround a message. Context provides the background that helps reveal the message's real meaning. Good communicators are similar to detectives. They look for clues that tell them how to interpret and understand a message.

Setting is the first part of context. It involves time, place, and occasion. You may say something at a certain place or time that you would not say at another place or time. You may be more honest about your feelings in your room than in a crowded restaurant during a birthday party. If your coach is rushing to an important meeting, you probably should not stop him to talk about last week's soccer game.

The people in the setting influence what is said and what is not said. You may decide not to talk about your bowling trophy when a member of the losing team is sitting at the next table. You probably will not make fun of the talent show in front of the director's son.

The way you see the setting and the other people involved will affect how you handle certain topics. The basketball game may not be the place to discuss your sister's serious illness.

All human communication takes place within an overall context. This context is an essential element of communication that touches all the other elements, influencing the messages, people, feedback, and channels people use to communicate.

SUMMARY

This chapter discussed the essential elements of communication. Good communicators pay attention to verbal and nonverbal messages. Communicators must be aware of how people's perceptions affect communication. Finally, communicators must be aware of the importance of channel, feedback, and context in communication.

CHAPTER REVIEW

THINK ABOUT IT

1. What are the six essential elements of communication?
2. Give an example of each of the categories of nonverbal communication.
3. How does noise in the channel affect communication?
4. Why is feedback important in communication?

TRY IT OUT

1. Role-play various stereotypical nonverbal messages that you associate with the following people. Show how each person would walk or stand. See if other students can identify the role you perform. (It may help you to imagine these persons doing specific things when you role-play them.)

football coach	politician	large person
two-year-old	smart six-year-old	old person
burglar	police officer	ballerina
teacher	street person	principal
wrestler	student	chef

2. Describe a situation from your past in which actions spoke louder than words. Carefully describe the verbal messages expressed during the situation. Then describe the nonverbal messages that seemed to carry the real meaning.

3. Observe a speaker addressing an audience. Record the kinds of positive and negative feedback the audience members gave the speaker. Note how the speaker responded to the feedback. Describe any noise in the channel that interfered with the sending and receiving of messages.

4. In a small group, redesign your school to make it more comfortable for you. Consider the spatial arrangement and environmental factors. How would you change the cafeterias and classrooms? What rooms would you add and what would the purpose of each added room be? How might the nonverbal changes affect verbal communication?

PUT IT IN WRITING

1. Record the slang words or expressions you hear throughout one day. Tell whether the words are familiar to everyone or to just a few.
2. Create a body language booklet. Find pictures in magazines, newspapers, and comic books to illustrate ten of the following emotions or attitudes:

happiness	love	compassion	grief
fear	boredom	conflict	disgust
disappointment	hurt	approval	affection
surprise	irritation	disapproval	joy
fatigue	relaxation	sadness	confidence
anger	excitement	emphasis	shyness

Use a page for each emotion or attitude. Label the picture. Then write a brief explanation of the facial expressions, posture, and gestures that indicate to you why the picture shows emotion or attitude. Share your booklet with your classmates. Do your classmates perceive the pictures in the same way you do? Why or why not?

SPEAK ABOUT IT

1. Create your own communication model. Use a collage, mobile, or poster. Explain it to the class.
2. Describe a situation in which you were involved where actions spoke louder than words. Carefully describe the verbal messages expressed during the situation. Then describe the nonverbal messages that seemed to carry the real meaning.

The Work of Speaking and Listening

After completing this chapter, you should be able to

- describe the steps of vocal production.
- define *listening* and distinguish it from *hearing*.
- describe the four steps in the listening process.
- describe the four types of listening.
- describe the three barriers to good listening.
- list the guidelines for good listening.

KEY WORDS

articulators

pharynx

diaphragm

resonators

external barriers

speaker barriers

hearing

self-barriers

larynx

trachea

listening

vocal cords

The spoken word belongs half to those who speak, and half to those who hear.

This French proverb is another way of saying that speaking and listening are two parts that form the whole—communication. To become skillful at communication, you need to know how to create sound properly and how to give meaning to the sounds you hear. In short, you need to know about the work of vocal production and listening.

VOCAL PRODUCTION

Every day you get out of bed and begin to make an amazing number of different sounds. You may yawn, grumble, giggle, talk, yell, or sing. But do you know how your voice makes these sounds? To do their work well, singers, actors, and politicians learn how their voices produce sound. Most other people know little about vocal production.

When a friend telephones, you can usually tell instantly who it is by listening to his or her voice. Even if three friends

were to call and say the exact same words, you would recognize each speaker's voice. How do people produce the sounds that become vocal tones and words? The production of sounds and speech is a complicated process. It is so automatic that people are usually unaware of it. The three major elements in vocal production are (1) breath and sound, (2) resonance, and (3) articulation. The first part of this chapter will look at each element separately.

BREATH AND SOUND

The production of sound begins with the breathing process. The breathing process provides the air needed for sound production. Besides the lungs, the process involves the **diaphragm**, a muscle that separates the chest from the abdominal cavity. When you fill your lungs with air, or inhale, the diaphragm expands. When you let air out, or exhale, the diaphragm contracts and forces the air from your lungs into your windpipe, or **trachea**. Most of the time you perform this process without thinking about it.

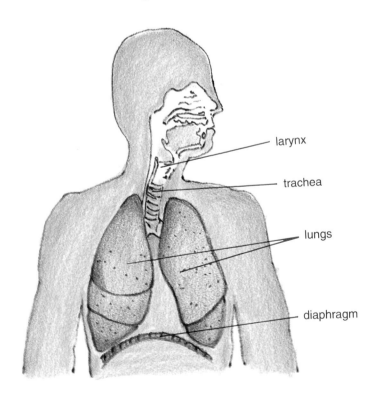

Breath Control

What do you find yourself doing when you need to hold a musical note for a long time during choir practice? Or when you have to give a speech to a large group without a microphone? Usually you try to take in a large amount of air. You then control the flow of air from your lungs to create a sound that lasts for the right length of time.

Most people try to take in a deep breath and let it out slowly. Often they do it incorrectly and waste a lot of energy with poor results. When some people hear "Take a deep breath," they suck in their stomachs and raise their shoulders.

But this does not get more air into the lungs. When you inhale, the diaphragm needs to move down and out as the air fills up the lungs. The shoulders should remain level. Even though people are usually self-conscious about holding in their stomachs, good breathing may make them swell out like pears. Also, it is more effective to breathe through the nose to avoid gulping air.

INTERACT

Choose a partner and stand face-to-face. Watch each other take in deep breaths (inhale) and slowly release the air (exhale). If you see your partner's shoulders rising, say so. Press gently on your partner's shoulders while he or she inhales. Place your fist above your own belly button as you inhale. As you inhale, you should feel your hand being pushed out as your diaphragm moves down and out. Do this only three or four times because it can make you feel faint. Try breathing properly a few times each day until this process becomes more natural for you.

Sound Production

As you exhale, air leaves your lungs and passes into the windpipe, or trachea. The trachea is the tube that carries air, just as the esophagus carries food. At the top of the trachea, air passes into the **larynx**, also called the voice box. The larynx contains your vocal cords.

The **vocal cords** are two elastic folds with a slit between them. As air is pushed upward through this slit, the cords vibrate when certain sounds are made. When you hold the neck of a balloon before knotting it, you can hear slight noises as air escapes. Your fingers act very much like the folds of the vocal cords, opening and closing to create the air flow.

Not all speech sounds depend on the vibration of the vocal cords. For example, some consonant sounds, such as *p, s,* and *ch,* have no voiced tone. When you make them you allow air to pass through your vocal cords without vibration. However, when you make voiced sounds, your vocal cords vibrate. Voiced sounds include *b, z,* and *j.* You can try making these sounds to see how this works. Be sure you make the sound rather than say the letter.

OBSERVE

Place your three middle fingers gently against your throat. Make the *p* sound and repeat it. You should not feel any vibration in your throat. Now repeat the experiment with the following pairs of sounds: *b/d, g/k, v/f.*

Pitch. The length of the vocal cords affects the **pitch,** or highness and lowness of sound. The longer the cord, the lower the voice; the shorter the cord, the higher the voice. Men usually

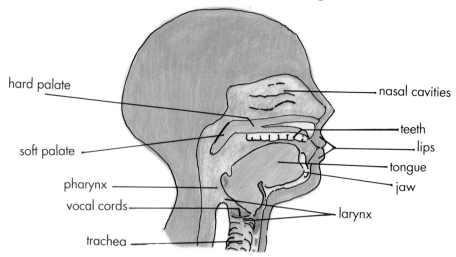

have longer vocal cords than women, which is why their voices are lower.

Tension also can affect the length of the vocal cords. When you are very nervous, your neck area becomes tense and your vocal cords tighten up. This tension may create a higher pitch or a more strained sound. If you are relaxed, the sound will be lower and less strained.

Singers, actors, and speakers are very aware of how they use their vocal cords. They wish to produce the proper sounds and keep their voices relaxed. They are careful not to strain their voices through yelling or speaking too long or too often. (Proper use of the voice is discussed in Chapter 12.)

RESONANCE

The sound produced by the vocal cords moves upward in the throat to resonating chambers. The **pharynx**—the muscular sac between the mouth and the esophagus—the mouth, and the nasal cavities act as hollow chambers, or **resonators**, to increase the sound. (If you have ever been in a cave, you know how a sound increases as it bounces off walls.) The thin soft sound that comes from the vocal cords becomes louder as it moves through the resonators. Many instruments such as the bassoon and French horn are actually complex resonators for the air flow produced by the player.

Just as an instrument creates different notes when the player changes the shape of the resonator (by covering and uncovering holes or pushing keys), the sound of the human voice is affected by the size of the resonating chambers and by the tongue, lips, and jaw. For example, if you do not open your mouth wide enough and if your jaws are tense, the sound may not be relaxed or pleasant.

JOURNAL ENTRY

I have a friend who is hard of hearing and who had to learn to read lips. It's amazing to see how Charlie can figure out some very complicated words just by watching my lips and face. I know it must be hard when he is first introduced to someone and has to read that person's lips.

ARTICULATION

Speech occurs when articulators form sounds into words. The **articulators** are the tongue, teeth, jaw, hard and soft palate, and lips. These parts of the vocal mechanism affect the final formation of words. Try forming the sounds s, d, v, and r, and pay careful attention to the position of your lips, tongue, and teeth.

Articulation Errors

Most articulation errors occur because of laziness or carelessness. You may hear *jest* for *just*, *git* for *get*, *ax* for *ask*, *comin'* for *coming*, and *Linder* for *Linda*. Some people substitute one sound for another. They may substitute *t* for *th* as in *nort* instead of *north*, or *in* for *ing* as in *goin'* instead of *going*. Other people may leave sounds out, dropping the *g* in *recognize* or the *d* in *friend*, for example.

Articulation is very important to making sure that your message is understood. While listeners usually can figure out what you mean, they may get tired or distracted. Careful, accurate articulation is easier for listeners to follow.

INTERACT

With a partner take turns reading the following tongue twisters as clearly and quickly as you can.

A big bad bear bit a brown and black bug.
She sells seashells by the seashore.
Peter Piper picked a peck of pickled peppers.

IMPORTANCE OF VOCAL PRODUCTION

Effective speech begins with good vocal production. It is important to develop correct habits for creating sounds so that you can make yourself understood in many situations.

When you travel across the United States, you find certain words pronounced in different ways. When you travel around the world, you find sounds in some languages that do not exist in the English language.

Most people take vocal production for granted. Skillful communicators learn how to improve their voices and make themselves more easily understood by listeners.

THE LISTENING PROCESS

What is listening? Is it the same as hearing? You may be surprised to learn there is a difference. **Hearing** is the act of receiving sound. When you hear something, you are aware of sounds. Listening involves hearing, but it is much more complicated than just picking up sounds.

Listening is the four-step process of receiving, interpreting, evaluating, and responding to messages. Hearing is only part of the first step in the listening process. Although you may listen to nonhuman sounds such as car motors, air conditioners, or singing birds, the focus in this chapter is on listening to other people. This includes messages sent by people to other people in face-to-face situations and messages sent through the media.

RECEIVING

The first step of the listening process is receiving. It involves hearing and seeing. You use your ears and eyes to gather information, or sense data. Your ears take in the vocal tones and words, such as, "Did you know about the party at Jenny's house?" or "There will be a final band rehearsal at 3:30 this Friday." Your eyes read the nonverbal signals to get the full message. You watch facial expressions, gestures, and eye movements.

INTERPRETING

Once you have received a message through your ears and eyes, you have to use your own experience to interpret what you just heard. An effective listener tries to interpret the speaker's message to truly understand what the speaker intended to say.

Suppose you hear the question, "Did you know about the party at Jenny's house?" You may interpret it as meaning "Did *you* know there was a party? No one told me about it." Or you may interpret it as meaning "Did you know what really happened at that party?" There may be still other meanings. The nonverbal cues will give you helpful information in figuring out the meaning.

EVALUATING

After you have interpreted the message, you have to evaluate it carefully. You have to connect that message to your ideas or feelings about the subject of the message. You have to decide if you agree or disagree, or if you need more information.

For example, depending on how you interpreted the message about Jenny's party, you may need to consider whether or not you should tell the other person why he wasn't invited, or you may want to know why he is asking. While each person is talking, you begin to think, "So what?" You will ask yourself, "What do I think?" or "How do I feel?" or "What do I need to know?"

RESPONDING

Almost all messages require some type of response. A lack of response frustrates most speakers. The listener who gives no verbal or nonverbal feedback makes a speaker feel invisible. The speaker expects a verbal or nonverbal signal that you "got" the message.

As a listener you are faced with sending a response. You may say, "She only had the basketball team members over," or you may nod your head to indicate you knew about the party.

The listener's response is important for effective communication. If the speaker gets no feedback, he or she has no connection to you.

TYPES OF LISTENING

An effective listener uses four types of listening. They include informative, empathic, critical, and creative listening.

Each type of listening requires effort and awareness. A competent listener is comfortable using all types.

INFORMATIVE LISTENING

An important part of communication is getting information, or doing *informative listening*. Many people have problems at

NOTE TAKING

Competent communicators listen with their ears and their eyes to take classroom notes effectively. Following are some guidelines for note taking:

1. *Decide what kind of notes you need to take.* Think about the teacher and the subject. Do you need only a few key words on each topic because the material is also in your history book? Do you need to write down most of what the teacher says because you have no textbook or because the material is not covered in your book?

2. *Pay special attention to what the teacher highlights.* Look at what the teacher writes on the board or screen, since this is a clue to what is important. Listen carefully to what the teacher emphasizes or repeats. Example: "So by this time there were thirteen colonies. Not eight, not seventeen, but thirteen." Also listen carefully to what the teacher says is important. Example: "Remember this formula because you will need to use it again."

3. *Follow the teacher's outline format.* Try to get the whole picture before you start to take notes. Example: "There are six styles in this experiment" or "We will review the criteria for becoming a senator." Use clues the teacher gives. Example: "So the second step is the addition of salt."

4. *Make your own comments as you write notes.* Tie the points to your own life or your opinions. Star or circle ideas you think are important.

5. *Review your notes after class.* Correct your spelling or clean up messy handwriting. Underline or circle ideas you think are important. (Colored pencils might help with this.) Write down any reactions you have to the material or clues to help you to remember. Examples:

"similar to Brazil" or "gopher story." Draw arrows or lines to connect related points.

6. *Remember the "don'ts."* Don't try to write down every word. Don't try to write down the stories and examples, just label them. Example: "Andrew Jackson horse story."

home, work, or school because they do not listen carefully for information they need. Often they do not ask the right questions to find out what they need to know.

Informative listening involves listening to information, directions, or news. You are listening for information when you take notes in class, when you take telephone messages for another family member, or when you pay attention to a demonstration speech on how to make chocolate chip brownies. During television or radio broadcasts you also listen for information about weather, news events, and political issues.

Informative listening is the basis for the other types of listening. Unless you understand a message accurately, you cannot analyze the other person's ideas or respond to the other person's feelings.

EMPATHIC LISTENING

Empathic listening involves listening to another's feelings. It is not easy to just listen when others are talking about feelings. Sometimes you want to solve their problems. Sometimes you want to interrupt with questions or ideas.

Listening to negative feelings requires patience and caring. Talking to a friend who is angry or sad can be difficult. Eye contact or touch is often a better response than words. As a camp counselor, baby-sitter, or hospital volunteer, you may hear many people talk about their feelings. This will give you the opportunity to engage in empathic listening.

Someone who is upset may just need another person to be there. The listener does not have to solve the problem. The listener simply has to respond to demonstrate understanding of the problem and the feelings it is creating. For example, you can't solve your friend's family problems, but you can listen and show you care about your friend.

Apply

Read the following comments and identify the feeling being expressed in each. Then imagine how you might respond if a good friend made these comments to you.

"What do you do when your folks get in a fight? Do you just pretend you don't hear anything? I never know whether to hide in my room or just help by doing stuff downstairs."

"Hey! Guess what! I came in first in the 440."

OBSERVE

Think back to the last time you listened to someone's feelings. What kinds of feelings do your family and friends ask you to listen to? How do you respond? When is it easy to respond? When is it difficult? Share your stories with your classmates and listen to their stories, too. Have you all had similar experiences or problems?

CRITICAL LISTENING

Critical listening means examining a persuasive message and making decisions about your findings. After examining a message, you need to respond actively. Perhaps you may need to ask questions to obtain further information.

Critical listening involves separating fact from opinion and checking out the source of a message. A *fact* is a statement that can be proved or disproved. An *opinion* is a statement that is based on a belief or feeling. It is a judgment. For example, you can prove that the temperature in Dallas, Texas, was 85 degrees yesterday. Yesterday's Dallas temperature is a fact. You may also believe that it was a beautiful day in Dallas yesterday, but that is an opinion. You cannot prove the opinion. Someone else might feel that 85 degrees is too hot to be considered a beautiful day.

A critical listener hears the other person's ideas first; looks for facts, opinions, disagreements, confusion; and then figures out how to respond effectively. Whether you are an audience member during a persuasive speech or a participant in a debate, your mind should be working constantly.

Apply

What questions might a critical listener ask when responding to the following statements? (Keep looking for facts and opinions.)

- Remi says there will be only two slots open on the track team and one is already promised to Darren.
- The election was a joke. Forty-five percent of the citizens did not know who was running.
- The Hatfields have three cars. They are very rich.

All these statements should be questioned by a person interested in how true they are. Critical listeners always keep alert and ask questions. It's hard work, but it's worth it.

CREATIVE LISTENING

Creative listening means using your active imagination as you interpret a message. This is sometimes called *recreational listening*. You probably enjoy listening to music. Your imagination creates pictures or stories to go along with the music. Often when you listen to others, your mind does similar things. A storyteller helps you create mental pictures. You can find yourself in a medieval castle or on a new planet in just a few seconds. A comedian makes you see the world in new and surprising ways. You use your imagination when you watch a play or listen to a comedy album. In all these cases the speakers stir up your creativity while you listen.

You may become more actively involved in other kinds of creative listening. If you have done role playing, you know how carefully you have to listen to respond to the other people in the scene. Whether you and a friend are working on a science project or creating a computer game, listening to each other makes the work more imaginative. As you listen to your friend's ideas, you may find new solutions to problems that come up.

Sometimes you can see new ways to do things based on what other people say. Suppose you are building a model of the planets and one group member wants to glue the rings around Saturn. Another person wants to create a complicated hanger so the rings can come off. If you take the time to discuss your ideas and hear each other out, you may come up with a third approach—using magnets or Velcro to remove the rings. Creative problem solvers have very fine listening skills.

INTERACT

Try out creative listening by doing a soap opera role play. With a partner, try to portray two imaginary characters in a particular situation. Act out the situation so the class can understand who the characters are and what is going on.

As a class, you might try a role-play tag. Start with two characters and a particular situation. After a couple of minutes, someone from the class tags one of the characters and steps into the role play. After a couple more minutes, someone else tags the other character and steps into the scene. Continue the role-play tag until everyone has had a turn being an actor. Afterwards, discuss the role that listening played in the role-play tag, as people created characters or had to adapt to new characters.

BARRIERS TO LISTENING

A person who has normal hearing is not necessarily a good listener. Many different things can prevent a speaker's message from being received. These are called barriers to listening. The three major barriers to listening are external barriers, speaker barriers, and self-barriers. A discussion of each barrier follows.

EXTERNAL BARRIERS

External barriers are situations in the environment that keep you from paying careful attention to the speaker. Such distractions may include a bee flying around your head, a fire engine siren wailing outside, or a ringing telephone. Coughing, whispering, or giggling can distract you in the classroom. (These are examples of noise in the channel discussed in Chapter 2.)

External barriers can be temporary and unusual, but they also can be ongoing or permanent. If you go to school near a busy airport, you may hear the sound of jet engines pass over your classroom every afternoon. This is a temporary distraction. If you live near noisy neighbors, this may be a long-term or permanent distraction. Sometimes you can change the distractions by shutting the windows. Other times you have to learn to listen in spite of them.

External barriers exist outside the speakers and listeners but can greatly interfere with communication. Good listeners recognize the distractions and ignore or remove them.

SPEAKER BARRIERS

Speaker barriers are characteristics of the speaker that interfere with listening. They include appearance and manner, prejudice, and believability.

Appearance and Manner

Some speakers turn off their audiences through their appearance or by their manner of speaking. Appearance may interfere with the message. If you are distracted by a speaker's clothes, jewelry, or hairstyle, you may miss the main point of the conversation.

Some people constantly use filler words such as "you know," or "like." Others look at the floor or tap their fingers during a conversation. These habits distract listeners, who remember the annoying habit rather than the message.

Prejudice

Speakers who appear narrow-minded or prejudiced also turn off listeners. Listeners have to work hard to concentrate on the message. You may learn not to be put off at once by someone who appears to brag. You may remember occasions when you

judged someone too quickly and later discovered how much you missed. Usually these experiences help you to keep an open mind the next time.

Believability

Listeners need to believe that the speaker knows his or her subject well. A speaker with low believability may create barriers to listening. A speech on "How Karate Can Change Your Life" should not be given by a student who has taken only three karate lessons. A seriously overweight doctor is not an ideal person with whom to discuss weight loss. Listeners may not respect these speakers' opinions.

What makes people believable when they are talking? In some cases, a person's formal or informal reputation precedes a message. A speaker may be introduced like this: "Dr. May Falk, a specialist in sports medicine, will talk about how athletes stay healthy. Dr. Falk is head of the sports medicine program at Fairlawn University." This formal introduction makes the speaker believable. Informal reputations often serve to influence believability. You may think of someone as a bigot, liberal, burnout, or brain. Such labels tend to influence how you react to what they say.

Sometimes a speaker establishes believability during a conversation. Comments such as, "When I ran the marathon..." or "When I play the saxophone..." show knowledge about the subject. When you hear two people trade baseball statistics or argue about computers for half an hour, you begin to see them as believable speakers on their subjects. On the other hand, people who talk about topics they know little about tend to create a barrier between themselves and their listeners.

SELF-BARRIERS

Self-barriers are personal attitudes or behaviors that interfere with listening. You can keep yourself from being a competent communicator. Internal distractions, lack of knowledge, personal prejudices, and your desire to talk may get in the way of listening.

Internal Distractions

Your thoughts, feelings, or physical state can interfere with listening. If you failed a test last period or just had a fight with a friend, you may be unable to pay attention in class. Thinking of next weekend's party can also cause you to tune out the speaker.

Your physical state may interfere with your ability to give full attention to someone else. Headaches, toothaches, stomach cramps, or lack of sleep are internal distractions. If you are in pain, will you be able to give full attention to a friend's conversation with you?

Lack of Knowledge

Sometimes you will find that no matter how hard you try to listen, you cannot understand what the speaker is saying. Your past experience or classes may not have prepared you for a discussion of rocket boosters, coin collecting, or gospel music. Sometimes speakers use a special language that you cannot understand. For example, if you do not understand terms such as *hard drive, double sided–double density, 640K,* or *laser printer,* you will have trouble understanding a basic discussion of computers.

Good listeners take the risk of asking questions to find out what they cannot understand. They will also try to learn to interpret new words and nonverbal symbols to be more effective listeners in the future. Sometimes you may have to say, "I don't understand now, but I'll try to learn more about it."

Personal Prejudices

Your beliefs also may keep you from really hearing what another person has to say. People have their own beliefs on certain subjects. Their beliefs may reflect their studies or upbringing. Yet many believe they know everything about a certain topic. They don't think they can learn anything new by listening carefully to others. This leads to closed minds and creates barriers to communication.

Apply

Sometimes you create a barrier just because you believe a subject is uninteresting. Which of the following subjects is likely to cause you to close down mentally?

modern poetry	the NBA playoff schedule
recent Broadway shows	the space program
rodeo riders	badminton
modeling careers	country and Western music

Some of these topics may meet with a ho-hum from you. Yet many people are fascinated by these topics and enjoy listening to a discussion of them.

Sensitive topics can cause barriers to good listening. Each of us has strong feelings about discussing values with anyone, particularly with people we don't know well. If a person you just met asks you about your religion, you may put up a barrier. But you and a trusted friend may feel very comfortable talking for hours about your religious beliefs.

Sometimes you will tune out after hearing a speaker take a particular position, saying to yourself, "I hold the opposite view. Why should I bother to listen?" This often happens with national political topics, such as nuclear energy or welfare. But it can also happen on issues of personal taste, such as your choice of clothes, sports teams, or music. If you don't listen to points of view different from your own, you may learn more and more about one point of view but remain unaware of others.

Desire to Talk

Many people would rather talk than listen, especially if they have to listen carefully. You probably know someone who may appear to be listening but is really waiting to talk. And you can probably remember arguments in which all you could do was wait for the other person to finish. In these situations, very little listening is going on.

Sometimes people compete to "top" another person's joke or story. You can recognize such a listener in the person who says, "You think that's bad, wait till you hear this. . . ." Usually this competition takes the fun out of a conversation because the speakers seem to be listening only to themselves.

People who find themselves always trying to get in the next word need to learn the value of controlling their talking. Good listeners try to listen until a speaker is finished. Then they start to respond.

Every speaker and listener has the responsibility to try to communicate with the other. Communication breaks down when barriers go up and one or both persons stop trying to reach each other.

OBSERVE

Listen to your classmates at the lunch table for fifteen minutes and record all the barriers that keep them from listening to each other. For example, list the distracting noises that compete for attention. Or note how certain people tune out when a particular subject is mentioned.

GUIDELINES FOR GOOD LISTENING

The following guidelines are used by people who work at their listening skills. These guidelines can help you develop your own listening skills.

1. *Watch for nonverbal clues.* Often speakers tell us what is important through nonverbal messages. A speaker's

hand gestures may stress a point. A speaker's face reveals his or her feelings about a subject. When a speaker's voice gets louder or softer, it may be a signal to pay special attention. Good listeners look for nonverbal clues.

2. *Try to see things from the speaker's point of view.* Whether or not you agree with another person, you will be a better listener if you try to understand what is going on inside the other person. If your friend is angry at people who were calling him or her names, you need to imagine how you would feel if someone called you those names. If you are listening to a speech on outdoor adventure activities, you might try to imagine how exciting it would feel to ride a motorcycle or climb a mountain. Good listeners try to put themselves in the speaker's shoes.

3. *Avoid distractions.* When you enter a classroom you may have a choice of whether to sit at a window seat or next to your best friend. If you really wish to pay attention to the teacher, you may avoid both your friend and the window. You may choose to sit close to the front of the room. In many settings you can choose to pay attention to distractions, or you can choose to avoid or ignore them. Believe it or not, you can even choose to ignore the train whistle, the crawling spider, the noise in the hall. Good listeners do!

4. *Listen for the new and unusual idea.* What makes you pay special attention to a speaker? Something that forces you to take notice. It may be a funny story or it may be the way your name is said. Any change will tell you, "Pay attention!"

   Good speakers change the pace. They may switch from facts to stories, put up a chart, or tell a joke. Even in everyday conversation, change will force you to take notice. If your friend normally calls you "Katie," but suddenly you hear her call loudly, "Katherine!" you will pay closer attention. If your friend changes to a higher voice or a funny accent to tell a story, it will grab your attention and make you listen. As a listener you will remember the unique and creative.

5. *Listen for repetition.* If information is repeated several times, you are more likely to remember it than if you

hear it only once. From conversations to formal speeches, repetitions send the signal "Important!" Many famous speeches use repetition. Martin Luther King, Jr., used repetition in his famous "I Have a Dream" speech.

So let freedom ring from the prodigious hilltops of New Hampshire.
Let freedom ring from the mighty mountains of New York.
Let freedom ring from the heightening Alleghenies of Pennsylvania.
Let freedom ring from the curvaceous slopes of California.
Let freedom ring from Stone Mountain of Georgia.
Let freedom ring from Lookout Mountain of Tennessee.
Let freedom ring from every hill and molehill of Mississippi, from every mountainside, let freedom ring.

You use repetition in everyday life as well. If someone making cookies says, "When making gingerbread cookies use light molasses. Remember, *light* molasses," you are more likely to remember the correct kind. If it is important for a sweater to be washed in cold water, repeating that fact draws attention to it.

Good listeners create opportunities for repetition. They may prompt the speaker to repeat by asking, "Where did you say I turn for the hobby shop?" They may even say, "Tell me that again" or "Would you mind repeating the directions?" Hearing information more than once helps fix it in your mind. Ask for repetition if you need it.

6. *Get prepared.* People have something on their minds at all times. Many good listeners make a deliberate effort to clear their minds so they can concentrate on a conversation. For example, you may have to stop thinking about your English test in order to be able to listen to your friend's description of a fight with her sister. If you can't clear your mind, you will either miss important information or keep asking questions such as, "What did you just say?"

When you are about to listen in a formal situation, such as a class or a speech, you can prepare by arriving on time, sitting where you can see and hear the speaker easily, and getting your notebook ready ahead of time.

7. *Respond to the speaker.* Nothing is worse than talking to someone and getting no reply. It makes the speaker feel invisible. Good listeners find a way to show the speaker that they received the message. It may be in the form of a nod of the head, a laugh, or a comment. Perhaps a listener will respond by doing what the speaker requested, such as taking out the garbage or voting for a certain candidate. The journal entry praises a student's brother for responding.

JOURNAL ENTRY

I find it easier to talk to my older brother because he listens and doesn't say anything until I ask him a question. I can talk or ask him anything, and he will give me an answer if he knows it. If he doesn't know the answer, he finds one and then tells me.

8. *Apply the ideas to yourself.* As a listener you should try to answer the question, "How does it relate to my life?" If you can apply information to yourself, you are more likely to remember and use it. Usually *you* have to do the work of connecting the information to yourself. If the speaker is discussing jewelry making, you may think, "I could make something like that for birthday presents." A speaker discussing training for cross-country runners may provide you with information you could use on a diet.

Apply

How might you find a way to apply three of the following topics to your life?

Raising dogs for fun and profit
How music videos are made
Gangs in our high schools

Why do people get divorced?
Quilting in pioneer days
Brothers: how to cope with them

It's not always easy to find the connection, but any idea you can apply to your own life will make it easier for you to listen to that topic.

9. *Listen for structure.* Most speeches follow a structure or order somewhat like a road map; for example, "First point, second point, third point, fourth point." The structuring and ordering of information keeps the listener from getting lost. The structure helps good listeners look for clues that indicate where the speaker is. A listener may say, "That's the end of that story" or "Now she's heading for the punch line." If you listen for the speaker's clues, you can follow what is said more easily.

10. *Review and preview the points.* Careful listeners review in their minds the points a speaker has made. For example, you might think, "Roberto has talked about the history of Alaska and the geography of Alaska. Now he seems to be getting into the major industry there." This kind of thinking keeps you in touch with what was said and what is to come. In some cases a speaker will tell what the next points will be.

Listeners have one advantage over speakers. This advantage allows them to be active while listening. It is called *thought speed*. Most people can speak at a rate of 120 to 180 words per minute. Yet people can listen at a rate of up to 400 words per minute. That's a big difference! Thought speed refers to the extra time listeners gain because they can process words faster than speakers can produce them. The good listener uses the extra time to practice the listening guidelines that are appropriate. Better listening is a very important part of better communication.

GUIDELINES FOR GOOD LISTENING

1. Watch for nonverbal clues.
2. Try to see things from the speaker's point of view.
3. Avoid distractions.
4. Listen for the new and unusual.
5. Listen for repetition.
6. Get prepared.
7. Respond to the speaker.
8. Apply the ideas to yourself.
9. Listen for structure.
10. Review and preview points.

SUMMARY

This chapter covers vocal production and listening. Vocal production involves breath and sound, resonance, and articulation. Skillful communicators learn how to use their voices properly and carefully. Listening involves a four-step process: (1) receiving, (2) interpreting, (3) evaluating, and (4) responding. There are four types of listening: informative, empathic, critical, and creative. Good listeners avoid the three barriers to listening (external, speaker, and self-barriers) and use the guidelines for good listening.

CHAPTER REVIEW

THINK ABOUT IT

1. What are the three elements of vocal production?
2. Describe the proper way to breathe.
3. What are the four steps in the listening process? Give an example of how one message goes through these steps.
4. Describe the four types of listening and their importance.
5. Describe the three barriers to listening. Give examples of each.

TRY IT OUT

1. Role-play examples of barriers to listening. Try to act out these situations and others:
   - A teenager who has distracting habits tries to talk to some friends.
   - Two students are talking about what a good time they each had at the dance, but neither is responding to what the other is saying.
   - A young person is talking about music videos to an older relative.
2. Say each of the following sentences aloud and change the meaning by emphasizing different words.
   - I thought not. (surprise)
     I thought not. (agreement)
     I thought not. (sarcastic)
   - Did you get a B in English? (Thought you'd get a D.)
     Did you get a B in English? (Thought it was math.)
     Did you get a B in English? (Thought you'd get an A.)
3. Listen to conversations on television or radio or in public places. Record examples of five articulation errors you hear. Also find two or three variations in pronunciation that occur because the speakers are from different parts of the country.

PUT IT IN WRITING

1. Think about the different places in which you need good communication skills in your own life (home, school, work, sports events, clubs, church). Choose one of these places, and think back to when good listening was an important part of your activity there. Describe one time when the listening was effective and one time when it was not. Also, describe why good listening did or did not take place.
2. Keep a listening log for twelve hours. Keep track of how much time you spend listening to TV, radio, your parents, your friends, and your teachers. Then write one paragraph for each of the following questions.
   - How much of what you heard in those hours can you actually remember?
   - What did you really listen to?
   - Why did you listen to these things and not to others?
   - How might you listen better, so you can remember more of what you hear?

SPEAK ABOUT IT

1. Describe to your classmates an incident in which a barrier to listening caused problems for you.
2. In small groups, take turns presenting short speeches that present instructions. The listeners should be able to follow the instructions as they are being presented. (Example: how to do a dance step.) At the end of each speech, check how closely the directions were followed. Also analyze who was responsible for the successes and failures—the speaker, the listener, or both?

CHAPTER

4

THE COMPETENT COMMUNICATOR

KEY WORDS

communication acts

competent communicator

communication strategies

rituals

competency steps

visualize

After completing this chapter, you should be able to

- define *competent communicator*.
- describe the five communication acts.
- provide examples of speaking and listening for each of the five communication acts.
- explain the four competency steps and describe how a competent communicator uses each of them.

Almost everyone can talk and hear, but good communication takes effort. People who communicate well are called **competent communicators**. The word *competent* means "well qualified and capable." Competent communicators have knowledge and skills in the area of communication. You recognize these people because they always seem to know what to say or do in any situation. They also know how to improve their knowledge and communication skills.

Competent communicators do not have a secret formula. Rather, they do two things: they develop a number of ways to deal with new communication situations, and they follow certain steps in order to reach their communication goals.

Apply

If someone asked you "What are the reasons you communicate?" which of these reasons would you give?

- to get information I need
- to tell someone something
- to find out how to do something
- to learn things I didn't know before
- to persuade someone to do, or believe, something
- to show someone I care about him or her
- to make up my mind on a debatable subject
- to enjoy myself by talking with others
- to test new ideas

All of the above statements express good reasons for listening or speaking to other people. They are communication acts.

COMMUNICATION ACTS

There are five **communication acts**. They describe the major reasons for communicating. The five acts are (1) sharing information, (2) discussing feelings, (3) managing persuasion, (4) following social rituals, and (5) using imagination.

These communication acts involve you as a speaker and as a listener. For example, as a speaker you may act as a persuader, and as a listener you may try to analyze another person's persuasive message directed at you. Competent communicators are skilled in using all the communication acts. In this section of the chapter, you will look more carefully at each one.

SHARING INFORMATION

As you know, an important part of communication is sending and receiving information. Many people take this communication act for granted. Then they find themselves with problems at home, at their jobs, or in school, because they did not present their information well or listen for information carefully. They may mix up the steps or omit important information when giving directions for things like making chili or describing the location of a movie theater. Perhaps they do not ask the right questions to find out what they need to know.

Often speakers assume, "I told you. Therefore you should understand." Yet, if the speaker is unorganized in presenting information, the listener cannot get the right message. Competent communicators organize their information very carefully to help their listeners get the main points.

In so many areas of your life, you need to share information. Incorrect or unclear information can result in frustration or serious confusion. You know how frustrating it is to get the wrong order in a restaurant or to wait outside the wrong store for a friend.

You probably experience many little communication breakdowns each week because of careless speaking or listening. Communicating to share information serves as the basis for all speaking and listening. Unless you send a message accurately, you cannot get your point across and you cannot truly understand another person's ideas.

Apply

Read the following short examples in which the same ideas are presented in two different ways.

Imagine that you are a student in a first-aid course. Someone is explaining how to help a choking victim by using the Heimlich maneuver. Decide which explanation you would prefer to follow if you had to save a life.

A

If you have a friend who is choking, you can help him. You have to get behind him and put your arm around him. It doesn't matter if you are taller or shorter than he is. Then make a fist and push the fist inward under the ribs. Oh, use the fist thumb side in, and be sure to push upward also. Keep doing this until he stops choking.

B

If you have a friend who is choking, you can help the person by following some simple steps. I will now describe what to do if the victim is standing up. First, get behind the victim and place your arm around the victim's waist. Second, make a fist with that hand and place it, thumb side in, below the bottom of the victim's ribs and just above the navel. Third, grasp your fist with your other hand and press inward with a quick upward motion. Fourth, keep repeating this movement several times until the object comes out of the victim's mouth.

Although both explanations contain similar information, explanation B is clearer. It presents the information in steps and includes all important information, such as the victim should be standing. Explanation A is unclear, unorganized, and omits important information.

INTERACT

Prepare a set of directions telling how to do a task, how to get to a certain location, or how to prepare something. Some examples are the following: how to perform a dance step, how to get downtown, and how to make a peanut butter sandwich. Present the directions to the class. Check how well your classmates listened to the directions by asking them to repeat what you said. Note any similar problems people had and try to see if the problem lies with the directions you gave.

DISCUSSING FEELINGS

Discussing feelings involves personal effort and risk for both speaker and listener. Talking about feelings requires you to reveal information about yourself. When you share your feelings with a friend, you might gain a stronger friendship, or your friend might try to change the subject or avoid you. Often people become uncomfortable and do not know how to respond when a conversation moves into a discussion of feelings. Yet sometimes a person who is talking about his or her feelings just needs someone to listen.

Most people are not used to saying "I feel...." They may have learned to talk about ideas and to keep feelings to themselves. Even many adults cannot communicate that they are proud, happy, sad, angry, or disappointed because they have learned to control their emotions and cannot talk about them. When asked "How do you feel about the accident?" a person might answer, "I think it is terrible" or "I feel that we need to take a tougher stand on drinking and driving." These are not really statements of feeling, since a feeling has not been expressed. A person who is comfortable talking about feelings might say, "I feel angry" or "I feel sad."

The following journal entry shows how hard it is to communicate feelings when a person does not try to respond.

JOURNAL ENTRY

When I feel that I have hurt my dad's feelings and I want to say I'm sorry, he just sits there in silence. He won't tell me what he's feeling. That gets me mad and by this time I don't care if he is hurt anymore.

Apply

Complete the following sentences for yourself and see how easily you can connect a feeling with an event.

I feel excited when....
I feel happy when....
I feel embarrassed when....
I feel frustrated when....
I feel angry when....
I feel scared when....
I feel disappointed when....
I feel jealous when....
I feel silly when....

Think about how you respond when someone else talks about feeling happy, sad, angry, or frightened. Do you let the person talk, or do you try to change the topic? Some listeners who get uncomfortable say, "Oh, you don't really feel that way" or "You shouldn't feel like that." These kinds of responses do not allow the speaker to talk freely. Other listeners take over the conversation by immediately responding with their own feelings instead of letting the other person speak. Competent communicators are able to talk about their feelings and to listen to other people's feelings.

MANAGING PERSUASION

In our society it is not enough to exchange information or to share feelings. You must be able to manage persuasive messages. These are times when you need to listen carefully to the persuasive messages you receive. There are times when you need to persuade others. One student listed the following as examples of her own use of persuasion:

I try to persuade my

- brother or sister to drive me places.
- friends to go to a certain movie.
- teacher to let me turn a paper in late.
- best friend to visit my dad and stepmother with me.
- uncle to take us camping.
- coach to let me go to Saturday's meet.
- parents to increase my allowance.
- brother to go bicycle riding with me.

Persuasive messages are a part of everyday life. You need to be able to present information persuasively, to argue, and to come to agreement with other people. You may wish to change another person's beliefs or actions. For example, you may want

to talk a friend into quitting smoking or persuade him or her not to shoplift or skip school anymore. You also need to evaluate persuasive messages, such as deciding whether to loan a friend your favorite tape.

To become a competent communicator, it is very important to analyze persuasive messages directed at you so that you can make careful judgments about how to respond. You may need to question or argue with the speaker. Analyzing the message requires thinking about it, sorting out points, and looking for both good ideas and problems. The competent communicator understands the power of persuasive messages.

OBSERVE

Think of five kinds of persuasive situations that you have observed or experienced in the last week. Did a fast-food salesperson try to persuade you to buy one more item? Did your sister offer to do your homework for a week if you would lend her your tapes for her party? Were you persuaded to buy a product or make a decision? Why or why not? Discuss your situations in class. How might a competent communicator act in these situations?

FOLLOWING SOCIAL RITUALS

Each culture or society has its own social **rituals**, or information rules, for interaction. There are rituals for greetings, for saying good-bye, for small talk, and for telling secrets. There are also rules for talking. For example, in a conversation you should not do all of the talking or stand very close to the other person. Neither should you talk or listen with your eyes closed. You should look at the person with whom you are communicating.

There are many informal rituals people follow every day. Your mother may have a certain way of waking you up. You and a friend may have a secret handshake or code words you use to communicate secretly. If you play a team sport, you and your team members may use rituals to get each other mentally prepared for a game.

Some rituals for communicating apply to certain settings. In a classroom, students usually raise their hands when they wish to talk. One student does not answer all the questions. The teacher usually talks to start and to end the class. Very personal information is discussed with the teacher in a one-to-one situation. These are only a few of the classroom rituals. You can probably list many others.

In a store, customers can ask questions about a product but not personal questions of the salesperson. It is unacceptable for salespeople to shout at or express anger to customers. Both customers and salespeople are expected to say "Thank you" when the sale is completed.

Although most people learn their society's rituals at home and in school, some people never do learn them. When a person acts differently from the rest of the group, other people may make fun of him or her. Often the student who stands too close to others, shouts out in class, or discusses very personal information in public gets teased or avoided. If that person really understood the unspoken social rules, he or she might choose to stop breaking them.

Apply

Think about the following communication rituals and decide how you would explain them to a person unfamiliar with them.

- introducing a stranger
- asking to talk in class
- ending a friendly conversation
- telephoning to talk to a friend
- asking for the time of day
- bidding in an auction
- asking someone to dance
- leaving a friend's party

Formal social rituals in a society are highly predictable. They are repeated over and over again in the same way. When you recite the Pledge of Allegiance or when you recite familiar prayers during a religious service, you are taking part in a formal social ritual. Groups that use parliamentary procedure to run their meetings are participating in a formal social ritual. What other formal social rituals can you think of?

Each culture has different social rituals. Americans tend to expect listeners to maintain eye contact or look at them most of the time. They also expect listeners to respond by nodding, smiling, frowning, or in similar ways. These signals show that the listener is thinking about what is being said. In other cultures, good listeners do not look at the speaker's eyes; instead, they look down as a sign of respect. Their faces may not show much emotion because it is not expected. In some cultures people stand almost nose to nose when conversing. People who use the social rituals they learned in one culture may find the rituals are unacceptable in another culture.

In every society, persons are expected to act in certain ways and to avoid other actions. Competent communicators understand the social rituals and usually follow them. If they do not follow a ritual, it is because they choose to be different. Competent communicators are alert to new rituals and know when to follow them. Although engaging in social rituals may not be the most critical area of speaking or listening, the person who is effective in social rituals may develop relationships that lead to more important conversations.

OBSERVE

Choose a social ritual and observe some people engaging in it. Predict ahead of time the communication you expect to see. After watching the ritual, describe in detail two or three examples of predictable communication. Also, describe any communication you found surprising or inappropriate.

Making and Acknowledging Introductions

Social rituals involve making formal introductions. Many people avoid this ritual because they are afraid they do not know the correct way to introduce someone. If you remember some simple rules when introducing someone, then you can use these rules for all introductions.

Remember to speak clearly and courteously. If you have an interesting remark about the person you are introducing, include that in the formal introduction.

The key to making formal introductions is to remember age, sex, and rank.

Rule 1: Always mention the name of the oldest person first, then the name of the person you are introducing. Then introduce the youngest person to the oldest.

Example: "Mrs. Van Schoick, this is my sister, Natalie. Natalie, this is my algebra teacher, Mrs. Van Schoick."

You could then add: "Mrs. Van Schoick is the sponsor of the math club. Natalie will be in your class next year and hopes to be in the math club. She has always enjoyed math."

Rule 2: Mention the name of a woman or girl first.

Example: "Mrs. Dahm, I'd like you to meet my dad, Edward McKinney. Dad, this is my English teacher, Mrs. Dahm."

or: "Katy, I'd like you to meet my brother, Thomas Gordon. Thomas, this is my good friend, Katy Gavin."

Rule 3: Mention the name of the person who has a higher rank or position of authority first.

Example: "Mrs. Jan DiCarlo, may I present Mrs. Mae Knight, our new historian? Mrs. Knight, this is our PTA president, Mrs. Jan DiCarlo."

Formal introductions should be handled with courtesy and politeness. Older people should be addressed by their title, and not by their first name. Generally, it is customary for men to extend the right hand to shake hands. Women may or may not shake hands.

Introductions can be awkward, but with confidence and a friendly attitude you can master this social ritual.

Making and Receiving Telephone Calls

One ritual that is important in our interpersonal skills is making and receiving telephone calls. Many times, people do not know the person to whom they are talking on the phone. Therefore, impressions depend entirely upon the voice and manners of the person speaking.

There are several key things you should remember for courteous and effective phone conversation.

Making Calls

1. Call at a convenient time. Try to avoid mealtimes and late-night calls.

2. Identify yourself to the person who answers the phone, and then ask for the person you are calling.
    Example: "Hello, Mrs. Wilkinson, this is Jamie Hall. May I speak to Kara?"

3. Keep the conversation short and try to get to the reason for calling. If it is a social call, chat for a brief time and then end the conversation. Remember that there are others who may need to use the phone.

4. If details are given, you may wish to repeat these details or have the receiver recite the information back to you to make sure all information is clearly understood.

5. End the conversation. Remember, if you made the call, it is generally up to you to end the call.

Receiving Calls

1. When receiving a call, answer quickly and pleasantly. "Hello" is a pleasant way to answer the phone. "Yes," "What," and "Yeah" are generally considered poor manners.

2. Listen attentively and avoid interrupting or being impatient. If you cannot talk at that time, ask the caller if you can return the call at a later time. Example: "I am sorry, we just sat down for dinner, may I call you back in a half hour?"

3. Speak clearly, and with verbal responses such as "yes," "no," or "I understand." Grunts or phrases such as "uh-huh" are considered impolite.

4. If the caller wants to speak to someone who is either not home or is unable to come to the phone, ask the caller if he or she would like to call back or leave a message. It is discourteous to say "Who is this?" or "What do you want?" It is courteous to say "May I take a message or say who called?"

5. Thank the person for calling.

Business Calls

If you have to make a business call or formal call, you need to make a good impression. Keep the conversation short, to the point, and courteous.

1. Identify yourself and state your business.
2. Have all information at hand so that you may refer to your notes if needed.
3. Be brief and polite.
4. If you have a complaint, be specific with your facts and reasons. Do not be impatient or irritable. If you do not receive satisfaction, ask to speak to a supervisor and then begin again.
5. End with a thank you or some statement of appreciation of the person's time.

Remember, telephone conversations are important to communication. Be polite, brief, and smart.

USING IMAGINATION

A very important area of communication involves using your imagination. One way of creating through imagination is through dramatic situations. Older brothers and sisters may tell stories to a toddler. Actors and actresses create roles in plays by using their imaginations. When you role-play in a historical debate, you are creating an imaginary situation. The person who retells a scary situation communicates the fear to the listeners. You have probably entertained your friends by telling tales of your family vacation. Or you may have entertained your family by telling stories about funny events in school. You may also have read poetry at a school assembly or recited the words of a famous speaker in a camp program.

As a listener you often enjoy speakers using their imaginations. Examples might include your father telling his corny old jokes, your grandmother telling her stories of the Old Country, or your friends playing verbal games. The actors performing in your favorite TV show, friends reciting their own poetry, or the community theater putting on a production are other examples of people using imagination. Although you need the same skills for any other listening situation, you may be more relaxed if you are listening for enjoyment.

Apply

When do you find yourself in situations involving dramatic imagination? Do you enjoy telling jokes or stories? Do you like to do magic or watch TV comedians? Add to the list of examples that follow.

- doing puppet shows
- reading a story to children
- joking with friends
- talking about a TV show
- reading for the blind
- describing a rock concert
- explaining why homework is late
- rapping

Imaginative communication occurs in many other situations besides storytelling or drama. When you and a friend are working together to solve a problem, creative communication occurs. You may suggest one idea, and your friend may use your idea to create a second, which then leads to a third idea. Actually you may be feeding each other's imaginations. When you make predictions, you are using your imagination too. You can make predictions about transportation in the year 2020, or about what clothes will be like in the future. Good listeners like to hear how other people put ideas together. It stimulates their thinking.

Imagination allows you to entertain, to create new worlds, to predict. It is a special part of your communication abilities. Competent communicators value their own imaginative ability and that of other persons.

INTERACT

In a group of four or five classmates, pick one of the five communication acts. Then make up a situation that involves this communication act and role-play the situation for the class. Ask the audience to identify your communication act.

COMPETENCY STEPS

Competent communicators work to gain knowledge and skills to become effective at communicating. They grow in competence through meeting other people, dealing with new situations, and watching others talk. Over time, they develop plans of action for dealing with various situations. Competent communicators follow four specific **competency steps**:

1. Thinking of strategies
2. Selecting a strategy
3. Acting on the strategy
4. Evaluating the strategy's effect

THINKING OF STRATEGIES

A competent communicator has various communication strategies that can be applied to one situation. **Communication strategies** are the verbal and nonverbal messages created to reach a specific goal.

The older you get the more ways you have to cope with communication difficulties. Each year you have learned new strategies for handling certain events or problems. For example, when you were a three-year-old and your parent told you it was bedtime, what did you do? You may have cried, begged for a nighttime story, or asked for a drink of water. By the time you were ten, you had added more strategies. You may have reasoned with your parents, "I don't have to get up early tomorrow." You may have compared yourself to your friend, saying "J.P. doesn't even have a regular bedtime." You may even have tried persuasive strategies, "I have to study my spelling. You don't want me to flunk, do you?"

By now you have developed even more strategies, although you probably don't disagree about bedtime as frequently. Your strategies now probably involve curfew.

Apply

To gain a later curfew, which of the following strategies have you used?

1. I plead for an extra half hour.
2. I inform my parent(s) I'm too old for this type of curfew.
3. I explain that my friend's parents do not give her or him a curfew.
4. I try to convince my parent(s) that this is a very special occasion.
5. I volunteer to help around the house tomorrow.
6. I promise I will never ask for a curfew change again.
7. I threaten to go live with my best friend's family.
8. I remind my parent(s) how responsible I have been in the past.
9. I stop speaking to my parent(s).
10. I slam doors and sulk around the house.

Did the strategies you used leave both you and your parent(s) satisfied?

Strategies do not apply just to your relationships with adults. You can be a more effective communicator with your

friends if you have a number of different ways of handling difficult situations. For example, if you have a friend who gets laughs by making fun of you, how could you handle it? You could ignore the situation and hope it will go away. What else could you do if that doesn't work? You might try the silent treatment, but your friend might not understand your silence. You might say, "Quit making fun of me in front of other people. I don't think it's funny." Or you might say, "It hurts my feelings when you make fun of me. I wish you would stop it." You might consider threatening a loss of your friendship: "If you don't stop making fun of me I'm going to stop being your friend." Finally, you might consider how to tease your friend back and hope that this will solve the problem.

The competent communicator thinks up a number of possible ways to deal with a situation. The greater the number of strategies, the more choice there is in dealing with a problem.

SELECTING A STRATEGY

Once you have thought of a few ways to handle a problem, consider the specifics of *that* situation. Think about the who, what, where, and when:

- *Who*—When considering "who," you need to think about what you know about the person. You also need to think about your past relationship and possible future relationship with this person.

- *What*—When considering "what," you need to think about the importance of the topic to you and to the other person.
- *Where*—When considering "where," you need to think about how the place or other people will affect your discussion of the topic.
- *When*—When considering "when," you need to think about whether this is a good time to discuss the topic.

All these add up to how you act or use the best strategy for a person, topic, place, and time.

Now look at how these factors might affect a curfew discussion between you and your mother after you have moved to a new city. The situation is that you want to come home one hour later from a trip to the amusement park.

The "who" is your mother. You know the following about her: She often gives you rules similar to those of your friends; she is not acquainted with many adults in this neighborhood; she can be flexible about curfew for special occasions.

The "what" is a trip to the amusement park. It's not a once-in-a-lifetime experience, but it's not an everyday event either.

The "where" and "when" are not fixed, and you have control over them. For example, you might be able to talk about them in the car on a weekend or in the kitchen after dinner. You would also consider whether you want to be alone with your mother or in a group of your friends. You may consider when your mother is likely to be tired or cheerful.

Now that you have thought about the who, what, where, and when, you are ready to make a move. Because your mother likes to know what other parents do, you might make the comparison. "Jarella's and Sally's parents let them stay out an hour later than I'm allowed." Because you know she can be flexible about special events you could call this a special trip. You might consider briefly telling her that you will move in with a friend's family if she doesn't let you do what you want. But you then may decide that your mother will find this funny rather than realistic. Of course, you could promise never to ask for a curfew change again, but that may also be unrealistic.

You may decide "where" should be the car and "when" should be a time you are alone together and your mother is cheerful.

INTERACT

Examine the following situations and think of the who, what, when, and where that would affect the communication strategies you choose to use. Share these in a group of four.

Situations:

1. (Walking home after school)
   Responding to a stranger who wants you to search for a lost dog

2. (In the hall between classes)
   Asking a friend to lend you five dollars

3. (At the dinner table)
   Asking your parents if you can go to a rock concert

4. (In school cafeteria line)
   Finding out why a friend has not talked to you for a week

5. (As bell rings for class)
   Explaining to a teacher why your homework is late

Remember that after you consider the circumstances—the people involved, the topic, and any other important facts—you will select a strategy for those you thought about.

ACTING ON THE STRATEGY

Do you ever know exactly what you should say or do but then you never go ahead and really say or do it? Most people find they do not carry out all their plans. They may think of some good strategies and even select the one they consider the best. And then they stop.

Selecting the strategy doesn't do much good until you act on it. It is one thing to plan to tell a friend that he or she hurt your feelings and another to actually say, "You hurt my feelings" or "I want you to stop teasing me."

Apply

How often have you planned to do some of the following but never carried through with the behavior?

- volunteer in class
- ask a salesclerk for more information
- tell your mother or father how wonderful she or he is
- compliment a friend for something well done
- thank a teacher for help
- apologize for talking badly about someone

Competent communicators learn to follow through with their plans.

PREPARING TO BE A COMPETENT COMMUNICATOR

This simple three-step skill called Peer Pressure Reversal* will get you out of tough situations and still let you be part of your peer group.

1. *Check out the scene.* Checking out the scene involves two steps. First, look and listen for anything unusual or strange in the way your friends are talking or behaving. Are they in an off-limits place, or are they trying to bribe you into doing something wrong? Second, ask yourself: "Is this trouble?" If the situation would break a law or get someone in charge mad, you are facing a trouble situation.

2. *Make a good decision.* To make a good decision, you need to think about two things. First, weigh both sides. Your friends will tell you about the positive consequences: you must rely on yourself to consider the negative consequences. The risks involved are usually not worth it. Second, you must make a firm decision so that the pressure won't cause you to act weak. If you take a risk, be prepared to accept the consequences. If you decide against the trouble, you might just convince your friends not to take the risk either.

3. *Act to avoid trouble.* There are many ways to refuse a friend's suggestion including saying no politely and firmly, leaving, or giving a true excuse. You can suggest a better idea and walk toward it and your friend will often follow you! Some people can say "No" in joking ways, such as "I wish I could, but it's my night to walk the goldfish." And if a friend dares you, learn to return the challenge, "Are you scared to do it by yourself?"

When using Peer Pressure Reversal, remember to stay in control, look the person right in the eyes when talking to him or her, and get out of the trouble in 30 seconds or less.

*Scott, Sharon. *Peer Pressure Reversal, How to Say No and Keep Your Friends.* Amherst, MA: Human Resource Development, 1986.

Many Olympic champions report they **visualize**, or picture in their minds, every single move before actually performing. Swimmers see every stroke in their minds and imagine a perfect, winning race. Basketball players visualize perfect foul shots, experiencing each muscle movement in their minds. Just as athletes use visualization to practice before competitions, competent communicators often rehearse in their minds what they will say. For example, you can rehearse what you will say to someone else and try to imagine how the other person will respond. Many fine public speakers visualize delivering their whole speech, over and over again, imagining each word and gesture. Visualization is a kind of mental rehearsal.

Active rehearsal occurs when you role-play a situation or practice a speech out loud. You and a friend may practice ways to apologize for forgetting to invite a friend to a party. You may practice your sales pitch for selling candy bars to raise money for the school trip. The speaker who practices the persuasive speech out loud is rehearsing. But until the speaker talks to the audience, it is all planning. You must take the final step and act on the plans. Until you talk to your mother about curfew or apologize to your friend, it's all imagination and rehearsal. Remember that nothing will happen unless you act on the strategy.

 OBSERVE

Record two experiences of hearing people discuss what they should have said or done. Very often people will say, "I should have told him no," or "I wish I had asked about the price."

Describe two situations in which you or a friend knew what strategy to select but didn't act on it. Describe what kept you or your friend from acting on the strategy.

EVALUATING THE STRATEGY'S EFFECT

Now that you have carried out a strategy, can you relax? The answer is no. The final step is to make a judgment—to decide whether the strategy worked well. Basically you have to reach a conclusion. You can think in terms of the following: the effect on you, the effect on others, the result, and the conclusion.

Even though you do not evaluate every word or action, you need to evaluate important communication events. For example, if you had three different strategies for an apology and chose one, did both you and the person you apologized to feel good when you were done? Or, if you chose a joke to introduce your speech, did the class find it funny? When you communicate in important situations, you need to look at the effects and the results. Then you can decide if you would repeat the strategy in a similar situation or if you would do something else the next time.

You need to consider your beliefs about right and wrong when choosing, using, and evaluating a strategy. A competent communicator does not hurt another person on purpose.

SUMMARY

This chapter discussed the competent communicator, a person with knowledge and skills who communicates well. Competent communicators can use their knowledge and skills to (1) share information, (2) discuss feelings, (3) manage persuasion, (4) follow social rituals, and (5) use imagination. To use these communication acts well, competent communicators follow four steps: (1) thinking of strategies, (2) selecting a strategy, (3) acting on the strategy, and (4) evaluating the strategy's effect.

CHAPTER REVIEW

THINK ABOUT IT

1. What is a competent communicator?
2. Define and describe the five communication acts.
3. What are the four competency steps used by competent communicators? Give one- to two-sentence descriptions of each step.
4. When selecting a strategy, what four specifics of the situation do you need to take into consideration? Write a sentence or two explaining each.

TRY IT OUT

1. To help you enhance the imagining function of communication, picture yourself in the following situations and answer the questions.

   - You are walking through the woods on a spring day. The sun is shining. What do you see and feel?

   - You have done poorly on an exam. Your teacher asks to see you. You open the door to the classroom and walk in. The teacher is sitting at the desk. What happens next? Describe the classroom. How hot is the room? Where do you sit? What does the teacher say? What do you say? How do you feel?

   - Your best friend returns home after living in another community for three months. As soon as you see each other, what do you say? How do you feel? How do you act?

2. Interview a classmate about how he or she handled a problem communication situation. Ask that person to describe what he or she did at each of the competency stages. Then have your classmate interview you while describing a problem communication situation.

3. Describe two communication rituals you observe as part of your daily life. Describe the setting and the words people speak or the nonverbal messages they send. For example, you could describe how people greet the bus driver each morning; how you say good-bye to your best friends on the phone; how your club meeting starts each week.

PUT IT IN WRITING

1. Giving or getting information is an important communication act. Using the questions below, interview your grandparent or an older member of your community. Write two or three paragraphs describing what you learned from the interview.
   - What was the world like when you were growing up? For example, how much did a candy bar cost? What did teenagers do for fun? What were the rules your parents set? What was school like? What world events were occurring? Who was president of the United States?
   - If you could live your life over, what would you change? Why?
2. Describe a situation in which you had to persuade a friend to do something, such as lend you tapes or money. Then write a sample dialogue in which you act as a competent communicator and are persuasive.

SPEAK ABOUT IT

1. Using the information you gained from interviewing your grandparent or an older member of the community, present a short speech to your class in which you share the most interesting piece of information you gained.
2. Go to the library and find information about rituals of other countries. Choose a ritual and describe it to your class. For example, in China "face" is of vital importance, and codes of behavior to avoid "losing face" are also important.

PART 2

COMMUNICATION WITH SELF AND OTHERS

CHAPTERS

Communication and Your Self

Communication with Others

COMMUNICATION AND YOUR SELF

KEY WORDS

intellectual side of self

self-concept

self-esteem

physical side of self

social side of self

After completing this chapter, you should be able to

- define *self-concept* and *self-esteem*.
- list the four parts of self-concept.
- describe the physical, social, and intellectual sides of yourself.
- describe how self-concept, self-esteem, and communication skills are related.
- list four of your communication strengths.
- list three areas of communication you need to improve.
- describe ways to improve your self-concept.

I am an old-looking bicycle.
I can do more than people give me credit for.
　　—Frank

I am a knife.
I can be sharp and witty at times.
At other times, I can be
dull and boring.
　　—Richard

I am a chameleon.
I am constantly changing colors. One
minute I'm pastels and very happy;
then the next minute
I'm red and angry.
　　—Debbie

If you were to compare yourself to something, what would it be? What would that comparison say about you?

The way you see yourself affects every part of your world, especially the way you communicate. To help you understand the connection between how you see yourself and your own communication skills, in this chapter you will consider (1) your self-concept; (2) how self-concept, self-esteem, and communication are connected; (3) your communication skills; and (4) ways to improve your self-concept.

SELF-CONCEPT

Almost everyone wishes he or she were different and better. Few people are satisfied with the way they are. Most people think, "If I could only be smarter, thinner, funnier, better looking, or richer, my life would be happier." Most people also want to be better at doing things: "If I could dance more gracefully, talk more easily to new people, score more baskets, have more money, or get more A's, life would be terrific." Often it boils down to "If I could only be like so-and-so, my life would be wonderful."

You are not alone in having these thoughts. Many people look at their lives and ask questions such as

- Who am I anyway?
- Why can't I fit in?
- Why can't I be like so-and-so?
- Why am I the only one who seems to feel like this?

You may have other questions you could add to this list. You spend a great deal of time thinking about yourself and how you fit into your world—your family, school, religious organization, or community. These are important thoughts. They help you decide who you are. These thoughts help form your self-concept.

What is self-concept anyway? Your **self-concept** is your picture of yourself, formed from the beliefs and attitudes you have about yourself. Your self-concept is composed of how you see yourself; how you would like to be; how you think others see you; and how others actually see you.

Silly
Yahoo
Laughing
Venturous
Impartial
Appreciative

Rowdy
Attentive
Mischievous
Outgoing
Sensitive

—**S**ylvia **R**amos

Rough
Outgoing
Gifted
Extraordinary
Ridiculous

Dashing
Amiable
Vivacious
Intricate
Lazy
Artistic

—**R**oger **D**avila

HOW YOU SEE YOURSELF

Although you can use words such as *smart* or *dumb* and *happy* or *sad* as labels for your whole self, they are very general. Most of the time you find yourself saying things like, "I'm good at sports but lousy at math" or "I'm usually cheerful except when my mom and dad fight." Or perhaps you say, "I'm lazy except when I can earn money for working."

As you probably know, you have many different sides. Each affects your answer to the question "How do I see myself?" You may like some parts of yourself better than others. How coordinated are you? How attractive are you? How do you see yourself as a friend? As a son or daughter? Are you a hard worker? What kind of math or English student are you?

If you were to compare thoughts with your friends, it is likely that you'd come up with many similar ideas. You share similar ideas and concerns because you are all living your teenage years. That means a lot of self-exploration is going on. When a group of students was asked what it's like being a teenager, here is what some of them said:

- "Being a teenager is like being David when the whole world is Goliath."
- "Being a teenager is like walking a tightrope without a net."
- "Being a teenager is like jumping into the sea and not knowing how to swim."
- "Being a teenager is like skydiving without a parachute."

Apply

Look at the following list and pick out the sentences that express how you see yourself most of the time.

- I am sad.
- I am lovable.
- I am lazy.
- I am energetic.
- I am clumsy.
- I am honest.

- I am helpful.
- I am smart.
- I am capable.
- I am dumb.
- I am happy.

- I am a mess.
- I am a loser.
- I am not okay.
- I am okay.
- I am attractive.

How satisfied are you with your answers? There are sixteen descriptions, eight positive and eight negative. Did you pick out more positive or more negative statements? What kind of picture do you have of yourself?

OBSERVE

On a separate piece of paper, list six to ten adjectives that you would use to describe yourself. Try not to use the adjectives that appear in the sentences above. Complete the sentence, "I see myself as..."

Sides of Self

Questions regarding how you see yourself are important to answer as you try to understand more and more about yourself. Most of the questions you ask about yourself can be put into three areas related to your physical, social, and intellectual sides.

Physical. The **physical side of self** includes how you look, and how you use your body for physical activities such as playing sports, doing work, or doing creative movement. As you consider your physical self, think about your height, weight, hair color, voice quality, body build, ease of movement, and facial features.

Read the following journal entry and identify the parts of this writer's physical self-concept:

JOURNAL ENTRY

I think that my overall personality is pretty good. I'm usually in a good mood. On first impression, I think I wear pretty nice clothes and look pretty nice. I have been listening to myself while I write this entry and I sure sound stuck up! One thing I don't like about myself is that I wear braces and have freckles and wear glasses. I know how "your looks don't count, it's what's inside that does," but sometimes I don't believe that. After writing this, I have come to the conclusion that I have both bad and good points. After all, no one is perfect!

Intellectual. The **intellectual side of self** includes how you handle ideas, values, and beliefs. Your intellectual side is your thinking self. As you consider your intellectual self, think about such things as school work, honesty, religious beliefs, reading and study habits, and curiosity.

In the following journal entry, a student describes his love for new knowledge, a part of his intellectual self.

JOURNAL ENTRY

I was talking with a friend the other day and he asked me why I like to experiment in model rocketry. Ever since the beginning of time, man has thirsted for knowledge, and some scientists even think that's why man has his appearance, and such a large capacity for his brain. People also ask me why I read so much and so fast. Books open a whole new world and usually give a thought or a question to ponder when you finish.

Social. The **social side of self** involves how you relate to other people. As you consider your social self, think about comfort in large groups, comfort in small groups, concern for other people, popularity, friendship, and people with whom you like to talk.

In this short entry a student writes about a major social problem.

JOURNAL ENTRY

I don't consider myself popular, and right now I'm having lots of trouble finding out who my *real* friends are and where I should be. *Should* I be with the popular group? Right now there are really two popular groups, and I don't know if I want to belong to either of them.

The physical, social, and intellectual parts of one's self are very important to self-concept. In addition to a view of "who I am," everyone also has an idea of "who I would like to be."

HOW YOU WOULD LIKE TO BE

If you are like most people, you have dreams or desires about how you wish to be. You may wish you were a famous person such as Michael Jordan, Bonnie Blair, Hammer, or Paula Abdul. You may even wish you were one of your friends or classmates. Do you dream about being like someone else, famous or not? Who would that person be?

You may wish to reach a goal. What are some goals you have for yourself? You may wish to act differently: "I wish I could be friendlier, smarter, funnier." "I wish I could make Mom's life easier." "I wish I could be more organized and less lazy." "I wish I weren't so sensitive." What things do you hope to be able to do?

Very few people are satisfied with the way they are. Most people think, "If I could only be like so-and-so, my life would be so much better." What's often surprising is that so-and-so also wishes to be like someone else.

Look at the following model and try to think of similar examples that apply to you and your friends.

Ginger wants to be popular and cute like her classmate Mary.

Mary wants to be more intellectual and get better grades in school, like Jose.

Bill wants to be easygoing and carefree like Ginger.

Tom wants to be wealthy and have expensive clothes like Bill.

Jose wants to be athletic and strong like Tom.

Although you may have dreams, goals, or plans for things to be different, it's nice to feel good about who you are now. As you know, each day and each year you become slightly different. Hopefully, you are like the following student who seems quite satisfied with who he is but hopes for a few changes:

JOURNAL ENTRY

If I could be anyone in the world, I would probably want to be me, still. I would just want to have more "in" clothes and be able to play in the band. That would be OK with me. I would never want to be a popular person because they never have any privacy to do what they want to do. I would still like to be myself because I like the way I am.

HOW YOU THINK OTHERS SEE YOU

If you asked your best friend, mother, and math teacher to list four adjectives that describe you, what would each say? Here's what one student expected:

best friend	mother	teacher
worried	popular	friendly
caring	nice-looking	silly
smart	active	average
funny	forgetful	athletic

You will never know exactly how others think of you. Yet most people are affected by what they think other people think of them. How often have you heard someone say, "Oh, so-and-so doesn't like me"; "So-and-so thinks I'm really cool"; "So-and-so acts like I'm dirt"; or "Did you see how so-and-so smiled at me?"

If you think that a certain person is terrific and you hear that he or she likes you, how do you feel? How do you feel about yourself if you discover that this person doesn't like you? Thinking someone likes you can make you feel happy. Thinking someone dislikes you can upset you.

Often people guess about the meaning of the messages others send them. Look at the following journal entry in which the writer does just that.

JOURNAL ENTRY

My biggest fear is people making fun of me. I can't stand being laughed at. I really want people to like me. I guess that's kind of insecure. I don't know. I just can't stand it if a girl refuses to dance with me. I'm sure she doesn't like me.

This student assumes that because a girl refuses to dance with him she does not like him. This is possible, of course, but there are other reasons why a girl may refuse to dance. She may be afraid of being teased or of making her boyfriend angry. She may not know how to dance to the kind of music being played or she may be dizzy and not want to dance at all. If the boy assumes he is being refused because he is not liked, his self-concept may be affected. But it's not always necessary to assume the worst!

HOW OTHERS ACTUALLY SEE YOU

The student who made out a list predicting how others viewed her decided to see if she was right. She actually asked her best friend, her mother, and one of her teachers to list four adjectives describing her. The following are the results of the survey:

best friend	mother	teacher
funny	friendly	studious
caring	sloppy	cheerful
pretty	moody	creative
sincere	nice-looking	polite

Compare this list with the girl's own predictions. (See page 107.) How accurate were her original ideas?

Sometimes you know exactly what others think of you because they have told you. You may have asked for their opinions, or they may have told you voluntarily. Here are two examples of such comments:

My friends have told me I have a bad temper. I've gotten better at controlling myself. When people insult me, hurt me, or cheat on me, I just laugh it off. If it's really bad, I just go home and cry, then forget about it.

One thing that is really getting me down is my ex–best friend. Last year we were the best of friends. The only thing I didn't like about her was she always told me what she didn't like about me. So one day I told her what I was mad at her about. She got real mad and hasn't talked to me since.

In these two cases, people were direct about their thoughts. It wasn't hard for the students to know what these people thought of them.

There are times when you may need to separate comments about yourself from evaluations of your work or ability. For example, getting a bad grade in science does not make you a bad person, nor does having your friends tell you that you have a bad temper. But it may mean that you have to work on your grades or learn to control your temper. Often, one person's ideas about you may be completely different from another's because not everyone will see you the same way. For example:

Juan thinks of himself as being witty and outspoken.
His friends think Juan is humorous and talkative.
The teacher thinks Juan is disruptive.

Your self-concept reflects your picture of yourself. You may decide it is a very positive picture or a very negative picture. This affects your self-esteem.

SELF-ESTEEM

Self-esteem is your opinion of yourself based on your self-concept. Depending on your opinion of yourself, you may have high self-esteem or low self-esteem. You may like the person you think you are, or you may wish that person were different.

For example, if you see yourself as popular and you like being popular, you will feel good about yourself and have high self-esteem. If you don't believe you are popular but want to be, you may have low self-esteem. People who like themselves, that is, who have high self-esteem, feel productive, capable, and likable. Those who have low self-esteem feel worthless, incompetent, and unlikable.

SELF-ESTEEM CHECKLIST

Use this checklist to assess your self-esteem. Which statements *never* apply to you? Which statements *sometimes* or *frequently* apply? Which statements *always* apply?

1. I am comfortable with my appearance.
2. I welcome new experiences.
3. I am satisfied with my ability to make friends.
4. I am able to talk about my feelings with some other person.
5. I can handle helpful criticism.
6. I am willing to stand up for important beliefs.
7. I am willing to learn from my mistakes.
8. I am willing to try new challenges.
9. I can laugh at myself when I do something foolish.
10. I can be proud of a job well done.

COMMUNICATION AND THE SELF

Communication, self-concept, and self-esteem are closely related. Communication affects your self-concept and self-esteem, and your self-concept and self-esteem affect your communication. Look at this statement from both sides.

COMMUNICATION AFFECTS SELF-CONCEPT AND SELF-ESTEEM

From the moment of your birth, people started talking to you and about you. These messages have continued ever since. After many years of receiving messages from other people, you have learned how you think other people see you and how they actually see you. Therefore, much of your self-concept has been built on verbal and nonverbal messages from others. A good self-concept and high self-esteem are created through positive messages; a poor self-concept and low self-esteem are created through negative ones.

Apply

Look at the following comments. Decide which might lead toward a good self-concept and which to a poor one.

- "What a beautiful baby!"
- "He has his father's ears, poor thing."
- "I can always count on you to complete your work on time."
- "Gerry is very irresponsible."
- "She thinks she's so smart!"
- "Where did you get that shirt?"
- "You're on the team? They must take anyone."
- "Try out for the talent show. We need a good pianist."
- "I really missed you when you were sick."

Messages like these tell how others see someone. If most of the messages are negative, the listener might develop low self-esteem. If most are positive, he or she is likely to develop high self-esteem.

Read the following self-description and see how encouraging comments affect the writer of this journal entry:

JOURNAL ENTRY

I am the dew on the grass. People don't notice me much, but I am always there, listening. Sometimes, when I have encouragement from my friends, I shine.

When this young woman feels noticed, she has a positive self-concept and she "shines." She may talk more, smile more, perhaps even argue more. This change leads to the second point.

SELF-CONCEPT AND SELF-ESTEEM AFFECT COMMUNICATION

If your self-concept is positive and your self-esteem is high, how are you likely to communicate differently? What kinds of messages do you send when your self-concept is poor and your self-esteem low?

INTERACT

Look at the following words and phrases. Which do you think describe someone with a good self-concept? Which describe someone with a poor self-concept? Discuss your ideas in a small group.

- gives compliments
- interrupts
- teases
- acts rude
- smiles
- complains
- agrees with everyone
- avoids eye contact
- speaks very softly
- always stops talking when someone interrupts
- apologizes

Communication is so complex that a single behavior cannot be matched with a level of self-esteem. Someone who avoids people, apologizes constantly, and seems uncomfortable sharing ideas may have low self-esteem. If you have a good self-concept, you may risk trying new things, talk more in class, or try to meet new people. You probably have confidence in your ability to do well.

The point is simple. If you believe you are dumb, unattractive, or unfriendly, your poor self-concept and low self-esteem may make you avoid many social situations. If you see yourself as smart, attractive, and friendly, you will be comfortable speaking and listening in different situations.

Usually your self-esteem remains the same over a long period of time. But on some days you do feel better about yourself than on others. You notice those days and people around you do, too.

The link between self-concept and communication is very important. Remember that your communication affects your self-concept and self-esteem, and your self-concept and self-esteem affect your communication.

OBSERVE

Select a person you know well, perhaps a family member or close friend. Describe how you know when this person is feeling "up" or "down." How does this person's communication change as his or her self-esteem changes?

JOHARI WINDOW

One way to consider what you are communicating to others is to use the Johari window. This four-part box diagram, created by Joseph Luft and Harry Ingham, represents the awareness people have of themselves and others. The diagram may be developed in stages.

In the first stage, imagine (1) what you know about yourself and (2) what you are not aware of. For example, you know your personal history, your likes and dislikes, your dreams and fears. But you may not know what a particular person thinks of you. You may not know your scores on certain tests or that your friends describe you as moody and smart.

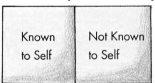

Then imagine a second stage, including (1) things about you that are known to others and (2) things about you that are not known to others. For example, many people may know your nickname, your favorite foods, your interest in animals and computers. No one may know that you worry about your mother's health, or that you would love to be a famous singer.

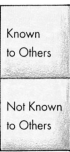

Now, put these stages together into the full Johari window.

THE JOHARI WINDOW

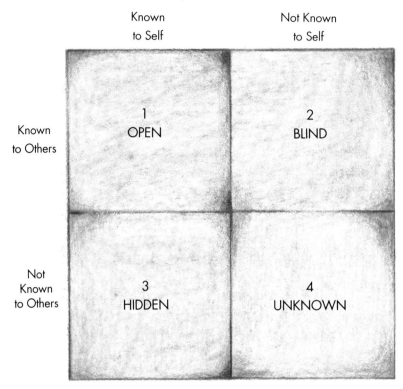

Quadrant 1. The open area refers to behavior and motivation known to an individual and others.

Quadrant 2. The blind area, where others can see things in an individual of which that person is unaware. This is sometimes called the ''bad breath'' area, but it also refers to positive things.

Quadrant 3. The hidden area, which represents things the individual knows but does not reveal to others (for example, a hidden agenda, matters about which the individual has sensitive feelings, or private and very personal information).

Quadrant 4. The unknown area represents what the individual does not know about himself or herself and what others do not know about the individual, at least not yet.

Your Johari window sections change shape depending on the person or pressures to which you are responding.

Look at the Known to Self part of the diagram (quadrants 1 and 3). Look at the windows below and answer the following questions about the people they represent.

- Which person has shared more about himself or herself in a communication situation? A or B?
- If B chose to disclose more information about himself or herself, how would the window change?

A   B

Here are some other windows with the Known to Self and Not Known to Others sections filled in.

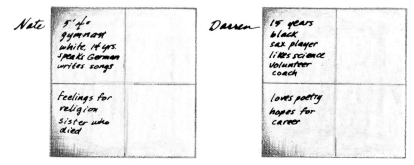

You can think about your window in relationship to people in general or in relationship to certain persons. Your self-esteem affects how much you are likely to share about yourself with others. People who feel good about themselves may share more with others.

How much are you willing to share about yourself? How much do you allow others to probe you about yourself? Take a few minutes to analyze your self-disclosure—how much information you are willing to share with another in order to improve communication. Draw your own Johari window and think about how you share information with others and how others see you.

Think about your self-disclosure behaviors and the things that affect your communication about yourself.

IMPROVING SELF-CONCEPT

One thing in life you can be sure of is change! You will continue to change, as will your friends, family, and other people around you. Some changes you can control; others you cannot. For example, your mother or father could receive a job transfer to another state and your family would have to move. Or you might grow two inches next year and become a better basketball player as a result. These changes are not under your control but they may affect your self-concept. You can make some deliberate changes to improve your self-concept. You may decide to work very hard in math to receive a better grade. You may plan a new haircut and buy new clothes to change your appearance. If a change in self-concept is desired, you may wish to consider the following guidelines:

1. Evaluate yourself honestly.
2. Set realistic goals.
3. Support yourself.
4. Support others.

EVALUATING SELF HONESTLY

Improving self-concept starts with an understanding of the physical, intellectual, and social areas of the self. A realistic understanding involves looking at both personal limitations and strong points.

All people have to learn to live with some limitations. Look at the following lists one student made of her personal limitations and personal strengths:

Limitations

1. I have wispy hair.
2. I have to study hard even to get a passing grade in science.
3. I have a hot temper and get angry quickly.
4. I am shy at parties.
5. I can't afford the kinds of clothes other people have.

Strengths

1. I am loyal to my friends.
2. I find it easy to work with computers.
3. I can draw very well.
4. I listen well to my friends' problems.
5. I can talk easily in front of groups of people.

A realistic evaluation of self is the first step in improving self-concept. Remember these mottos: "Know your limits but don't let them control you" and "Know your assets and value them."

SETTING REALISTIC GOALS

Once a person has a realistic picture of himself or herself then it is possible for that person to decide on one or two things to change. Not *twelve* things, but one or two! Not *fix,* but change. It's important to be realistic.

If Max is five feet, ten inches tall, he cannot be a successful jockey but he can ride horses for fun. If Benita can't carry a tune, she is not likely to get the lead part in the school musical but she can sing with her friends. Setting realistic goals saves unnecessary self-criticism. For example, if you have a bad temper, a goal such as "I will never lose my temper again" would be unrealistic. But a goal such as "When Ravi bothers me again, I will leave the room or change the subject" may be realistic because it is specific. You could do it.

If someone is nervous about giving speeches in class it would be unrealistic to set a goal of never being nervous again. Instead the person may say, "I'll prepare my speeches more carefully and I'll try not to be so nervous."

Read the following example of one student's goal setting:

Limitation:

I have trouble remembering other people's names when I meet them.

Unrealistic Goal:
I will concentrate on names of new people and never forget anyone's name.

Possible Realistic Goals:

I will try to say a person's name out loud when we are introduced to help me remember.

I will try to find a way to connect a new person's name to something else to help me remember it.

INTERACT

With a partner, look at the following unrealistic goals and decide how each could be changed into a possible goal.

- I'll never fight with my brother again.
- I will not be shy anymore.
- I will get 100 percent on all my English tests.
- I'm going to win the next science fair.

SUPPORTING SELF

Did you ever hear the expressions "Don't blow your own horn" or "Don't brag about yourself"? Many people find it difficult to praise themselves. Yet, people need to pat themselves on the back when they do things well. Most people are good at finding all the bad things about themselves but they have to learn to name the good things.

People need to support or praise themselves for making small steps in the right direction. For example, someone might say, "Well I still got angry at Andy, but I didn't swear at him as I would have a few months ago" or "I got three of my foul shots although I missed four. Last year, I could hardly ever make one. I'm getting better." Self-praise takes practice but it's worth learning.

SUPPORTING OTHERS

People who accept themselves also accept others. When people feel good about themselves they are able to be positive and helpful to others. Yet often people don't say the good things they are thinking about others.

Often you think someone is smart, helpful, funny, or good at doing something. You may think "Conrad gave a great speech" or "Cory is such a good artist" or "If I have a problem I can always talk to Jane." But do you ever tell Conrad, Cory, or Jane? People need to be supported when they have done something well or been helpful to another person.

There is an adage that says "We are not another's keeper, but another's maker." Each person has the ability to influence how others see themselves. Each person has the power to help or hurt others. Praising others may help them improve their own self-concepts.

As you work to improve your own self-concept and that of others, remember the words of the Greek writer, Epictetus, "First say to yourself what you wish to be; and then do what you have to do."

SUMMARY

Throughout this chapter you looked at the role of the self in communication. Self-concept is made up of four parts: (1) how you see yourself; (2) how you would like to be; (3) how you think others see you; and (4) how others actually see you. Self-esteem is your opinion of yourself based on your self-concept. Your self-concept and self-esteem affect communication and vice versa. To improve your self-concept, you should follow these four guidelines: (1) evaluate yourself honestly; (2) set realistic goals; (3) support yourself; and (4) support others.

CHAPTER REVIEW

THINK ABOUT IT

1. Describe the difference between self-concept and self-esteem.
2. What are the four parts of self-concept?
3. Give an example of how self-concept and self-esteem affect communication.
4. How can one's self-concept be improved?

TRY IT OUT

1. Make a collage using various words, pictures, and slogans to communicate your communication strengths and weaknesses. Share your collage with a partner. Describe at least one strength and one weakness as represented on your collage.
2. Suppose you were to bury a time capsule about yourself to be opened ten years from now. Make a list of the things that are representative of you at this time. In a few sentences explain what these things would tell about you ten years from now to someone who didn't know you.
3. Write a bumper sticker that describes how you see yourself. Place all the bumper stickers written in your class on one desk and ask someone to read them aloud. Have classmates guess who wrote each one.

PUT IT IN WRITING

1. Write a three-paragraph journal entry describing your physical, social, and intellectual sides.
2. Keep a daily diary for a week. Write about how the following topics affect your self-concept.

- Popularity
- Proud moments
- Parental or teacher conflicts
- Peer pressure
- Fears

3. Complete the sentence, "I am a...." Then write a two- to three-sentence description similar to those on the opening page of this chapter.

SPEAK ABOUT IT

1. Present an impromptu speech in a small group of five to six students. Tell about one of the following:

- My most embarrassing moment was when....
- The happiest day of my life was when....
- My proudest day was when....
- My most valuable possession is....
- My favorite toy as a child was....
- If I could get enough money, I'd....
- My children will never have to....

2. Present to your class one of the incidents you wrote about in number 2 of "Put It in Writing."

CHAPTER 6

COMMUNICATION WITH OTHERS

KEY WORDS

constructive criticism

empathy

first meetings

interpersonal communication

stereotyping

support

After completing this chapter, you should be able to

- define *interpersonal communication*.
- describe the characteristics of friendship.
- describe the stages of friendship and the communication patterns at each stage.
- define the communication building blocks of friendship.

Friendships are like seeds. When nurtured they grow; when neglected they die.

Friends are like rubber bands. If you stretch them too far, they'll snap back at you.

Friends are like crayons. They come in all colors.

Friends are like mirrors. You can see your true self through them.

A competent communicator uses a variety of interpersonal communication skills to build and maintain relationships with others. As you interact with community members, teachers, neighbors, family members, and friends, you develop interpersonal relationships with many different kinds of people. Friends learn how to speak and listen to each other in order to strengthen their relationship. This chapter focuses on using interpersonal communication skills to build friendships.

FRIENDSHIPS

What would life be like without friends? Friends are people with whom you share things and develop a special kind of communication. People often take friends for granted until a friend moves away or becomes a better friend to someone else. The students who wrote the opening statements capture some of the importance of friends and friendships in their lives.

FRIENDSHIP AND COMMUNICATION

Friendship requires a special type of communication called interpersonal communication. **Interpersonal communication** is sharing meanings in order to build and maintain long-lasting relationships. Merely communicating with persons such as the grocery store clerk, bus driver, or neighbor is not interpersonal communication. Interpersonal communication refers to one-to-one sharing between friends. Although you may have friendships with your parents, other family members, or other adults, in this text, friendship and communication with people close to you in age will be emphasized. It is through communication that friends share their joys and problems while at the same time building a stronger friendship.

CHARACTERISTICS OF FRIENDSHIPS

What qualities do you look for in a friend? A magazine survey asked people to tell how important the following qualities are in a friend. The percentages next to the quality show the number of people who said that quality was important or significant. All these qualities are tied to communication.

Qualities	Percent responding
Ability to keep secrets	89
Loyalty	88
Warmth, affection	82
Supportiveness	76
Honesty	75
Sense of humor	74

FRIENDSHIP COMMUNICATION CHECKLIST

Use this checklist to help you think about how you talk with your friends. Which statements *never* apply to you? Which statements *sometimes* or *frequently* apply? Which statements *always* apply?

1. It is comfortable for me to talk to other people about personal things.
2. I often ask others how they feel about what I'm saying.
3. I am often able to put myself in the other person's place, and I imagine what he or she is feeling.
4. I often check whether others really understand what I'm saying.
5. I can be trusted with other people's secrets.
6. When I feel hurt I tell others how I feel.
7. I am usually able to say what I mean.
8. Other people come to me with their problems.
9. I try to be honest with my friends.
10. I stick up for my friends when others make fun of them.
11. If friends criticize my actions I think seriously about their comments.
12. I am sure to find time to spend with my friends.

When you think about your responses to the above checklist, you realize that good friends don't just happen. People *learn* to be good friends.

Secrets

To keep a secret, or a confidence, you must know which messages to keep. Keeping a friend's confidence says you are a friend. Here is what one student wrote in her journal about the importance of keeping a confidence:

JOURNAL ENTRY

I have found one friend I can trust. I can tell Melissa anything and she will never tell anyone. Not even her sister. Last year Dawn blabbed my secret all over school. Melissa would never do this. She is a true friend.

Loyalty

A good friend does not ignore old friends after making new friends. There is an old song that says, "Make new friends, but keep the old. One is silver and the other gold." Through loyalty you can develop many long-term friendships.

JOURNAL ENTRY

I thought that Liz would be my friend forever. We had such great times together. I told her everything. I thought that she told me everything too. Recently, I have been noticing a change in her feelings toward me. She doesn't want to talk as much. She seems almost embarrassed to be around me. It has been getting worse. I feel so cheated. Is there something wrong with me? Why has she suddenly become tired of being my friend? I don't understand how she could do this to me.

Warmth

Nonverbal clues tell you a lot about which people are friends. Usually you can sense warmth between friends. They may sit close together, tease each other, do things together, or share lunches. The way they include each other or talk about each other tells you they are good friends. Usually you can sense the warmth in a relationship by paying close attention to nonverbal messages.

Support

Good friends support each other. *Support* refers to messages that make people feel good about themselves. Friends may support each other in arguments. They may help each other with homework or worry when the other one is sick. If one wins a prize, the other is happy. When asked how friends support each other, some students replied:

My friend Eric always congratulates me when I beat him in basketball. He is pleased that I'm getting better.

I always encourage my friend who gets upset with herself when she can't do something. I tell her she can do it. The last time she tried out she got a part in the school chorus!

Honesty

"Friends are like pins. They are pointed and sharp." Sometimes only a friend will tell you the truth. If you are being a snob, you may need a friend to set you straight. If you tease too much, a friend may tell you it hurts. Your friend, and only your friend, may tell you that you are too stubborn, selfish, careless, or stuck up. A good friend tells you for your own good and stays with you as you change. A poor friend criticizes you to hurt you.

Humor

Being a friend may mean putting up with bad jokes. Friends can laugh with each other and sometimes at each other. They enjoy having fun together. They act silly and kid around together sometimes. Friends cannot be serious all the time.

Friends are many things to each other. They contribute to each other's self-concept and self-esteem. Friends show each other loyalty, warmth, supportiveness, and honesty. They keep secrets and laugh together. Friends make you feel good about yourself, which helps build a strong self-concept and high self-esteem. If you have a friend with some of these qualities, you are very lucky. Not all people have all of these qualities, but most of those who do are capable of being true friends.

STAGES OF FRIENDSHIP

Think about your friendships. How did each begin? What made you decide to continue a friendship after your first meeting? Generally, friendships progress through fairly predictable stages. These stages are first meetings, becoming acquaintances, becoming friends, and sometimes becoming best friends. Friendships move gradually from stage to stage. You are not acquaintances one day and best friends the next. A detailed discussion of friendship follows.

FIRST MEETINGS

Any of the following statements might be the beginning of a friendship between two people.

Dad, I'd like you to meet my coach, Mr. Darrel.

Hi. Are you new here?

Excuse me. Can you tell me how to get to room 201?

First meetings are the beginning stages of relationships. They can be compared to auditions or tryouts for a play or music group. New people go through tryouts to see if they want to get to know each other.

Physical appearance and any previous knowledge you have about a person affect first meetings. It's unfortunate but true that people pay close attention to appearance in first meetings. Certain clothes, hairstyles, or shoes may help you decide whether to talk to someone. You may never know who ignored you or approached you because of how you looked.

Sometimes you know about a person before you have met that person. You may have heard that Antonio is funny and smart. When you meet Antonio, you may make time to talk with him. If you heard that Heather is stuck up, when you meet her you may not waste your time trying to talk with her.

When you meet someone for the first time, you probably follow some social rituals. The rituals may include:

- Sharing your names, schools, and classes
- Talking about interests and hobbies
- Making small talk
- Avoiding arguments
- Avoiding sharing very personal information

Communication at first meetings is based on stereotypes. **Stereotyping** is labeling people as part of a group and treating them as if they possessed only the characteristics of that group. For example, if you meet a person at a party who belongs to a group different from yours, you may evaluate that person according to what you know about the group, rather than the person. People evaluate others based on their social or cultural groups. The following comments show how hard it can be to be judged according to a stereotype:

JOURNAL ENTRY

Just because I'm on the football team people think all I can talk about is sports. Whenever I meet new people they always want to talk about playing football.

I have to be very careful about what I eat because I have diabetes. As soon as other people find this out they think I'm weird or something.

The first time you meet someone, you form an impression or picture of that person. This picture helps you decide whether you wish to get to know the person better. If both of you have positive first impressions, you may be on your way toward a friendship.

INTERACT

In small groups, discuss which stereotypes are sometimes applied to:

- cheerleaders
- straight-A students

- football players
- chess club members
- student council members
- female athletes
- drama club members
- teachers
- wealthy students
- poor students

Add examples from the types of groups found in your school or community. Discuss how these stereotypes affect the way people relate to members of each group.

BECOMING ACQUAINTANCES

You relate to most people you know at the acquaintance level. Acquaintances are not strangers, but they are not really friends. You may say hello in the school hall, you may play together on the softball team, or you may sing together in the chorus. Some family friends, teachers, or store clerks may be your acquaintances.

Your communication with these people follows a set pattern. Comments such as, "How's it going?" or "Hi, how are you?" may begin your conversations. After that you may have very predictable conversations. Often you discuss the same things each time you meet. The same questions may be asked. For example, "Which team is going to win the championship?" or "How's your sister's new baby?" or "Have you been to any good movies lately?" These conversations are pleasant but not very personal.

You may know something about the person's family, school activities, or hobbies. You may know, for example, that the person in the "jock" group is also a good musician. The "rich" person may be an expert at bicycle repair. Because you know more about an acquaintance than someone you meet for the first time, you don't use stereotyping as much.

Although acquaintances may not share very personal information, they may discuss opinions on many subjects. Comments like the following keep the conversation going: "I'm sure glad Pat won the student council election" or "This is going to be a great weekend for racing. I can't wait."

People at the acquaintance level have few ties to each other. If you run into an acquaintance, you will have a pleasant conversation. Neither of you will make an effort to spend time together. Sometimes acquaintances move on to become friends. Then the relationship and level of communication change.

BECOMING FRIENDS

Friends have a special relationship. Friends talk more often to each other than do acquaintances. They talk for longer periods of time and about many different topics. Friends share personal information with each other. You know what makes your friend get angry, sad, or frustrated. You discuss your friend's family, interests, and past experiences. You share some worries and happiness with each other.

Friends develop special communication abilities. Sometimes they finish each other's sentences. They may have code words or nonverbal signals that only the two of them understand. For example, a certain look may mean "Let's get out of here." Friends can talk about experiences that other people may not share. Comments such as, "Remember the night your mother..." or "That's like the time at the dance when...." Sometimes friends use a short version of a message because they don't have to explain very much to each other. The statement "My Dad says Saturday can be another fishy day!" may not mean much to most people. But to two friends it could mean "My Dad says he will take us up to the lake next Saturday and let us go fishing with him in the boat." Friends can change their communication rapidly. They may be silly one minute and serious the next.

Many times friends will talk to each other about being friends. Each may say how important the other is in comments such as "You can't move. Who will I talk to?" or "It's great we are in four of the same classes" or "If you're not invited, I'm not going either. Friends stick together."

Most outsiders know when two people are friends. They see and hear messages that tell them that two people have a close relationship.

OBSERVE

Describe a good friendship between two people you know. As an outsider how can you tell these two are friends? How do they talk to each other and about each other? What nonverbal messages show they are friends?

BECOMING BEST FRIENDS

If friendships are special, best friendships are very special. Usually a person has one best friend, although sometimes a person may claim two or three people as best friends. It is impossible to have many best friends because friendships need privacy and time. You tell your best friend secrets. You share deep feelings and worries with each other. You are able to read your friend's nonverbal messages very well. One look at your best friend's face and you can tell if he or she is angry, upset, or excited.

Best friends do all the things friends do with verbal and nonverbal messages and more. They can often predict what the other will do or say and are right most of the time! Sometimes people say that two friends look or sound alike. They may use the same gestures or expressions, or laugh the same way. Comments such as, "You sound just like (your best friend)" make you feel good.

Best friends spend many hours together. They may talk on the phone every day and may spend hours at each other's houses. They develop a history in their relationship. They may share possessions such as clothes, tapes, or jewelry.

Best friends look out for each other. They do things for each other that they would not do for someone else. One student's journal entry described how best friends solved a problem of winning and losing:

JOURNAL ENTRY

My brother Matt and his best friend Mike both entered the Arbor Day Five-Mile Race last year. They were in the same age category. They got out in front early and ran together. I could see that they were still together when they got near the finish line. I kept waiting for one to break out ahead. Instead they just kept coming together. As they ran up to the line they both stopped. They looked at each other, laughed, and both stuck one foot across the line at exactly the same moment. The park district had to plant a tree to honor each of them because they both won.

Often other people recognize a pair as best friends. You hear comments like, "If you want Ed to come, you'd better invite Marco also" or "Vicki says she's going. That must mean Becky will be there too."

A family member sometimes feels like a best friend. You might be able to talk with your mother, father, or brother about what is important to you. Sometimes you may not have a best friend, but a few months later you may have two.

Best friendships take effort. You have to make time to see each other and to talk to each other. Each of you has to be willing to listen when the other needs to talk. You have to reach compromises on many plans or ideas.

CHANGES IN FRIENDSHIPS

Just as you and another person can move forward through the four stages of friendship, you also can move backward. You may know someone at school who used to be a close friend, but now you hardly even speak to each other.

As the quotation at the beginning of this chapter says, "Friendships are like seeds. When nurtured they grow; when neglected they die." Sometimes people neglect a best friendship. They get involved in new activities, find new people, or join new clubs. As the relationship changes, the verbal and nonverbal messages change. While you once shared secrets, you may now talk about the math test. You ignore each other's nonverbal clues. You don't spend much time together. The relationship becomes more distant. Best friends become just friends. Friends become acquaintances. People around you sense the change. Sometimes the two people can move their relationship up the stages again, but in other cases neither person wants to bother. Most people remain acquaintances. A few lucky people get to be best friends. Some friendships don't last very long.

OBSERVE

Select three friendships from books or television and decide at what stage each friendship appears to be. Describe the communication behavior of the people and tell why you think they are at that stage.

INTERPERSONAL COMMUNICATION SKILLS

JOURNAL ENTRY

My sister has tons of friends. Everyone likes her. I think it is because she tries to be thoughtful and she tries to be fair. She can really keep a secret, so people tell her all their troubles. She can even tell people negative things about themselves and they don't get mad.

Some people seem to make friends easily. Others see friendship as a mysterious thing. Using your communication skills can help you build friendships. There are six building blocks or communication skills you can use to build a strong friendship. These skills include: (1) sharing personal information, (2) sharing feelings, (3) empathy, (4) listening, (5) support, and (6) constructive criticism. A discussion of each follows.

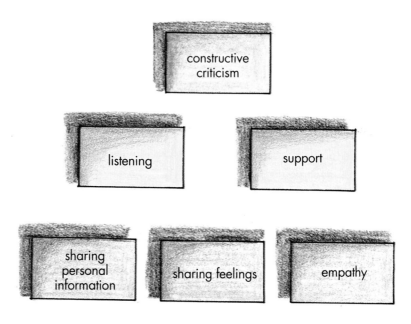

SHARING PERSONAL INFORMATION

Sharing personal information means telling someone private information about yourself. You choose to share this information; no one forces you to do so. You also take a risk, because if your friend told other people your secrets you might be hurt or embarrassed.

Many people wear masks much of the time. They appear happy, tough, or unfeeling when they really feel sad, scared, or upset. When people slowly drop their masks for one another, they get to know each other well. True friendship does not require masks, because friends accept each other. There is a sense of being oneself with another person. People sometimes hesitate to drop their masks, fearing that, "If you really know who I am, you won't like me anymore." One student describes the problem in putting on a certain mask:

JOURNAL ENTRY

If you put on a false front, you may find some friends, but you'll always have that question in the back of your mind if they like you or if you like yourself. I don't think it's worth it.

When good friends share personal information, their relationship usually gets stronger. There are some guidelines to help the sharing process work well.

Guidelines for Sharing Personal Information

Competent communicators know that sharing information happens over time and requires both people to be involved. These guidelines help many friendships develop slowly and well:

1. *Don't overtalk.* The person who tells *all* and tells it quickly can ruin a possible friendship. If the first time you meet someone, you hear all about his or her troubles, old best friends, travels, and so on, you will be uncomfortable. People who talk about themselves too much and too quickly will have trouble making friends.
2. *Don't undertalk.* The person who listens to everyone else but never says anything personal can also ruin a possible friendship. You may realize that a new person

knows all about your family and friends, your interests, and your plans for the future. If you know almost nothing about this person, you need to ask yourself, am I talking too much? Is this person unwilling to talk to me? Undertalking keeps the relationship from continuing through the friendship stages.

3. *Choose the information you wish to share wisely.* Even best friends do not have to share *everything.* You do not have to answer every question someone asks you. You can decide when and with whom you wish to talk about personal things.

SHARING FEELINGS

Feeling statements describe your emotions, a very personal part of you. Many people cover up their feelings with thought statements, because a thought statement is less personal. For example, it is less personal to say, "I think the director cast a good show," than "I'm so glad I'm going to be in the show." Often people hide their sadness, anger, or jealousy by talking about a subject but never sharing their feelings about it. Feeling statements let your friends see parts of you that you don't often share. As people get to know each other better, they share their feelings more openly.

Apply

Look at the following quotes and pick out those you think are feeling statements and those you think are thought statements:

1. "I'm so happy I'm going to be in the school play. I really wanted a part."
2. "It seems like the director cast a good show. I'm going to play a scientist."
3. "I get so jealous when I see how easy it is for Stephanie to sight-read music."
4. "It seems that some people have a natural talent for reading music. Not me."

The first and third statements are emotional statements. The second and fourth are thought statements.

OBSERVE

In your journal, keep a record for three days of feeling statements you hear. For example, if you hear someone say "I'm so angry at the bicycle repair shop...," write "I'm angry." After three days count how many feeling statements you actually heard and describe the types of feelings you heard most often expressed, such as sadness, joy, fear, anger.

Sometimes your good friends use nonverbal clues to show how they are feeling. Suppose you ask your friend, "How are you?" and your friend looks away and quietly says, "Fine." If you are paying attention to your friend's voice and eyes, you will know he or she is not really fine. If you pay attention to nonverbal clues, you can help your friend put into words what is going on. The better you know people, the easier it is to find out how they are feeling by reading their nonverbal cues.

JOURNAL ENTRY

A lot of adults seem to have trouble talking about feelings. We used to have a joke in our family about "Are you mad, glad, sad?" but only the kids really used feelings words. Most adults I know keep their real feelings inside.

EMPATHIZING

A newspaper column discussed the story of a twelve-year-old seventh-grader. The boy returned to his desk after lunch one day to find a printed card that said "Most Unpopular Student Award." Some classmate had filled in the boy's name under the title.

Think about this situation for a minute. If this happened to your best friend, how would he or she feel? How would you feel if it happened to you? After the newspaper article was published, many adult readers wrote in to say they felt bad for

the boy. The article reminded them of when they or their children were teased in school. Because they could still remember their own feelings when this happened, these adults had empathy for the student.

Empathy is the ability to put yourself in another person's place and understand what that person is feeling. You can show empathy for a friend when you have had a similar experience or when you understand the feelings your friend is having. Good friends try to put themselves in the other person's shoes and empathize. In the following journal entry, one student describes just such a situation:

JOURNAL ENTRY

I would have lost my mind without Jay last summer. After I broke my leg, I lost my place on the soccer team, and I was stuck home for most of the summer. Everyone else told me how lucky I was the car accident didn't kill me. Only Jay seemed to know how really sad and angry I was. Jay always made me feel he understood what I was feeling.

A skillful communicator tries to see the world from a good friend's point of view—and then show the friend that he or she is not alone in those feelings, that someone else understands.

LISTENING

"Sometimes the best thing a friend can do is just sit and listen." The student who wrote this discovered something important about communication in friendships. Good friends should be able to count on each other to listen to feelings and personal information.

You may have heard the expression, "You have to read between the lines," which means figuring out what is implied but not actually stated in a written text. The same idea can be applied to spoken words. It's called "listening between the words," and it means hearing what is implied but not actually said.

Many people do not say what they mean, particularly when they are talking about negative feelings. As a listener, you hear a part of what is in the speaker's mind. But you don't get the whole story directly. The better you know someone, the easier it is to put his or her remarks into context.

For example, if you heard someone say, "I'm certainly not up for spending Thanksgiving at my father and stepmother's. I wish the day would just disappear," you might interpret the remark in a number of ways. Some interpretations might be:

I'm jealous of my father's time with his new wife.

I feel guilty leaving my mother on Thanksgiving.

I feel uncomfortable in their house. I just don't fit in.

I feel sad not spending Thanksgiving with my mother.

Only if you knew the speaker well would you be able to interpret the correct feeling. You would know that the original statement about Thanksgiving was a surface statement. The strong feelings were below the surface and could only be understood by "listening between the words."

INTERACT

Write three messages that contain implied meanings. In a small group read your statements to each other. Each person should try to identify possible meanings by "listening between the lines."

SUPPORTING

Your hair always looks so nice. I hate you.

How come your brother is the only coordinated one in your family?

These and other put-downs are heard every day. Some people think it's clever to make fun of others. Some people seem to feel better about themselves when they cut someone else down. Often such messages hurt friendships. Look at this journal comment:

JOURNAL ENTRY

Just this morning Carlos and I were trying to insult each other, and I really hate it when he gets me worked up like that. When he insults me, I try to defend myself but I guess that's only natural. I don't know if he's trying to get back at me or at someone else, but it seems like he loves to call people names and tries to cut them down. People who belittle others are just insecure themselves, but their comments still hurt.

The opposite of cutting someone down is supporting someone. **Support** refers to messages that make people feel good about themselves. These messages may include compliments, good wishes, appreciation, or congratulations on a job well done. They may be directed to the person, or they may be said about the person when he or she is not there. Look at the following examples:

Your hair always looks nice.

I heard you got the only A on the history test. You deserved it.

I appreciated your help on the pep rally.

Although some friends enjoy themselves by kidding around, there are times when a direct message of support is important. Good friends are willing to give direct compliments or recognize a friend's achievements.

What friends say about each other to different people is a real test of friendship. What do you say if you hear someone cutting down your good friend? Do you ignore it, or do you defend your friend? Do you ever cut down your friends when they are not with you? When friends support each other, they help build each other's self-esteem. When they cut each other down, they may lower each other's self-esteem. Friends have a great deal of power over each other.

CONSTRUCTIVE CRITICISM

All friends must deal with differences between them. No one is perfect, and people will upset each other by things they say or do. Some friends never really say what is bothering them and keep annoying each other until the friendship dies. Other friends are able to tell each other what they do and don't like.

Apply

Look at the following questions and decide in which case Susan is acting as a better friend.

Susan to Consuelo
Brittany makes me so mad. She borrows my sweaters and

ruins them. She's always asking if she can wear my earrings or use my purses. Then she forgets to return them. She's a real slob, and I'm not letting her use my things again.

Susan to Brittany
I don't want to hurt your feelings, but I need to tell you something. I get upset when you borrow my sweaters and return them with stains. And I don't like it when I have to remind you to bring back things like my earrings. I would appreciate it if you would clean things that get messed up and return the other stuff when you said you would.

In the first case Brittany may never know how she upset Susan. Brittany has no reason to change unless Susan tells her how she feels. Yet Susan is complaining to Consuelo about Brittany. In the second case Susan has told the right person. Brittany now knows there is a problem. Susan has told her what to do to solve the problem.

Guidelines for Constructive Criticism

Good friends need to give and receive constructive criticism from each other. **Constructive criticism** involves stating what is bothering you and making suggestions for change. The purpose of constructive criticism is to remove the problem and make the relationship stronger. The following guidelines can help you give constructive criticism:

1. *Talk in terms of "I."* Think how you feel when someone says, "You were very rude to me." Do you feel differently if the person says, "I felt ignored when you kept interrupting." In the earlier example Susan told Brittany she got upset about certain behavior. She did not say, "You are a real slob," or "You ruin my stuff."
2. *Describe the behavior; don't label the person.* Instead of saying someone is "rude" or "mean" or "dumb," describe the behavior that upsets you. Comments such as the following tell your friend exactly what is upsetting you: "You said we would go to a movie Friday night, and then you made plans to go over to Terry's house"; "When we were at the party, you did not talk to me."
3. *Avoid name calling.* Calling people names or giving them negative labels does not help solve a disagreement. If

you call people names, they do not hear your true message. This shuts out any constructive criticism or communication.

4. *Stick to the present.* Don't criticize by dragging in past history. If you are upset about how someone treated you last weekend, don't remind that person of what made you angry last month or last year. Storing things up and then telling someone everything at once is not fair. No doubt, when someone does this to you, you get quite angry. No one likes to find out that a friend has been holding a grudge.

INTERACT

Work with a partner and develop two scenes based on a single interpersonal situation, for example, a friend who is angry at another friend for breaking weekend plans. First, play out your scenes using "you" messages and labels. Then replay the scene using "I" messages and descriptions. Each participant should describe how he or she felt in each scene.

All these guidelines and ideas depend on time. If you don't spend much time with your friend, it will be harder to share feelings and ideas with him or her. Too many people place other things above their friendships. For example, you might want to visit your sick friend Joseph but also want to watch your favorite television shows the same night. You have to make a choice. Your friend Celina may want to tell you about a problem after school on the day you had planned to go shopping for new clothes. Again, you have to make a choice. Making time for your friends is important. It's hard to share personal things with people you see once in a great while.

SUMMARY

This chapter defines and discusses interpersonal communication and relationships. It looks at (1) characteristics of friendships, including the ability to keep secrets, loyalty, warmth, support, honesty, and humor; (2) friendship stages, including first meetings, acquaintances, friends, and best friends; (3) communication skills of friends, including sharing personal information, sharing feelings, empathizing, listening, supporting, and offering constructive criticism.

CHAPTER REVIEW

THINK ABOUT IT

1. What are the six characteristics of friendship? Briefly describe each in one or two sentences.
2. What are the four stages of friendship? Describe and give an example of a relationship you have observed at each stage.
3. Give an example of stereotyping.
4. Describe the six communication building blocks, or skills, of friendship.
5. Define and describe *interpersonal communication.*

TRY IT OUT

1. In groups of three or four classmates, discuss your beliefs about friendship. Use the following questions to guide your discussion: What is the importance of friendship? What qualities should a close friend possess? What actions can ruin a friendship?
2. In groups of three or four classmates, describe situations in which you or a friend have been stereotyped. Discuss how the stereotyping affected communication between the stereotyped person and others.
3. In a group of four or five students, discuss one of the following statements in relation to the key word that precedes it.
   Empathy: Do not judge a person until you have walked a mile in his or her shoes.
   First Meetings: It's unfortunate you only have one chance to make a first impression.
   Listening: Listening between the words helps you find the real meaning of the message.
4. Using the statements at the opening of the chapter as a guide, create three two-sentence statements about friendship. Each one should start "Friendships are...."

PUT IT IN WRITING

1. Pretend you have a pen pal in a foreign country who will come to live in your community for a year. Write your pen pal a letter describing how good friends communicate with each other in your culture.
2. Look at some want ads in your local paper. Write a want ad for an ideal friend.
3. Write a paragraph describing a time when constructive criticism given by a friend helped you or someone you know make a friendship stronger.

SPEAK ABOUT IT

1. In a one- or two-minute speech, describe your ideal friend.
2. Find a poem about friendship, or write one of your own. You might follow a pattern such as cinquain poetry. Read your poem to your classmates.
3. Tell the class a short story about a turning point in a friendship. You may use your own experience or describe an incident from a friendship you read about or heard about.

PART

3

GROUP COMMUNICATION

CHAPTERS

Communication in Groups

Forms of Group Discussion

CHAPTER

7

COMMUNICATION IN GROUPS

After completing this chapter, you should be able to

- define *group* and *group discussion*.
- describe the characteristics of groups.
- list steps in problem solving.
- describe the duties of a leader and leadership styles.
- describe small-group speaking and listening responsibilities.
- evaluate a small-group discussion.

KEY WORDS

brainstorming

clique

criteria

group

group norms

group problem solving

group purpose

moderator

role

subgroup

150

We talked for an hour and we didn't get anything decided. Everyone was talking all at once and no one wanted to listen to anyone's ideas.

We were supposed to cover several agenda items at the student council meeting, but we got in a disagreement over the dress code and pretty soon we ran out of time.

At the Scout meeting last night, we made several major decisions about our troop's goals for the year.

All your life you have been part of different groups. Some groups you have belonged to may have worked well together and accomplished a lot. Some groups may not have worked well together. You may have belonged to 4H, a track team, speech team, student council, computer club, or swing chorus. Much of daily life involves moving from group to group.

Yet groups do not automatically work well together. Members and leaders need to be competent communicators in order to act effectively in groups. This chapter introduces the characteristics of groups, describes effective problem solving in groups, discusses communication skills needed by group members and leaders, and shows you how to evaluate groups.

CHARACTERISTICS OF GROUPS

What makes a bunch of people a group? Are people in the school hall a group? Are people in a crowded elevator a group? Are holiday shoppers in the mall a group? There is a difference between crowds or bunches of people and groups. A **group** consists of people who

- share an interest in the same things or share a common purpose.
- communicate easily and regularly among themselves.
- participate in planning and decision making.
- feel connected to the other members.

Do people always know how to act within a group? Are there rules or guidelines for members? In most cases members have to figure out how the group works while they are part of it. Competent communicators consider the following characteristics: structure, purpose, norms, roles, and subgroups.

GROUP STRUCTURE

Group structure is the amount of organization a group needs to carry out its business. There are two basic types of structure, *formal* and *informal.*

Do you see a difference between the student council and the dance committee? Or between the school board and the parent talent show committee? Groups with set rules for communication are highly organized and have what is called a formal structure. You know which persons will take certain responsibilities and you know the order of meetings. In most cases groups such as student council and school boards are governed by rules or procedures. For example, there may be established procedures for handling speaking to the group. Usually one person runs the meeting and each meeting follows the same pattern. As you will see in the next chapter, groups run according to parliamentary procedure have a formal structure.

Groups with an informal structure are less organized and do not follow set rules. Each meeting might be organized differently. These groups find ways to run a meeting without many rules and regulations. Friendship groups or groups that organize quickly for a specific purpose may not need much structure.

JOURNAL ENTRY

Two of the students in our school were burned out of their home. A group of teachers, parents, and kids got together to raise money and collect food, clothing, and furniture for the family. We operated as a group for about three weeks but no one really took over. Everyone called each other and took on certain projects. In three weeks they were in a nice apartment and the group stopped working together.

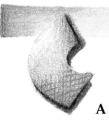

Apply

Look at the following conversations and decide which group has a formal structure and which has an informal one.

A Travis: The agenda for tonight's meeting will follow the usual order. We will hear the secretary's report, the treasurer's report, and the social committee report. Then we will finish old business and move on to new business.

Aimee: What about the fund-raising for the spring trip?

Travis: That comes under new business. We will get to it later.

B Travis: Well, we better get started. What do we want to talk about first?

Aimee: I think we need to get started on raising money for the spring class trip. We have to plan car washes, popcorn sales, and a minimarathon.

Travis: That's a good idea. Let's get a committee organized today in order to divide up the work.

As you can tell, conversation A showed the formal structure. There is a very specific way to carry on the meeting and Travis insists that the order be followed. Conversation B illustrates the informal structure.

Many groups have neither a totally formal nor a totally informal structure. If you think of a line that runs from formal to informal structure, you might place some groups in the middle. Also, groups that are usually formal may become more informal at times and vice versa. For example, as the date for the dance gets nearer, the dance committee may become very formal in order to get its work done on time.

GROUP PURPOSE

A **group purpose** is the group's reason for existing. Just as group structures range from formal to informal, group purposes range from all work to all social activity. Groups with a work purpose attempt to complete a task or reach a goal. The main purpose of a social group is to enjoy one another's company and have fun. Most groups do not fall into one purpose or the other but are a combination of both. Think about the purposes of groups to which you belong. Are the meetings set up for members to work, socialize with friends, or do both?

Many groups involve some working and some playing. Often groups faced with a problem have little time for socializing. For example, if your school athletic program was going to be dropped due to lack of money, some parent-student groups might try to raise money quickly. These people would come to meetings to work hard.

Some groups are formed to allow members to enjoy each other's company. Although the group members may do work, there is social time to laugh, talk, or have fun together. For instance, a swim team or marching band group may involve fun and work. A Scout troup works for badges and has fun on campouts. Spanish club members work to improve their ability to speak Spanish, but they also enjoy parties with Latin music and food. What groups have you joined because you wanted to be with the other people?

GROUP NORMS

Certain behaviors are expected in some groups. Each of the following statements describes the way members of a group know they are expected to act:

"When we have a swim team meeting, the coach locks the door as soon as we start. If you're late, you don't get in."

"When you criticize someone else's performance on the speech team, you have to discuss what the performer did. You can't just say 'I liked it' or 'I didn't like it.' "

Group norms are the ways that people are expected to act as group members. All groups have norms. Most groups have both general norms and communication norms. General group norms might include:

- how to act or dress
- whether it's OK to arrive late or leave early
- how hard to work
- whether taking a break is acceptable
- who can be part of the group

Groups have norms for speaking and listening. Particular communication norms within a group might include:

- whether it's OK to disagree
- how to disagree
- what topics are safe to talk about
- how much to talk
- how to talk about certain people

For example, the school newspaper staff may expect members to meet all deadlines. Group members who wish to talk loudly may be expected to move to another room if others are working on stories. People may not be allowed to leave until the plan for all the pages is finished, even if it gets late. Members will learn how to disagree with another's idea for an article. There may be inside jokes about names of people who are involved with the paper or about people in the school.

OBSERVE

Spend an hour with a group you know. Try to identify some of the general norms and the communication norms followed by members of the group.

GROUP ROLES

A **role** is a personal pattern of communication that characterizes one's place in a group. Think of a group in which you often find yourself. How would you describe yourself in that group: funny, serious, helpful, shy, angry? People tend to behave in predictable ways within groups.

Communication Roles

There are many roles people can take on in a group. These roles may be helpful to the group or they may hurt the group. The following list includes the most common communication roles.

1. *Experts.* These people know a great deal about a subject and are willing to share their knowledge with the group. If the experts start to take over and force ideas on other members, they may be looked at as "know-it-alls."
2. *Supporters.* These people support and defend the ideas of others in the group. Sometimes this helps a shy person's ideas to be heard and may encourage him or her to speak again. If supporters never offer new ideas or only support their friends' ideas, the supporters often become known as "yes-people," or "head-nodders."
3. *Questioners.* These people raise important points about ideas. They make everyone think twice before rushing

into decisions. They may spark discussion and new ideas. However, if the questioners raise issues about every topic, they slow down the group's progress and become "question hounds."

4. *Compromisers.* The compromisers can see how ideas could be combined into even better ideas. This is valuable because it uses other members' ideas creatively. However, compromisers also need to produce their own new ideas.

5. *Challengers.* These people are willing to argue or debate ideas rather than just accept them. They force the entire group to think more carefully. When they challenge everybody just for fun, they annoy other group members.

6. *Moderators.* These people keep the group process moving and try to see that everyone gets involved. They may remind the group of deadlines or help quiet members to participate. They may bring up group rules. When they try to police the group at all times, they lose their effectiveness.

7. *Tension Relievers.* These people keep things from getting too serious or boring. They may crack jokes, tease a member of the group, or make funny, supportive remarks. When they can't do anything but act silly, they are known as "clowns."

8. *Observers.* These people prefer to watch and listen during group meetings. They may feel uncomfortable in the group. They may be shy or they may just feel that they don't have anything to add.

INTERACT

In a group of nine or ten classmates, each person should choose a role from the list of group roles. Every role need not be chosen, and more than one person may choose the same role. The group should then select a school-related topic and discuss it. The class should identify the role or roles each group member is playing.

SUBGROUPS

Not all groups remain one single unit. Many groups have subgroups. A **subgroup** is a smaller group within a group. The rhythmic gymnastics group may have beginning, intermediate, and advanced subgroups. The student council may have a projects committee, a social committee, and a finance committee. Large social groups may include smaller groups of friends. These people may be closer friends because they live near each other, take the same classes, or have the same interests.

Subgroups allow people in work groups to work on specific jobs or to use special talents. For example, the finance committee can figure out the club budget. Sometimes the subgroup can become more important than the larger group. Members feel more attached to the subgroup and forget the goals of the larger group. For example, the social committee of the student council may get so involved in planning fun activities that members may lose sight of the larger group's governing goals.

Think about some large group of which you are a member. What are its subgroups? How well do the subgroups contribute to the large group's overall goals?

Cliques

A special kind of subgroup is called a clique. A **clique** is a subgroup of members who tend to associate with each other and avoid other people. Sometimes clique groups make nonmembers feel like outsiders. You may have cliques in your school.

One student expressed negative feelings about popularity and the "in" group in the following way:

JOURNAL ENTRY

Okay, I know I'm not popular. I'm sort of glad I'm not. Popularity does sort of make you a snob, because everybody not in your clique is supposed to be a nerd or stupid or any negative name they can classify you by.

When new people come to our school, the popular group tries to become their friend in order to prove to each other that they have a lot of friends. As soon as the new person has become their friend, they start to ignore that person. Sometimes they "accept" people into their group, and then try to make them feel out of place.

OBSERVE

Observe a group in your school. Describe in your journal the communication behaviors that indicate who is "in" and who is "out." Look at language, use of space, appearance, common interests, and how "outsiders" are treated.

As a competent communicator you need to be aware of a group's structure, purpose, norms, roles, and subgroups. As you learn about each of these group characteristics you will be able to select the best communication strategies to make your group work well.

STEPS IN GROUP PROBLEM SOLVING

Although some groups get together just to have fun, most groups have a task purpose. Very frequently the task involves problem solving. As a group member or leader you need to understand the process of group problem solving so you can use the process as you work in different types of groups.

According to an old expression, two heads are better than one. If this is true, do you think six heads are better than five, or seven better than six? Although there is no perfect number for a small group, several people can often solve a problem better than one person. But sometimes a group is unable to solve problems because members disagree, become lazy or stubborn, or spend too much time on one point. If a group does not work well, the situation may become frustrating.

One student describes the possible difficulties of working in groups as follows:

JOURNAL ENTRY

Sometimes you may never know what kind of a predicament you can get into when you're in a group. If everyone is shy, it's hard to communicate. If they don't work, you get stuck with all the work. If everyone wants to lead, there will be lots of arguments. Sometimes it's very hard for a group to work together unless the members can communicate in an orderly way. That means people have to have self-control. That's not always easy!

Although working in groups is not always easy, it is worth the effort. Groups can be very good at problem solving if they work on the problem in an orderly way, if the leader and the members act as responsible communicators, and if the setting aids the group's work. Group discussion occurs when a small number of people are simultaneously involved in face-to-face communication to make a decision or reach a goal. Some group discussions do not fall within this definition because people use phones or mail to communicate with each other. Yet most types of groups use the face-to-face problem-solving

process. To understand how successful problem-solving groups work, you will next examine (1) problem-solving steps, (2) members' communication responsibilities, (3) leadership in groups, and (4) how to evaluate problem-solving groups.

Solutions don't happen by accident. They should represent the best thinking of the group members. Problem solving follows a series of steps:

1. Identify the problem.
2. Analyze the problem.
3. Set criteria for a solution.
4. Develop solutions.
5. Select a solution.

To help you see how the problem-solving process works, a problem related to extracurricular speech activities will be discussed at each step of the process.

IDENTIFY THE PROBLEM

To hold an effective problem-solving discussion, you have to identify a very specific problem. This first step has two parts. The first part requires narrowing the topic, and the second part requires phrasing it into a question.

Narrow the Topic

Topics like "Bicycle Safety" and "Lack of Involvement in Speech Activities" are unclear because they are too broad. For example, what would be included under "Lack of Involvement in Speech Activities"? Would you discuss types of activities? Values of speech and drama clubs? Finding new members? The words of a discussion topic must be clearly defined, and everyone must understand what they mean. The topic must also be limited to an area the group can manage. For example, the group may decide to discuss types of activities one week and values of drama activities another week.

Phrase the Topic as a Question

A topic must be phrased carefully, so everyone understands the exact problem. Whatever type of question is used, it should be stated simply, clearly, and fairly, and phrased to avoid getting only *yes* or *no* answers. Usually problems are phrased as questions of fact, value, or policy.

1. *Questions of fact ask about what is.* They require people to find the answers. The solution to the problem is found in the information contained in the answer. The answer should be the end of the discussion. Examples of questions of fact are:

    What are the bicycle laws in this county?

    What extracurricular speech activities exist in this school?

2. *Questions of value concern issues of good or bad, right or wrong.* They ask if ideas for things are valuable or not, useful or not. They depend on facts plus opinions. The answers to questions of value are based on facts and opinions. Examples of questions of value are:

    How well are bicycle safety laws enforced?

    How valuable are the school's extracurricular speech activities?

3. *Questions of policy ask what should be done.* They ask about change. Examples of questions of policy are:

    What bicycle safety laws should be enforced by the school?

    What should the school do to promote speech activities?

The discussion will vary depending on how the question is phrased. If the speech activities topic is phrased as a question of fact, the group has to decide exactly what speech activities are and how many there are in the school. The group may discuss whether forensics should be called a speech class, and they might list the Kiwanis Club Oratory Contest as a speech activity.

If the topic is phrased as a question of value, the group has to decide how valuable speech activities are. Members may speak from their own experiences or from the experiences of others in the school.

Finally, to answer a question of policy, the group would have to consider ways to promote the speech activities and then choose the best ideas. The policy question "What are the best ways to promote the school's speech activities?" will be used as the rest of the problem-solving steps are discussed.

INTERACT

In pairs or small groups, evaluate the following discussion questions. Identify each question as a question of fact, value, or policy. Then decide whether each question is acceptable or unacceptable. If it is unacceptable for discussion, rewrite it on a separate sheet of paper as an acceptable question.

1. How can we improve the grading system in the school?

2. Should students be allowed to leave school during their free periods?

3. Should extra credit be available to all students?

4. What should be done to reduce school absences?

5. How serious is the school absence policy?

6. How many students take part in the school lunch program?

7. What can the school do to improve cafeteria food?

ANALYZE THE PROBLEM

As a group member you need to understand the history, causes, and current state of a problem. When discussing the problem of increasing interest in speech activities, the group would need to know information such as what activities exist; how many students are involved; why these students are involved; how many students take speech classes; why other students do not get involved; and what attempts have been made to involve more students.

Perhaps the group did research and discovered the following information: Many students do not even know the speech program exists; those who are aware of the program are unclear about the amount of work involved; some students say the speech activities conflict with sports activities or take too much time. Having made these discoveries, the group may decide that some students do not choose to be involved but that others really do not know much about the speech activities. After analyzing the problem, the group needs to set up ways to find a solution.

SET CRITERIA FOR A SOLUTION

As a group moves toward solutions, its members have to consider what would make a solution workable. In other words, they have to decide what standards a solution has to meet. These standards are called **criteria.**

In value and policy issues, standards or criteria must be defined for terms such as *effective, valuable,* or *useful.* In the example given, the group must decide what makes a speech activity valuable.

Policy questions usually involve criteria for setting up a program. These may involve money, time, people, or regulations. For example, when discussing the best ways to promote the school's speech activities, a good solution may have to meet the following criteria:

1. *Money.* The principal will give up to $100 to promote the activity.
2. *Time.* Something must be done in the spring to create interest and to build the activity for the fall.
3. *People.* All students should be reached through the solution.

DEVELOP SOLUTIONS

At this point group members try to find all kinds of possible solutions. This can be done in a number of ways. Members may suggest ideas, and everyone may discuss them as they are suggested. Or members may brainstorm to uncover as many solutions as possible.

Brainstorming is a process of listing aloud as many ideas as possible before discussion. In brainstorming, it is perfectly all right to add to someone else's ideas. There are two main rules for a brainstorming session:

1. Do not criticize or evaluate any of the ideas until the brainstorming session is completed.
2. Write down all ideas as they are given—even ideas that are similar.

After the brainstorming session is finished, the group should evaluate all of the ideas.

Solutions to the speech activities problem might include:

- a letter to parents describing the activities and their benefits
- a school assembly demonstrating the activities
- after-school speech demonstrations showing teams and performers in action
- a school tournament that involves participation by many classes
- speech activity representatives talking in each class
- a parent-student meeting one evening
- giving speech activity members permanent hall passes

SELECT A SOLUTION

To decide which of the solutions is best, a group needs to ask three major questions:

1. Which of the solutions best meets the criteria the group set up?

2. What are the weaknesses of the solution?

3. What are the strengths of the solution?

Some solutions are unworkable or impractical to carry out. For example, the last solution given above is unusable. The school could not give permanent passes to the members of the activity group without giving them to all other students.

Some of the other solutions do not meet the criteria. The letter to parents may not reach the students and would be costly to mail. The tournament could not be held in spring because it would take too much planning time. The after-school and evening activities would only be available to a small number of students, those who do not ride buses or have jobs. The group may reject all solutions except those involving the assembly and room representatives.

When examining the criteria, both the assembly and the room representatives solutions fit the criteria. The solution involving room representatives might have the disadvantage of only one person talking about the activities. The solution involving the assembly, on the other hand, would have the advantage of having many students demonstrating debates or giving speeches or performing group interpretations. Therefore, the group may decide to plan an assembly for the entire school.

A lot of work goes into reaching a workable solution. Group members must give time and energy to go through the steps correctly.

OBSERVE

Within the next week observe a small group trying to solve a problem. It could be your friends deciding what to do Friday night, or it could be your club deciding how to spend money. Try to identify the five problem-solving steps. Describe the comments people made at each step.

GROUP MEMBER COMMUNICATION

I have a problem working with people in a group. Most of the problem involves communication. People won't be quiet, so others around them can't hear what is being said. Everyone wants to voice his or her opinion at the same time.

All in all I think that the biggest problem with working in groups is that some people do not respect and listen to others' suggestions. If everyone is polite and gets along, your group project will be successful.

Group members' communication can support the group goals and help the problem-solving process, or it can slow down the process. To be a competent communicator in a problem-solving group, you have to act as both a responsible speaker and a responsible listener.

SPEAKER RESPONSIBILITIES

Jeanne just talked and talked and talked.

Aaron kept asking these dumb questions.

Arletta didn't say a word during the whole meeting.

Each group member has specific speaking and listening responsibilities. Problem solving will be easier if these responsibilities are fulfilled. The following are effective speaking skills for group members.

Be Prepared
Nothing slows down a problem-solving discussion more than unprepared members. These members not only waste their own time at the meeting, but they are a burden to the other members.

Share Your Ideas Thoughtfully
Take your share of the responsibility in the group. No matter how informed you are, you will be of no value to the group unless you share your information. You need to contribute to the group, as much and as often as necessary, to help the group solve the problem. Make sure, however, that you do not talk too much or stray from the subject.

Apply

Read the following dialogue of a group discussion. Can you identify the speakers' mistakes? Who is the competent group communicator?

Jennifer: I think you should listen to what I think about what should be the theme of our social dance this spring. I talked to several people and we all agreed that we should use a Renaissance theme. Everyone could make costumes or rent them and we could have lords and ladies as the favorites. It's the perfect solution and everyone I've talked to agrees with me.

(Karen and John nod at her in agreement.)

Anne: Well, that sounds great for people who can get their parents to rent or make costumes for them. But, my mom can't sew and we really can't spend money on renting a costume. Maybe a '50s dance would be better.

Will: I think Jennifer's idea is great. If students don't want to wear a Renaissance costume they don't have to. They can just wear school clothes. Let's vote on Jennifer's super idea. (Karen and John look puzzled.)

Anne: I don't think it would be much fun coming to the dance unless you feel a part of it. I remember once not feeling a part of a party I went to and then I felt left out. It's kind of like last night's episode of "Beverly Hills 90210" when Luke felt out of place at Jason's house and then his sister told him to...

Jennifer: Look, if you want to wear a Renaissance costume, do it, if not, don't. Everyone agrees except a couple of people. Let's vote.

Tomás: Excuse me, Jennifer. We need to listen to everyone's opinion before we vote. I think a Renaissance idea is unique and clever, but I like Anne's idea too. I'd like to hear what Karen and John think before we make a decision.

You probably decided that Tomás is the only competent communicator in the group. He states his opinion and also encourages others to share their ideas.

Speak with Self-Respect

Sometimes a member complains, "No one ever likes my ideas." This may occur because no one hears these ideas. Don't mumble! Be loud and clear. When you disagree with someone, don't make fun of his or her idea. Just present your ideas firmly and clearly. Be willing to repeat your ideas to make your point.

Ask Questions

Knowing how to ask the right questions is as important as knowing the answers. Too often people don't ask questions when they need to—when something is unclear or when they need more information. Competent communicators know when to ask questions and do so.

Support Others

Encourage other members of the group to contribute and share their ideas. Be nonverbally supportive by smiling, nodding your head, or giving other signs of approval. When you support others, they feel good about themselves. They feel that their contributions are worthwhile, and they will want to continue to help the group reach its goal.

Responsible speakers contribute to the group in many different ways. They are well prepared, share ideas thoughtfully, speak with respect, ask questions, and support others.

LISTENER RESPONSIBILITIES

Everyone wants to talk and no one will take turns!

In our history class on current events day, I would try to talk but no one paid attention.

The proverb that opens Chapter 3 says, "The spoken word belongs half to those who speak, and half to those who hear." Often group members forget the second half of this bit of wisdom. Many times while one person is speaking, other people can't wait to begin talking themselves. They think about what they are going to say instead of listening to what is being said. Or they interrupt the speaker.

Apply

Look at the following quotes and decide which come from competent communicators and which come from group members who need to develop better communication skills.

Speaker 1: Ingrid, that's the dumbest idea I've heard today.

Speaker 2: We're running out of time. I'm leaving. Bye.

Speaker 3: We need to look at the cost of this plan more carefully.

Speaker 4: I forgot my notes. I think we have to tell the principal by November 20. No, maybe it's November 15.

Speaker 5: I think Chuck's idea could save us at least $50. We need to consider it carefully.

If you recognized that speakers 1, 2, and 4 need to develop their group communication skills, you're correct.

Effective Listening Skills

The following are effective listening skills for group members:

1. *Practice good listening.* You will remember that good listening takes work. Apply the listening guidelines you learned in Chapter 3 to your group communication.

2. *Avoid barriers.* Although many people may be trying to talk and things may be moving quickly, try to overcome speaker barriers and self-barriers.

3. *Use your thought speed.* Remember, while other members are speaking at 120 to 180 words a minute, you can listen at a rate of 300 to 400 words a minute. Use this extra time to think about the ideas you are hearing.

4. *Listen for connections.* As you listen to Leo argue for one solution and Marita for another, see how their ideas might be similar. Check out suggestions as they are made to see which might fit within the group's criteria.

5. *Give nonverbal feedback.* Don't shut down when you are not talking. Look at the person who is talking and give nonverbal support to ideas you find interesting. Make other members feel as if someone is listening. For example, make eye contact, nod your head, or smile.

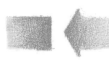

OBSERVE

Watch a small group operate and record the behaviors of the people who are not speaking. Are they remaining alert and involved? Are they giving positive or negative nonverbal feedback?

LEADERSHIP IN GROUPS

Some people fight to become leaders in groups. Others try hard to avoid leadership responsibilities. Both of these behaviors interfere with successful group communication. The quality of leadership strongly affects a group's ability to solve problems.

Good leaders are competent communicators. They have ways to speak and listen responsibly. They select the best strategy for each problem and act on it. Then they see how the members of the group act. Good leaders keep thinking, "How can I help this group do its best work at problem solving?"

BECOMING A LEADER

There are several ways a group member might become a leader. Leaders may be appointed or elected, or they may emerge from the group.

Appointed Leaders

Sometimes one person in authority chooses group leaders. A teacher may appoint leaders for classroom discussion groups. The president of an organization may appoint another officer, such as the vice president, to lead a committee. When a leader is appointed, the group has no control over the choice. Sometimes appointed leaders have trouble because they are not the group's choice.

Elected Leaders

Often sports teams select their own captains and extracurricular clubs elect their officers. It is very common for groups to elect their leaders. The job of elected leaders can be made easier because they have the group's support. One student describes the cooperation an elected leader might expect:

Our football team elects its captain, or leader, because the coach believes the team members will work best with someone they elected. Every week we have an hour in which the players and the captain discuss the team's problems. The captain encourages all players to talk about their feelings and share their ideas for new plays.

Emerging Leaders

Sometimes a group starts out without an appointed or elected leader, but over time a leader arises from the group because of how he or she has acted. A member may start to take charge and act as a leader. If the other members do not stop this person, he or she may emerge as that group's new leader. If you emerge as a leader, it could mean you are the only one willing to do the work. Or it could mean you have leadership skills that others respect.

LEADERSHIP RESPONSIBILITIES

Some people like the title *leader*, but not the work that goes along with the title. Being a responsible leader takes effort. Leadership responsibilities fall into the general areas of (1) beginning the discussion, (2) acting as moderator, and (3) closing the discussion.

Beginning the Discussion

The leader will begin by introducing the topic, introducing the members, or beginning the discussion. To introduce the topic, the leader may state the question or explain to the group or audience why the discussion is taking place. If group members do not know each other well, the leaders can hold an introduction period and introduce the group members.

In beginning the discussion, the leader may suggest who will speak first or what part of the topic will be discussed first. For example, "First we'll discuss the problem of playground destruction and then possible ways to stop it." Usually, appointed or elected leaders get things started. If there is no such leader, someone may emerge as a leader by taking over some of these duties.

Acting as Moderator

Leaders act as moderators for the discussion. **Moderators** keep a discussion moving and see that everyone's ideas are heard. Leaders will try to keep the discussion on track. It is important that members make comments that relate to the topic the group is discussing. If the group is analyzing the problem and someone suggests a solution, the leader could say, "That's an interesting point, Jack. Maybe you could bring that up again when we get to solutions." The leader also makes sure the members' comments are on the subject.

Leaders also make sure everyone contributes. The leader has to prevent one or two members from talking all the time and has to encourage quiet members to share their ideas. The leader may encourage quiet members who speak up by saying, "I'm really glad you said that. We hadn't thought of that idea."

Leaders also must watch the clock so the task can be completed before the group runs out of time. It's very frustrating to spend forty minutes on a problem and only ten minutes on how to solve it.

Closing the Discussion

Leaders end the discussion by summarizing the main points. They try to mention the main ideas that were discussed and announce any conclusions that were reached. They also thank the members for their contributions.

IMPROVING LEADERSHIP SKILLS

A good leader can always become a better leader. Competent leaders evaluate their own performances in order to improve their skills. You can use the checklist on page 176 to examine your leadership skills. Do not write in your book.

INTERACT

In a small group, discuss possible ways a group leader could handle the following situations:

1. Abdul, who has not done any research on the topic, constantly criticizes what other group members say.

2. One member shows interest in the discussion nonverbally but hasn't said anything.
3. Rebecca talks constantly. It is difficult for other members to get their ideas out.
4. Everyone is getting frustrated, although for varying reasons. Everyone is arguing. No one seems willing to listen to anyone else. If your grade didn't depend on this project, you'd never meet together again.

LEADERSHIP SKILLS CHECKLIST

Use this checklist to assess your leadership skills. Which statements *never* apply to you? Which statements *sometimes* or *frequently* apply? Which statements *always* apply?

1. I try to include everyone in the discussion.
2. I guide the group through problem-solving steps.
3. I try to help members compromise.
4. I am able to control excessive talkers.
5. I am able to draw out quiet members.
6. I watch the time.
7. I keep the group on the topic.
8. I encourage members to express different opinions.
9. I avoid talking too much.
10. I bring up the topic and close the discussion.

EVALUATING GROUP DISCUSSION

Decide whether the following statement is true or false:

The more small groups you are in, the better you become as a small-group communicator.

Hopefully, you said *false.* Having been in ten or twenty group discussions does not necessarily mean you are a better member or leader. All it means is that you have been in more groups!

Do you remember the steps a competent communicator follows? Competent communicators (1) think of communication strategies, (2) select a strategy, (3) act on the strategy, and (4) evaluate the strategy. Competent communicators must evaluate their group discussions. This allows members or leaders to retain helpful behaviors and change behaviors that do not work well.

The purposes of the evaluation are to (1) strengthen good points, (2) correct weak points, and (3) reduce mistakes. If you don't evaluate your group discussion by giving and receiving feedback with other group members or group observers, you will never know exactly how you are doing in the group.

GUIDELINES FOR EVALUATION

"Martina was good."

"J.P. could have done better."

These kinds of comments do not help group members. They are too general. When giving feedback to others, remember the following guidelines:

1. *Describe what you saw and heard.* Instead of saying "Tom was good," say, "Tom asked three good questions and made two useful suggestions to solve the problem." Don't say, "Geri wasn't a good group member." Instead say, "Geri talked to the person next to her instead of to the whole group. She made three jokes but did not make any suggestions for a solution."

2. *Limit your comments.* Don't try to evaluate everything. For example, say, "Jake contributed two or three things, but didn't dominate," or "Samara listened carefully and encouraged others." Do not make eight or nine comments. The person will never be able to keep track of what you are saying.

3. *Include strong points, weak points, and areas for improvement.* When giving feedback do not limit yourself to one type of comment. It is not useful to say, "I could not hear Kara." It is more helpful to say, "Kara paid careful attention to what was going on. It was hard to hear what she said. Next time Kara should speak more loudly and clearly. Then everyone can benefit from her good ideas."

Your group discussion should improve as you evaluate your own work and that of others. As a competent communicator you should strive to improve each time.

SELF-FEEDBACK CHECKLIST

Use this checklist to assess your participation in group communication. Which statements never apply to you? Which statements *sometimes* or *frequently* apply? Which statements *always* apply?

1. I worry about being wrong.
2. I ask questions to get attention.
3. I avoid interrupting speakers.
4. I am prepared with the necessary information.
5. I look at people when I speak to them.
6. I listen carefully to others' ideas.

7. I avoid disagreements.
8. My mind wanders when I'm not talking.
9. I try to include people who don't say much.
10. I am too willing to compromise.
11. I stick to the topic of the discussion.
12. I try to support others.

PROVIDING FEEDBACK

You can give feedback to yourself and to others to improve communication competence in groups. In order to examine your own behavior, you can create a checklist to chart your skill development. You might want to copy the Self-Feedback Checklist in the book or develop your own form. Evaluate your own communication each time you participate in a group discussion.

Your feedback to others should be based on a description of what you saw and heard. You can create forms to help you observe members in a group discussion. The sample feedback form on page 180 shows one way of recording group members' communication behavior. Each time a contribution is made, a check is placed in the appropriate space for each member.

SUMMARY

This chapter introduces characteristics of small groups and problem solving. Five important small-group characteristics are structure, purpose, norms, roles, and subgroups. Group members should be able to recognize these characteristics. Group discussion is most effective when the five steps of problem solving are followed: (1) identify the problem; (2) analyze the problem; (3) set criteria for a solution; (4) develop solutions; and (5) select a solution. Effective group problem solving means leaders and members must be responsible for the group's work and follow guidelines for responsible speaking and listening. Each member needs to know how leaders are chosen and what leaders' responsibilities are. Finally, your evaluation of the group and your communication in the group can tell you a lot about how well the group performed.

FEEDBACK FORM—GROUP COMMUNICATION

Directions: Place a checkmark in the appropriate column each time a group member contributes to the discussion. Add comments below.

Group Members	Agreeing	Disagreeing	Seeking information	Giving information	Seeking opinion	Giving opinion	Asking for solutions	Giving solutions	Encouraging others	Summarizing

Comments: _____

_____

_____

CHAPTER REVIEW

THINK ABOUT IT

1. Define *group* and list the characteristics of groups.
2. What are the five steps in problem solving?
3. What are speakers' responsibilities in groups?
4. What are listeners' responsibilities in groups?
5. What are the responsibilities of group leaders?

TRY IT OUT

1. In a group of six to seven classmates, talk about cliques. Use the following questions in your discussion:
   - Are there cliques in your school that are subgroups of other groups?
   - Is it possible to belong to more than one clique?
   - What are the different images various cliques have?
   - How realistic are the images?
   - How does it feel to be with members of a subgroup different from the one you usually spend time with?
   - What are the advantages and disadvantages of cliques or subgroups?
2. In a group of five to seven members, discuss either a topic of your choice or the topic, "Should the Student Council Be Given More Power in Determining School Policy?" At the end of fifteen minutes, discuss together: (1) What role did each group member perform? (2) To what extent did your group follow the five problem-solving steps?
3. As a class, brainstorm a long list of problems in your school and community. These can be problems of any sort. Then break up into small groups to address these problems. Your overall goal will be to do something about a problem you choose from the list. As a group, you have to figure out what you will do. You will also have to deal with group leadership and evaluate both your group's meetings and your own work in the group.

What specific problem will you address? Analyze it. At one time or another, you may have to ask questions of fact, value, and policy. Just be sure you know what you are discussing each time you get together (in class or on your own). Set up criteria for your solution, try to think up as many solutions as possible, and choose one. Then try it! See if you can solve the problem you worked on.

4. Evaluate a small-group discussion in which you took part. Choose either of the evaluation forms included in this chapter or make up one of your own. Then write a one-page paper discussing the strengths, weaknesses, and ideas for improvement of the group communication or of your own communication in that group.

PUT IT IN WRITING

1. Select one of the following topics and write two or three paragraphs describing the topic.
   - I Wanted to Be Part of the Group but Was Left Out
   - Our Group Made Room for One More Person
   - How Groups Make You Feel Welcome
   - The Group I Didn't Want to Join
2. List two groups to which you belong. Describe the norms of each group. Give an example of what might happen if a member in a group does not follow the norms.

SPEAK ABOUT IT

1. Present a two- or three-minute speech in which you give three reasons why group discussion is important.
2. Phrase three discussion topics—one of fact, one of value, and one of policy. Make sure these three topics meet the criteria on page 164. Present the three topics to your class, explaining why you think they are good topics.
3. Describe to your class why a particular group is an important part of the nation or the community. Explain why you consider this group effective.

FORMS OF GROUP DISCUSSION

After completing this chapter, you should be able to

- define *committee, panel discussion, symposium, forum,* and *buzz groups.*
- describe the roles of leader and participants in a committee, panel, symposium, and discussion.
- define *parliamentary procedure* and its four principles.
- describe the duties of the parliamentary officers.

KEY WORDS

agenda

buzz groups

committee

forum

majority

minority

minutes

motion

panel discussion

parliamentary procedure

second

symposium

183

Group discussion is important in our community. Several community members met with the city council, parks and recreation department, the PTA members, and interested kids from all our schools. The goal was to build Kids' Place (a large playground) in the largest park in our city. Everyone was allowed to express their opinions about the design and fund-raising, even the kids. The Kids' Place would have playground equipment for kids of all ages. One of the decisions made was to make it look like a large castle. The community children held discussion sessions in their schools and collected pennies from kindergarten through twelfth grade. Once the money was collected, volunteers from all over the city held discussions to arrange the work schedule to complete their plans. The community worked together around the clock for several days. We accomplished something very wonderful for our city. What was even more exciting, after we finished, several of the kids at our local schools got to be on "Good Morning America."

This student understands the importance of group discussion. Group discussion is used by school and community groups to examine issues and make decisions. Your life may be changed greatly by the decisions made by certain groups. Think about the decisions of groups in your school and community that affect your life.

The success of groups depends on the communication competence of the group members. Group members must use their communication skills effectively if the group is to complete its job. Group members must know the topic area well, decide on their views on the topic, listen, and speak responsibly. As you read this chapter, think about speaking and listening responsibilities and why they would be important in each of the groups discussed.

Although most problem-solving groups follow the steps described in the last chapter, different groups use different ways of conducting their business. This chapter discusses various group formats in which you may find yourself. These include special types of groups, such as committees, panels, and symposiums, and groups that use parliamentary procedure.

DISCUSSION FORMATS

Group members can use various formats to discuss, share ideas, and reach conclusions. These include committees, panel discussions, and symposiums.

COMMITTEES

At some time you've probably been a member of a committee. A **committee** is usually a subgroup of a larger group, and it is formed to take care of a specific task. If a large group has a problem or is discussing a topic on which it needs more information, the group may form a committee to study the problem further.

Suppose your class is planning a class trip. A committee could look into the possible places the class could go, figure the cost, find chaperones, set the date, and report their findings to the class. This committee could recommend an action for the group to approve. Other committees have the power to make decisions for the larger group. For example, your student council has the power to make decisions for the entire student body.

Often participants in a committee meeting sit at a round table so that all members face one another. Although an audience may be present, audience members do not take part in the discussion. Each committee member gives a report on the topic area. Following the reports, participants discuss the topic.

For example, suppose you are a member of a committee discussing course changes in your school district. First each committee member would report on the courses he or she thinks are necessary. Then discussion following the reports might focus on specific courses and the steps necessary to carry out the new courses.

JOURNAL ENTRY

At our school we have a committee made up of students who are against drugs. This is a subcommittee of our student council. We are allowed to plan a week called "Red Ribbon Week," in which red symbolizes being drug free. We plan activities and events for every day of this week. Our group usually has fifteen members, and usually we have more ideas than we can use. When we gather all our ideas together, we take them back to the student council and vote which activities we will use. We really enjoy sharing our ideas with each other.

Apply

Imagine that you have been assigned to one of the following committees. What kinds of tasks would you and the other committee members discuss and carry out?

- Minimarathon publicity committee
- Halloween dance decorations committee
- Parents' Night entertainment committee
- Candy sale planning committee
- Drug Prevention Week committee

PANEL DISCUSSIONS

A **panel discussion** is a discussion in which a subject is explored by the members in front of an audience. A panel discussion format allows the speakers to inform or influence the audience. Most panels have four to eight members. The members should be seated so they can see and be seen by the audience. Members of a panel make statements, ask questions, and comment on what other panel members have said. Most panel members have notes with information on them.

Usually a panel discussion has a leader, called a chairperson, whose job is to (1) introduce the panel members and the subject, (2) define important terms, (3) call on speakers during the discussion, (4) review points during the discussion, and

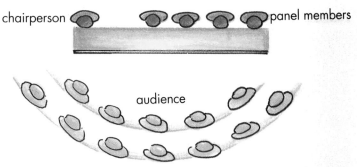

(5) summarize the main ideas. Most panelists remain seated so they can communicate with each other more easily and more informally.

Panel members are expected to be well informed about their subject areas. Preparation is important to successful panels. Usually the panel and chairperson meet to discuss who will speak about certain ideas. Panelists try to reach some agreement on their ideas before the end of discussion.

Panel discussions are popular in history and English classes. Students can use panels to discuss topics from different points of view. Many governing bodies use panel discussions to inform community members about issues of local concern. These panel discussions often occur before citizens vote on an issue.

The following is an example of a panel discussion about course changes:

Bob: Good afternoon. Welcome teachers, parents, and students. As you know, the officers of the student council have been asked to discuss what new courses are needed at our school. Each panel member will give his or her suggestions. Let me introduce the panelists. To my far right is Maria Vasquez, vice president. Next to her is John Holmes, treasurer. And next to me is Soon-ja Park, secretary. To my left is Mark Levy, social committee chair. Next to him is Nancy Henderson, service committee chair. I am Bob Marks, student council president.

As most of you know, every ten years the school reviews all the courses in the district. The school board appointed a committee of students and a committee of teachers to look at our courses and recommend changes. At this meeting we will share with you some of the student committee ideas. John, since you suggested this panel discussion, why don't you begin?

John: I've talked to a lot of students, and they think we need a course in video production. Since most students have VCRs at home, they're interested in learning how to make videos. This would also teach us what to look for as we watch videos at home.

Bob: Maria, you look like you want to say something.

Maria: How many students did you talk to, John? I talked to more than fifty and none mentioned video production. Most of the people I talked to wanted an additional class in computers. I know that would help me. My dad just bought our family a home computer and he wants me to set up some budgets. You can't get into the Introduction to Computers class unless you've been on the waiting list for a year.

John: Hey, that's a good idea. Mr. Finley says we should do our papers on the word processor so we can edit them easily. No one knows how to use it! And I don't want to go to summer school to find out.

Bob: John, please raise your hand when you want to speak. Mark has his hand up. Mark, go ahead.

Mark: I think both John and Maria have good ideas. I'd like to have more art courses besides painting or drawing. The people I talked to wanted jewelry making and paper sculpture.

John: I like that idea also.

Bob: Fine, but let's hear Nancy's ideas, since she's been waiting to speak.

Nancy: I talked to about fifty students and about ten suggested a course in woodworking. About twenty-five wanted more variety in English, such as classes in science fiction or mysteries. The rest had lots of different ideas.... *(The discussion continues.)*

This panel has offered some good ideas. Bob will summarize the ideas near the end and ask for final comments from the panelists. Notice that instead of formal speeches, a panel discussion is more like a conversation led by a chairperson.

INTERACT

Set up a practice panel that uses your own classmates' opinions. Some of you will act as panel members and the rest will act as interviewees. Have each panel member take ten minutes to interview a small group from the rest of the class about one of the following subjects or another subject of your choice. Give the panelists an extra five minutes to get organized and select a chairperson. The panel discussion should last for ten to fifteen minutes. Possible subjects:

- a new snack bar being made available in the cafeteria

- ways to improve the school grounds or building
- ways to raise money for new computers for the library

After the panel discussion, answer the following questions:

1. How well were your classmates' opinions represented?
2. How well did the chairperson direct the panel?
3. How well did the panel members express their ideas?

SYMPOSIUMS

A **symposium** is a discussion during which members give short speeches to an audience. A symposium is similar to a panel discussion. The main difference is that a symposium is more formal. Each person gives a speech and each speech represents a different point of view on the subject being discussed. Unlike the panel, speakers usually don't talk with one another unless there is a question-and-answer period following each speech. As in a panel, the leader introduces the symposium members and the topic. The leader also closes the symposium by briefly summarizing the speeches.

Suppose the panel discussion on course changes had been a symposium. Each participant would have spoken on part of the subject. John would have given a speech on a video production course; Maria, on the need for an advanced computer course; Mark, on art classes; and Nancy, on woodwork and various English classes. The speakers would present reasons why the courses they suggested are needed. They would also give facts, such as how many students want a certain course.

AUDIENCE PARTICIPATION

Sometimes audience members take part in panel discussions or symposiums. When the audience becomes involved, the discussion is called a **forum.** Audience members can ask questions of the persons presenting the information. Usually the questions are asked at the end of the panel discussion or symposium, but sometimes there is a question-and-answer period after each speaker's comments.

When the speakers use only half the scheduled time, audience members are sometimes asked to get into small groups, called buzz groups. **Buzz groups** are expected to discuss the ideas presented by the speakers and decide on some solution to the problem. The entire audience comes back together, and a representative of each buzz group reports on the group's solution. After a summary by the chairperson, the audience and symposium members discuss the proposed solutions and try to decide on the best.

JOURNAL ENTRY

Recently at one of the local schools, a forum was presented to discuss changing our school district from a nine-month school year to a year-round school year. The panel consisted of school board members from our school district and panel members from school districts in our state that had already changed to year-round schools. The forum was very informative, and parents and students had many questions that were answered.

OBSERVE

Attend a panel discussion or symposium in your school or community, or watch one on TV. Pay careful attention to the role of the chairperson. How well did this person keep the speakers in line? How well did he or she introduce speakers and summarize points? If audience members got involved, how well did the chairperson handle the audience participation?

PARLIAMENTARY PROCEDURE

Federal, state, and local governments use parliamentary procedure to conduct their business. **Parliamentary procedure** is a set of rules for running large group meetings. Groups, especially large ones, need rules to work effectively. Most large groups follow parliamentary procedure rules found in *Robert's Rules of Order Revised* by Henry Robert or in *Learning Parliamentary Procedure* by Alice Sturgis.

JOURNAL ENTRY

During our Washington trip our class observed a session at the House of Representatives. The members of Congress run their meetings according to parliamentary procedure. The Speaker of the House chairs the meeting and the members follow set rules for how to talk. It was complicated but interesting.

Parliamentary procedure began in the English Parliament many years ago as members tried to gain fair and equal opportunities to speak. American governmental groups use these rules to protect the democratic rights of all members to be heard. Today most student governments and large community organizations run their meetings according to parliamentary procedure.

PRINCIPLES AND PROCESS

Parliamentary procedure is based on the following principles:

1. The right of the majority (more than half) to decide
2. The right of the minority (less than half) to be heard
3. Decisions made according to a one-person, one-vote rule
4. The right of absent members' opinions to be included

According to parliamentary rules, the decision of the majority is accepted for the whole group—hence, the expression "majority rules." A **majority** is more than one-half of the votes. Even though the majority may win, the **minority,** or the group with less than half the votes, always has a chance to express its views. The leader of the group is elected by a majority vote and is expected to be fair and objective in running the meeting.

A vote can be taken by a ballot, by a show of hands, or by voice vote. In a ballot vote, each person receives a ballot and writes his or her vote on the ballot. Absent members may vote if they have previously turned in a ballot according to the group's rules. To vote by a show of hands, people raise their hands to indicate support for their position. If the show of hands seems close, there will be a count of the hands raised for each position.

In a voice vote, the chair says, "All in favor, say yes; opposed say no." If the majority of votes are *yes*, then the chair says, "The yeas have it," and the motion passes. If the majority of votes are *no*, then the chair says, "The nos have it," and the motion fails. If it is not possible to determine whether there were more votes for yes or for no, the chair may call for a show of hands. Those who do not wish to vote may abstain and the number of abstentions will be counted and reported along with the yes and no votes.

The parliamentary process helps people work in an orderly way because

- only one topic is considered at a time.
- all group members have a chance to speak their minds.
- all sides of a subject are heard.
- one or two people cannot shut off or dominate the discussion.

If a meeting is run according to parliamentary procedure, discussion of one topic must be completed before discussion of another topic can begin.

Under parliamentary procedure, all members are given a chance to speak. This means that all sides of a topic will be heard. Members may move to end discussion, but two-thirds of the group must agree to do so. Therefore, one or two people cannot take control of the discussion.

 **JOURNAL ENTRY**

Our community is debating whether to change the policies about teaching in the school system. A group of student representatives attended the last meeting, which was run according to parliamentary procedure. If you didn't understand the rules it was very hard to know exactly what was going on. We did get to talk for a short time, but we could have had more influence if we had known how to work according to parliamentary procedure.

ORDER OF BUSINESS

Most formal group meetings follow the same unchangeable order. Some groups print an agenda to make the order of topics clear. This standard order of business usually involves the following set procedures:

1. *Call to order.* The call to order begins the meeting. The chair says, "The meeting will come to order."

2. *Approval of agenda.* The chair asks the group to review the **agenda**, or plan for the meeting, and determine if there are other topics to be considered, or if it is necessary to alter the order of business. Any necessary changes are made and the agenda is approved as corrected.

3. *Reading of minutes.* The **minutes** are notes taken at the previous meeting of the group. The chair asks the group's secretary to read the minutes. After the secretary reads the minutes, the chair asks, "Are there any additions or corrections?" If there are no additions or corrections, the chair asks for a motion to approve the minutes. The chair indicates the minutes are approved or approved as corrected.

4. *Reports of other officers.* Besides the chairperson and secretary, many organizations have a treasurer and other officers. The chair says, for example, "The treasurer will give us a treasurer's report." The treasurer then reports the group's financial balance and accounts for money that was received or expended. The chair then calls for the treasurer's report to be received by the group. Each officer provides a report on his or her area of responsibility.

5. *Committee reports.* The chair asks each committee chair if the committee has a report to make. Each committee chair then gives a brief report of the group's work or indicates the group did not get together since the last meeting. Organizations with a large number of committees may request brief written committee reports to be passed out. The oral presentations may reflect only debatable topics.

6. *Old business.* Old business includes any issues that were not resolved at the last meeting or any updates on ongoing business. The chair asks, "Is there any old business from the previous meeting?" In large groups, the old business may be listed on the agenda. In this case, the chair says, "Let us turn to the old business."

7. *New business.* New business is any topic that has not been discussed previously. After completing the old business, the chair asks, "Is there any new business?" Any member is free to introduce new business. A member may raise his or her hand and state an issue for

discussion. For example, a student council representative may say, "Our school is the only one in this area without a video yearbook. I wish to bring this issue to the student council's attention."

8. *Announcements.* The chair or other designated speaker announces future events, including news about members. These announcements may be comments such as, "The science fair has been rescheduled for April 10" or "Mrs. Hiller is out of the hospital."

9. *Adjournment.* The chair closes the meeting saying, "The meeting is ended" or "This meeting is adjourned."

MOTIONS

I move we give $250 to the 'Mathletes' for their trip to Washington.

I move the adoption of the following resolution: "We the students of North High urge the school board to require foreign language classes."

A **motion** is a proposed action. A motion should be brief and clear, propose a specific action for the group to take, and state only one idea.

There are four types of motions: (1) main, (2) subsidiary, (3) privileged, and (4) incidental. Main motions introduce the topic that members wish to discuss. Subsidiary motions modify the content of a main motion or change the way a main motion is dealt with. Privileged motions are concerned with the immediate needs and comforts of the members; therefore, once a privileged motion is made, it is considered before any other motion. Finally, incidental motions deal with procedures involved in running the meeting.

Apply

Compare the following motions. Which ones are well-stated?

- I move our club have a skating party, sell candy, and have a bake sale to raise money.
- I move the hockey club have a picnic on the last day of school.

- I move the art club sponsor a contest for the poetry book cover.
- I move the soccer team get involved in a community project.

You're correct if you think that the second and third motions are the better motions, because they propose specific actions.

Before a main motion can be discussed, at least one other member must **second** it, or support it. After a motion is proposed, another member says, "I second the motion." If no one volunteers, the chair asks if there is a second to the motion. If no one will second the motion, there is no discussion of that motion.

To pass, a motion must be accepted by the majority of the voters. If members wish to change the main motion, they can make a subsidiary motion to amend it. If the members wish to discuss it at a later time, they can make a subsidiary motion to table the main motion. When a motion is tabled, it is usually put on the next agenda as part of old business. If the members want to have the main motion studied further, they can make a subsidiary motion to send it to a committee.

Only one motion can be considered at a time. If a member believes discussion has gone on long enough and he or she wants the motion voted on, he or she would say, "I call the previous question." If there are no objections, the chair calls for a vote on the motion. Two-thirds of the group must agree to close discussion.

DUTIES OF OFFICERS

When parliamentary procedure is used, each officer performs certain duties. The officers serve to keep the organization alive and responsible. Each position requires time and energy. Effective officers are competent communicators and understand the rules of parliamentary procedure.

President or Chair

If you are the president or chair of a club or organization, parliamentary procedure can help you lead the group effectively. It's your job to make sure the group accomplished something. The president's duties include:

1. *Keeping the meeting under control.* The president has to keep the members on the subject, make sure that everyone has an equal opportunity to be heard, and budget the time so that the group can complete its tasks.
2. *Making sure each main motion is finished.* The president is responsible for making sure each motion is voted on or set aside before a new one is introduced.
3. *Explaining the points if some members don't understand.* One of the president or chair's main duties is repeating questions and information so that everyone in the group can hear and understand them. If there are any questions about procedure, the president is responsible for answering them, or for asking the group's parlimentarian to answer them.
4. *Moderating the discussion.* The president does not participate in the discussion, but he or she makes sure that all the members know what is going on. The president recognizes and introduces speakers and makes sure that discussion continues in an orderly manner.
5. *Voting in case of a tie.* The president or chair only votes in order to break a tie. The reason for this is so that members won't feel pressured to support the president's side of an issue.

Vice President or Vice Chair

The vice president or vice chair assists the president or chair. The vice president's duties include:

1. Chairing the meeting when the president is absent.
2. Chairing certain committees as an assistant to the president.
3. Substituting for the president whenever necessary.
4. Completing any vice presidential tasks listed in the group's constitution.

Secretary

Most organizations or clubs have a secretary to keep records. The secretary's duties include:

1. Keeping the minutes or records of meetings.
2. Checking the attendance at meetings.
3. Sending out notices about future meetings.
4. Sending out letters as directed by the president or chair.

Keeping the minutes is an extremely important duty. Minutes include the date, time, and place of the meeting; the person who ran the meeting; the main points from the reading of the last meeting's minutes; all main motions presented at the meeting and what happened with them; and what time the meeting was adjourned.

Treasurer

The treasurer is the group's financial officer. The treasurer's duties include:

1. Keeping records of all expenses and incoming funds.
2. Paying the bills.
3. Collecting dues or other money.
4. Giving a financial report when required.

Parliamentarian

The main duty of the parliamentarian is to advise the president or chairperson on parliamentary procedure. Whenever questions arise about parliamentary procedure, the parliamentarian's job is to provide the correct answer. If any violations of parliamentary procedure occur, the parliamentarian is responsible for pointing them out.

Historian

The historian keeps records of the group's history. Often this record takes the form of a scrapbook that includes the group's special events and projects, past officers, awards, and so on.

Committee Chairs or Other Officers

Some groups may have committee chairpersons in areas such as publicity, fund-raising, or long-range planning. Each person's duties are spelled out in the constitution.

OBSERVE

Attend a school or community meeting in which parliamentary procedure is used. Write a report on the effectiveness of the chairperson and how the use of parliamentary procedure helped the meeting run smoothly.

KEY PARLIAMENTARY TERMS

adjournment	closing of the meeting
agenda	list of subjects to be discussed at a meeting; often indicates order of reports and topics of old business and new business to be considered
amendment	a proposed change in a motion. It is stated as ''I move to amend the previous motion by . . . .''
by-laws	list of rules governing the procedures to be followed by the group
call previous question	move to an immediate vote. Example: ''I call the previous question on this motion.'' Sometimes just stated as ''Question.''
chairperson (or president)	person who leads the meeting
constitution	document that describes nature and purpose of a group
floor (to have the)	to have been granted the right to speak. Example: ''I'm sorry, Tamara. Kyle has the floor right now. You may speak when he has finished.''
incidental motion	motion dealing with procedures involved in running the meeting
main motion	proposed item of business or action for the group to consider. It is stated as ''I move . . . .''
minority	one less than one-half of those people voting
minutes	written report of what happens at a meeting; usually prepared by the secretary. Minutes are considered for approval at the following meeting.

order of business	the sequence or order in which matters will be discussed; usually established in an agenda, but group may decide to change the order of business through a vote
parliamentarian	person responsible for making sure parliamentary procedure is followed; usually uses *Robert's Rules of Order Revised* or *Learning Parliamentary Procedure* for reference
point of order	objection to the discussion on the floor. Reasons for a point of order include a speaker moving to an unrelated topic, telling an inappropriate joke, and so on.
privileged motion	motion to deal with immediate need of members
quorum	number of members who must be at the meeting in order to conduct the meeting and make binding decisions
recess	to take a break from the meeting for a set period of time
request for information	question asked of the speaker or chair in order to clarify a point
second a motion	show of support for a motion. Example: "I second the motion."
secret ballot	written vote used for nominations and controversial topics
subsidiary motion	motion to change the main motion or way of dealing with main motion
table a motion	to put a motion aside to be discussed at another, usually specified, time. Example: "I move we table the motion until the next meeting." A motion cannot be tabled without a second.
two-thirds rule	rule that states two-thirds of the group must be in favor to close debate

PARLIAMENTARY PROCEDURE IN ACTION

The following script follows a meeting in which parliamentary procedure was used. Notice how parliamentary procedure is followed by the different group members.

call to order

Chair: The meeting will come to order.

approval of agenda

May I have an approval of the agenda?

Kirsten: So moved.

Jack: Second.

Chair: Any objections? _(Pause)._ There being no objections we will follow the agenda as proposed. Our secretary, Nancy, will present the minutes of the last meeting.

reading of the minutes

Nancy: The monthly meeting of the Community Service Club was called to order by President Mary Jones on Tuesday, March 6, 1992, at 3:15 in Room 102 of the Highland School. The minutes of the last meeting were read and approved. Treasurer Jeff Nielsen reported that the club has $87.12 in the treasury. Under old business, the group reviewed the problem of attendance at the soup kitchen. Under new business, Jeff moved that the Community Service Club sponsor a child in Central America. The motion was passed. Jeff is looking into the arrangements. The group also discussed fund-raising for the Thanksgiving food baskets.

Paul Vasquez moved to adjourn the meeting. The meeting was adjourned at 4:45.

Chair: Thank you, Nancy. Are there any corrections or additions to the minutes? _(Pause.)_ If not, the minutes are approved. Jeff will read the treasurer's report.

committee report
treasurer

Jeff: We spent $28 on food and table decorations for Parents' Night. We took in $135. Our current cash balance is $194.12.

Chair: Thank you, Jeff. May we have the committee report for our Student Council Banquet? Julissa?

committee report
banquet planning

Julissa: The best place that we could find for our budget is McKinney's Steak House. The dining room is large enough for all of us. The banquet dinners are a low price of $8.00 a person. We will report back to you next week on the date. The restaurant is checking its calendar for May 6th. We hope to have a set date by next week's meeting.

old business

Chair: Thank you, Julissa. On to old business. At our last meeting we discussed fund-raising projects for our Thanksgiving food baskets. Anyone have any new ideas? Margie.

main motion

Margie: I move we have a dance.

Chair: John.

second the motion

John: I second the motion.

discussion

Chair: It's been moved and seconded that we have a dance to raise money for our Thanksgiving food baskets. Is there any discussion? Sara.

amendment

Sara: No one ever goes to our school dances unless it's some holiday dance like Halloween or Valentine's Day. I think we need to make it a special dance. I move to amend the motion by changing "dance" to "turn-about dance."

Chair: Jeff.

Jeff: I second the amendment.

Chair: It's been moved and seconded to amend the motion by changing "dance" to "turn-about dance." Is there any discussion? Jack.

discussion on the amendment

Jack: I really like that idea, but I think we have to do some clever kind of publicity so everyone will know what a turn-about dance is.

point of information

Sue: Point of information.

Chair: Sue.

Sue: What exactly *is* a turn-about dance?

Chair: Sara.

Sara: A turn-about dance is one where a girl asks a boy to go with her instead of the boys asking.

Sue: Thanks.

Chair: Kirsten.

Kirsten: I think Jack's right. If we have good publicity, we could make lot of money.

Chair: Is there further discussion of the amendment? *(Pause.)* Does anyone have any objections? Donna.

Donna: Yes. I don't like those dances, and I know a lot of other people who don't either. It puts so much pressure on us to ask guys. At a regular dance anyone can ask anyone. Isn't that better?

Chair: Any response? Jack.

Jack: You just don't want to have to ask someone. How would you like it if you were a guy?

Chair: Donna.

Donna: No, that's not it. I don't mind asking guys to dance. I just don't like the pressure.

Chair: Sara.

Sara: I see what you mean, Donna. But I think the pressure is always there and that this special twist for just one dance might really interest people.

<u>vote</u>

Chair: Any more comments? *(Pause.)* Since there is no further discussion, all those in favor of amending the motion by changing the word "dance" to "turn-about dance" say yes. All opposed say no. *(Pause. Scans room.)* The amendment is approved.

Chair: Any discussion on the motion? Michael.

Michael: I don't think we should have a dance at all. Everyone is sick of dances. There's one almost every week, and they're all the same. I think we should think of something else, something that's really new and fun.

Chair: Other ideas? Sara.

Sara: Well, I think this is new and fun enough. A lot of people still go to dances, and we can make a lot of money for the Thanksgiving baskets, which is what we're supposed to do anyhow.

Chair: Michael.

Michael: I don't mean to offend you. I'm sure we can make money at a dance. I just wish we could find a more creative way to do it. I don't have any ideas yet, but if we defeat this motion, I'll work to come up with something better.

<u>calling the question</u>

Chair: Gail.

Gail: Let's vote, I mean call previous question.

Chair: Any objections to calling previous question on the motion? *(Pause.)* If there are no objections, let's vote. Any objections? *(Pause.)* None. It has been moved that we hold a turn-about dance to raise money for the Thanksgiving baskets. All those in favor say yes.

Group
Voice: Yes.

Chair: All opposed say no. *(No sound.)* Abstentions.

Ralph: I came in late. I'll abstain.

Chair: The motion passes. Rachel.

adjournment

Rachel: It's getting late; I move that we adjourn.

Chair: Chris.

Chris: Seconded.

Chair: It is moved and seconded that we adjourn. All those in favor say yes. All opposed, say no. *(Pause.)* The meeting is adjourned.

As you can tell from this sample meeting, effective parliamentary procedure depends on the group members' knowledge of the rules and their good communication skills. Group members must listen carefully to the chair and other speakers, or else they may become confused and unable to contribute. Speakers must form their ideas quickly and stay on the point in order to address the large group effectively.

INTERACT

Work with a partner to match the standard phrase to the following situations in a meeting:

1. Postpone the vote on a motion

2. End the meeting

3. Limit discussion of a motion

A. I move we adjourn the meeting.

B. I move this motion be amended by _____ .

C. I call the previous question.

4. Vote on a motion

5. Take a break

6. Start the meeting
7. Change a motion

D. The meeting will come to order.

E. I move debate on this motion be limited to 15 minutes.

F. I move we recess until 2:15.
G. I move we table the motion.

SUMMARY

This chapter describes various discussion formats and parliamentary procedure. There are a number of formats in which groups can share ideas: (1) committees, (2) symposiums, and (3) panel discussions. Members are expected to communicate in certain ways. Large groups often use a set of rules called parliamentary procedure to govern their meetings. Parliamentary procedure is based on certain rules and principles found in *Robert's Rules of Order Revised*. Parliamentary procedure helps keep order in large group meetings. It uses very specific terms and a specific order of business. Officers have certain duties.

CHAPTER REVIEW

THINK ABOUT IT

1. What is a panel discussion? A symposium? A committee?
2. Explain the role of the leader in each of the following group formats: panel discussion, symposium, and committee.
3. What is a forum? What is a buzz group?
4. Define *parliamentary procedure* and explain its four principles.
5. What are the duties of each of the parliamentary officers?

TRY IT OUT

1. Attend a meeting of a student club or the city council. Take notes to describe (1) the type of rules of procedure followed by the group (2) the effectiveness of the group in completing its work, and (3) problems the group members and officers had. As a class, discuss your findings and make suggestions for how the group could have used parliamentary procedure.
2. Select a possible school event, such as a talent show, fund-raiser, or dance. List possible committees that would plan and carry out the event. In small groups, select one of these imaginary committees and plan your committee tasks and create a planning report. Meet as a large group and share your planning reports.
3. Invite a school administrator to your classroom to discuss the importance of small groups in school life. Brainstorm a list of questions you might ask the administrator. Select the best question to begin your discussion.

PUT IT IN WRITING

1. After observing a classroom panel discussion or a symposium, write a two- or three-paragraph paper in which you summarize the panel's main points and evaluate the role of the leader and participants.
2. In many schools around the world, students do not get a chance to work in groups. Rather, they sit and listen to a teacher speak for most of the day. Write a letter to a pen pal from another country telling that person about the kinds of classroom and extracurricular group activities that are part of your education.

SPEAK ABOUT IT

1. With five to seven classmates, select a discussion topic. Present your discussion to the entire class in a panel or symposium format. After the discussion is completed, conduct a forum based on the discussion.
2. Hold a symposium to discuss one of the following topics:
- Eliminating Cheating in the Classroom
- Providing Better Food in the Cafeteria
- Making the School More Attractive
  After the discussion, divide into buzz groups. A representative from each buzz group should report the group's findings to the class.
3. After learning the rules for parliamentary procedure, pair up and instruct other classes or groups in the practice of parliamentary procedure.

PART 4

PUBLIC COMMUNICATION

CHAPTERS

Introduction to Public Speaking

Finding and Using Information

Constructing the Speech

Delivering the Speech

Creating the Informative Speech

Creating the Persuasive Speech

Learning About Debate

CHAPTER

9

INTRODUCTION TO PUBLIC SPEAKING

KEY WORDS

audience analysis

audience goal

public speaking

social ritual speech

speech to inform

speech to persuade

After completing this chapter, you should be able to

- define *public speaking*.
- give examples of situations in which people give public speeches.
- describe the two main purposes of public speaking.
- describe the guidelines for selecting a topic.
- explain the importance of audience analysis.
- list various types of information needed for an audience analysis.
- define and create audience goals.

Vote for Corelle Brown for Treasurer. She will keep good records of expenses....

I am pleased to welcome the players and parents to the fifth annual hockey dinner. Tonight we will honor....

As Halloween party volunteers, you will need to know how to apply makeup to the elementary school students. There are four basic steps....

These statements could be spoken by young people or adults to listeners who were voting in a school election, attending an awards dinner, or helping with a children's Halloween party. Speaking to groups occurs in many areas of life. In a recent survey of five hundred adults, over 60 percent said they had given at least one speech to an audience of more than ten people. Most had given four or more speeches over the past two years. Most of these speeches were presented on their jobs. Some were given in clubs or community groups.

There will be many times in your life when you will have to stand up and talk to an audience. The more practice you have had, the easier it will be.

PUBLIC SPEAKING AND YOU

Public speaking occurs when one person addresses a group for a specific purpose. You may find yourself delivering a message to audience members, or you may be an audience member listening to a speaker. In both cases you are an important part of the public speaking process.

You might think you will never have to give a speech. But when you think about the many situations that involve public speaking, you may change your mind. There are many situations in which one person stands up and talks to a group of people. Speeches may be short or long, formal or informal, funny or serious. Keep your eyes and ears open. You may be surprised to discover how many times people are called upon to speak in public.

Teenagers often find themselves in public speaking situations. Look at the following situations in which a student is asked to speak to an audience:

"It's your job to introduce the football team at the sports banquet."

"As part of the English assignment, you will be expected to give a short presentation to the class on the author you studied."

"You will have to give a short thank-you speech for the math award during the assembly."

"You must introduce the guest speaker to the class."

"We need three students to address the school board on the new student discipline code. Will you do it?"

JOURNAL ENTRY

We have a small zoo in our town, and I am a volunteer who works with the animals. I never thought I would have to give a speech, but in the summer when the camps come to the zoo on field trips, I have to talk to the children about the snakes. I explain to them the types of snakes we have, I show them many of the snakes, and then I answer questions while some of the children pet the snakes. I used to be terrified when I had to speak, but now it's just part of my job.

Some people think public speaking only involves giving long formal speeches to large audiences. Although this is one type of public speaking situation, speakers often talk to small, informal groups of people. As you grow older you will find even more situations in which you will be expected to talk to an audience. Look at the following comments that adults might make that involve public speaking. Some apply to work life; others to the groups adults join.

This looks like a tough jury. My closing arguments better be persuasive or my client will be in trouble.

The boss wants me to talk at the union meeting about the new safety regulations.

I'm talking to the Rotary Club tomorrow night about how I got started in sports medicine.

I have to give the report to the PTA on next year's budget.

OBSERVE

When do people you know make speeches? For one week list all the situations you become aware of that involve a person you know talking to an audience of ten or more people. Note the ages of the speakers and the reasons for their presentations. For example:

1. My teenage brother has to do an oral report in class next week.
2. My dentist will give a speech about clear braces at the next dental convention.

In addition to *giving* speeches, a competent communicator must evaluate speeches. Almost every day you are an audience member for a speaker. You listen to teachers, political speakers, religious speakers, and many others. You use your listening skills to evaluate these speakers and their messages.

This chapter discusses the purposes of public speaking, topic selection, audience analysis, and audience goals. Later chapters will describe how to create and deliver different types of speeches.

PURPOSES OF PUBLIC SPEAKING

The main purposes for public speaking are to inform and to persuade. Other reasons to give speeches are to entertain and to inspire. This text focuses on the two main purposes, informing and persuading.

SPEAKING TO INFORM

A **speech to inform** is designed to increase the knowledge of the listeners. The speech may introduce the audience to a new subject or present an in-depth look at a familiar topic. It may describe or demonstrate. A speech to inform tries to be fair and objective. Here are some sample titles of speeches to inform:

- How to Make Tacos
- What Is "The Food Web"?
- How to Play a Recorder
- How Do Electrical Circuits Work?
- Putting On Clown Makeup
- Safety While Sailing
- Fossils of Arizona
- Easy Bicycle Repairs

For each of these topics, the speakers describe or demonstrate something. Listeners would expect to learn new information or new skills.

Social Ritual Speeches

A special type of speech to inform is the **social ritual speech.** Social ritual speeches are short and follow a pattern, or set of rules. The following situations may involve social ritual speeches:

- Introducing the acts in a talent show
- Announcing awards
- Nominating a candidate for a school office
- Introducing a guest speaker
- Making announcements at meetings

Listeners expect social ritual speeches to follow certain patterns and may become annoyed or confused if the patterns are

not followed. For example, if the person introducing the guest speaker gives a fifteen-minute introduction, the audience will become annoyed. After all, the audience came to hear the speaker, not the person introducing the speaker!

SPEAKING TO PERSUADE

A **speech to persuade** is designed to convince the listeners to hold a certain belief or to act in a certain way. The speaker may inform the audience members and increase their knowledge as a means to move the audience to some belief or action. The speaker wants the listeners to think or act differently. The following are titles for speeches to persuade:

- Protect Our Children: Fingerprint Them!
- Drunk Drivers Deserve Tougher Punishments
- Homelessness Is Everyone's Problem
- Pen Pals Create International Understanding
- Teenagers Need to Watch Their Weight

In each of these speeches, the speaker would try to convince the listeners to agree with him or her or to take some action. Listeners must be aware of the strategies such a speaker would use to persuade them.

TOPIC SELECTION

Every speaker is faced with the question of what to talk about. You might ask yourself, "Should I describe my stamp collection, or should I demonstrate how to make apple pancakes? Should I convince the class members to attend the community pancake breakfast?" For most classroom speeches, you can choose your own topic.

In other school-related situations, you may be asked to speak on an assigned topic. If your school has assemblies related to various holidays, you may be asked to speak on social, religious, or political subjects related to the holiday.

In most speaking situations, you can choose a topic that is related to your interests or to a certain occasion. If the school board is considering changing the school discipline code, you may need to prepare a persuasive speech on the discipline topic for the school board meeting. To introduce the models in the church fashion show, you might be expected to give short descriptions of each outfit that is worn.

When you choose a classroom speech topic, use the following guidelines: (1) select a topic that interests you and (2) select a topic that will interest your audience.

INTEREST TO YOU

As a speaker you must select a topic that interests you. If you are not excited about a topic, it will be hard for you to keep your audience interested. If you are bored, you are going to bore your listeners! If you are excited, your audience will get excited.

Apply

Make a list of ten possible topics that interest you. You need not know everything about the topic right now because if you actually use the topic for a speech, you will do research. As you think of each topic, ask yourself, "Can I get excited about this subject?" Before you begin your list, think about questions such as these:

- What are my future goals?
- How do I like to spend my weekend?
- What is interesting about me?
- What do I worry about?
- What is unusual about my hobbies and interests?

INTEREST TO AUDIENCE

The second thing you must do as a speaker is select a topic that will interest your audience. Ask yourself if your listeners would find this subject interesting. After you find two or three topics that interest you, think about how your audience might react to each. One student considered the following topics interesting: diets, camping, music, baseball, astronomy, magic, and animals. This student made her decision on a final topic based on the topic she thought the class members would find most interesting:

I could talk on any of the seven subjects but I decided to speak about music because most of the other students in the class are interested in music. I limited myself to guitar music. I decided to describe how I compose simple songs on the guitar because I could play some examples.

AUDIENCE ANALYSIS

A good speaker always considers how to connect the audience and the message. **Audience analysis** is the information about the audience that helps the speaker communicate effectively. The analysis includes basic data, beliefs, and attitudes.

How often have you heard someone say, "The speaker was telling us things we already know" or "After five minutes most of the audience was half-asleep because the topic was so boring." To communicate you must know your audience well. This will help you select the right topic or the right words to keep their attention.

In a class you speak to the same group of students a number of times. Ask yourself what might interest them. In speaking situations outside of class, you may talk to many different audiences that you don't know as well. You will need to know something about each one in order to communicate effectively with them.

Apply

If you were to talk to an audience you did not know well, what information would you like to know about the members? Look at the two lists of audience characteristics and decide which contains the more important information.

List 1	**List 2**
gender	hair color
age	mother's first name
educational level	favorite color
cultural background	shoe size
religious views	phone numbers
political views	square dancing ability
income level	car model
reason for attending	scuba diving experiences

If you have concluded that the information in list 1 would be more helpful, you are correct.

In the next few pages, you will look at the kind of information that could be helpful as you do an audience analysis. This information includes basic data, beliefs or opinions, knowledge of topic, and expectations.

BASIC DATA

Often you need to know basic information about your listeners, such as age, gender, occupation, educational level, and income level. If you were talking about fossil hunting to second-graders, you could not use terms such as *sedimentary* or *trilobites*—at least, not without carefully explaining them. Information about the audience's age would help you choose the right level of scientific language and technical information. Knowing basic information about the audience would affect the way a speaker talks about the following topics:

- Crises Faced by Farm Families
- How to Child-Proof Your Home
- Best Pitchers in Baseball
- Careers in Cooking

One student describes how she adapts to her audience:

JOURNAL ENTRY

I am part of a team of students that talks to community groups about helping our school. When we talk to business groups, we ask for money or equipment. When we talk to senior citizen groups, people who don't have much money, we ask them to volunteer their time.

The more you know about your audience, the more ways you will find to connect the audience and your topic. Use examples and language that the audience will understand.

BELIEFS AND OPINIONS

It is important to know if most audience members hold specific beliefs or values related to your topic. Being sensitive to

an audience's political views or religious beliefs can help speakers avoid offending the audience. Some hunters will not appreciate a speaker who supports gun control. People who believe in government spending to support the poor will not listen kindly to a speaker who wants to cut the food stamp program.

Apply

Look at the following and decide which audience beliefs or opinions a speaker should try to learn about before giving a speech on these subjects.

- divorce
- smoking
- MTV
- the homeless
- the Middle East
- career planning
- school dress codes
- terrorism
- women's rights

These topics could be controversial. It is important to know how the majority of your listeners might feel about these topics.

KNOWLEDGE OF TOPIC

It is important to ask yourself, Am I introducing this audience to a new subject, or do most people know a lot about this topic already? If you plan to talk about a topic that is new to most audience members, you need to start with the basics. You may have to define words or terms, discuss unfamiliar ideas, or explain how something works. If most of your audience is familiar with the topic, you may need to take a new approach or go into great detail in order to provide fresh ideas or new information.

Apply

Look at the following topics and think about whether most of your classmates would be familiar with them.

- gun control
- soap operas
- prison reform
- South Africa
- opera
- soccer
- making maple syrup
- the history of radio

EXPECTATIONS

At a sports award dinner, what would you expect the main speaker to talk about? Most of the time audience members expect a speaker to do or say certain things, based on the occasion or on their knowledge of the speaker. The speaker needs to know what the audience expects.

Audience expectations may affect your choice of topic or how you talk about your topic. An audience that expects you to talk about student life in Spain may be surprised to hear a speech on soccer. An audience that expects you to give a humorous speech may be disappointed when you give a serious one. As a speaker you don't have to do exactly what the audience expects. But if you are going to do something different, you should tell the audience so beforehand.

INTERACT

Suppose you have been asked to speak to your local PTA on the topic of how to stop vandalism of school property. In a small group, discuss your audience's basic data, beliefs and opinions, knowledge of the topic, and expectations.

AUDIENCE GOAL

Although you know the general purpose for giving speeches, one question remains. Why does Henry or Jolyne or Maria actually give a speech? A few people give speeches to get attention or to prove how smart they are, but most give speeches to change their listeners in some way. The change may be very small, but good speakers want something to be different by the time their speech is finished. In addition to a general purpose—to inform, persuade, or follow social rituals—speakers want their audiences to do something. That is why they have an audience goal.

After you think about your purpose for giving a speech and your future audience, you must decide on your audience goal. An **audience goal** describes what the listeners should be able to do after the speech is completed. A speaker might phrase an audience goal in the following way: "After my speech is over, I want my listeners to. . . ." For example, if Tina is giving a speech on the value of playing sports, her audience goal may be: "After my speech is over I want my listeners to understand three reasons why playing sports is important: (1) developing physical coordination, (2) learning about teamwork, and (3) getting exercise."

An audience goal is always worded in terms of what the *listeners* should be able to do, not what the *speaker* will do.

Apply

Which of the following are stated as audience goals?

1. I will describe my trip down Grand Canyon.
2. The listeners will donate one Saturday morning a month to clean up the school grounds.
3. The listeners will hear about this year's top country singers.
4. The listeners will describe the problem of acid rain and give two possible ways to reduce it.

Numbers 2 and 4 are correctly stated audience goals. They describe what the listeners should be able to do after the speech is completed.

The audience goal helps a speaker decide what should be included in the speech and what parts of the speech should be given the most attention. For example, if you are giving a speech on "Halloween Safety," your audience goal might be: "I want my listeners to be able to list six ways to make Halloween safer in our community." With this goal, your speech should focus on the ways to make Halloween safer, rather than on the history of Halloween or other matters.

INTERACT

In small groups, select three of the following topics and create one correctly worded audience goal for each topic. Remember to write the goals in terms of what the listeners should be able to do.

chocolate chip brownies	stepfamilies
pollution	student government
jazz	backpacking
healthy hearts	NFL stars

SUMMARY

Public speaking is a two-way process that involves speaking and listening. There are two main purposes for public speaking—to inform and to persuade. Public speakers follow three important steps in preparing to speak. They select a topic, analyze the audience, and set an audience goal.

CHAPTER REVIEW

THINK ABOUT IT

1. Name at least three situations in which people you know give speeches.
2. What guidelines should a speaker use to select a topic?
3. What are the main purposes of public speaking?
4. What things should you look for when analyzing your audience?
5. Explain the importance of an audience goal and give one example.

TRY IT OUT

1. With two or three classmates, complete an audience analysis for your class. Be sure to consider basic data, beliefs and values, knowledge of the topic, and expectations.
   - What are the future goals of your classmates?
   - How do class members like to spend their weekends?
   - What do classmates worry about?
   - What kind of television shows or books do your classmates enjoy?
   - What is unusual about your classmates' hobbies and interests?
2. List four topics on which you might like to speak. Write an audience goal for each. Ask two or three of your classmates if they are interested in the topics. Have them explain why or why not.
3. For one week keep a list of all the situations in which you have been an audience member. Describe two situations when you thought the speaker analyzed the audience poorly. Explain why you did not believe the speaker was well-informed about the audience.

PUT IT IN WRITING

1. Interview three persons who give speeches regularly. Were the situations most often related to the person's job or to a social situation? Write a few paragraphs in which you analyze the importance of public speaking in one's life.
2. Pretend you are about to give a speech. Select a topic and imagine your audience. Describe your audience's basic data, knowledge of topic, beliefs and opinions, and expectations. Then create an audience goal based on your analysis.

SPEAK ABOUT IT

1. Attend a public speech. In a short speech, describe to your classmates the public speaking event—who the speaker was and where the speech took place, and so on. Also share one thing you learned about public speaking from attending the speech.
2. Present a one- to two-minute description of the most effective speaker you have ever heard. Tell your class about the setting and the audience. Describe the speaker's delivery style. Explain why this person was an effective speaker.

FINDING AND USING INFORMATION

After completing this chapter, you
should be able to

- explain a variety of ways to find
  information.
- obtain information through interviews and
  surveys.
- list various types of print materials used
  for research.
- record research information properly.
- describe various types of supporting
  material.
- explain the difference between fact and
  opinion.

KEY WORDS

fact

interview

opinion

research

supporting
material

survey

Student A: I'm talking about students' views on cafeteria food.

Student B: I'm explaining the need for a crossing guard.

Student C: I'm discussing and demonstrating karate.

Although it may come as a surprise to students A, B, and C, each of their speeches will require research. Student A will have to survey students to get their opinions on the cafeteria food. Student B will have to find out how many students cross the busy intersections. Student C may have already done most of the research by studying karate and by observing karate experts. If student C plans to include the history of karate, some interviews or a trip to the library may be necessary.

RESEARCH SOURCES

Effective speeches are built on a foundation of solid ideas and information. After you have a topic and an audience goal, you need to find the best materials to help your audience reach that goal. These materials are found through careful research. In this chapter you will learn how to use research skills to find and record the materials you need to support your speech.

What comes to your mind when you hear the word research? **Research** is a process of investigation that you use every day. For example, how do you buy a skateboard? You might ask your friends questions about the boards they own.

You may check the size of their boards and see if they have soft or hard wheels. You might look at ads in the paper or talk to a salesperson in the sports store. You might read a magazine article in *Consumer Reports* that rates skateboards. You may even try out your friends' boards. That's research!

The public speaker goes through a similar process. Imagine that you have decided on the topic and purpose of your speech and you have analyzed the audience. Now it's time to research the topic to find the supporting material you need to create your speech. To gather information, you may turn to (1) your own experience, (2) interviews and surveys, (3) written or printed materials, or (4) electronic media. A discussion of each of these sources follows.

PERSONAL EXPERIENCE

Competent public speakers often start their research by using their own experience. This is similar to what writers do. When you have to write an essay, you begin by examining your experience with the topic. Public speakers also start with what they already know, then move on to other sources of information.

Suppose you are giving a speech on your hobby, collecting baseball cards. Your speech could include a description of how you became interested in baseball cards and a list of your favorite players. You might demonstrate the way you rate and organize your cards. All of that information comes from you.

Your own experience also includes what you have observed. For instance, if you have seen people flying kites at the city park every evening between 7 P.M. and 9 P.M., you can describe what you observed. If you decide to give a speech on the violence in prime-time television shows, you would watch some shows and use examples of violence from them to support your point.

INTERACT

With a partner, brainstorm ideas for topics that come out of your own experiences. When you are finished, you and your partner should have an interesting list of possible speech topics.

INTERVIEWS AND SURVEYS

Who would you talk to if you wanted to know more about these topics?

- Saudi Arabia
- How the Human Heart Pumps Blood
- 1980s Rock Stars
- The Need to Exercise
- Movie Critics
- Old Superhero Comic Books
- Getting a Job as a Caddie
- Rules for Babysitting
- America's Twentieth-Century Presidents
- Writing a Play

Other people are valuable sources for research. You can quote other people during your speech. For example, you can say, "I talked to my grandmother about World War II, and she said..." or "I asked thirty-six people where they would like to have the spring dance. Nineteen said at the community center; ten said at school; and five didn't care." If you talk to other people, you will learn a lot. Two ways to use people as sources are interviews and surveys.

Interviews

Sometimes the best way to get information on a topic is to interview an expert. An **interview** is a conversation with the purpose of obtaining information. The best interviewers are well prepared. Here are some guidelines for conducting a good interview:

1. *Know your topic before the interview.* When you are familiar with the topic, you know what information you need from the expert. You also need to know the vocabulary related to the topic. Unless you know the technical terms, you might misunderstand them or interpret them incorrectly.

2. *Prepare specific questions before the interview.* The people you interview don't have time for you to make up the

interview as you go along. Prepared questions will help you get the specific information you want. Although you can ask questions that occur to you during the interview, you should have at least ten to twelve questions ready ahead of time.

3. *Set up the interview.* Don't drop in on your expert. Call ahead and arrange a time and place to meet. When you call, tell the expert what you wish to discuss. You might mail some questions ahead of time so he or she can think about them before you meet.

4. *Handle questions carefully.* When you ask a question, allow the person time to answer. If the answer does not seem complete, ask for more information or ask a more specific question. Avoid asking questions that can be answered by a *yes* or *no*. Ask questions that allow you to get to know the other person.

5. *Keep a record of the information.* During the interview take notes or record the conversation on tape. The disadvantage of taking notes is that you cannot look directly at the expert while writing. Taping the interview will provide you with a record of the expert's exact words. Be sure to ask permission to use a tape recorder when you make your appointment.

6. *Express your thanks.* Thank the expert for his or her time by sending a note after the interview.

Apply

Read the following part of an interview and pick out the problems Jay is going to have. Jay is interviewing mystery writer Rod Solomon on the books Solomon writes:

Rod Solomon: Hello Jay, come on in.

Jay: Hi Mr. Sullivan. Thanks for letting me talk to you. I'm going to tape this.

Rod Solomon: Well, I guess that's OK.

Jay: I want to know about the books you write.

Rod Solomon: Any one in particular you want to discuss? Did you read *The Pocket Watch Mystery?*

Jay: No. Did you write it?

Rod Solomon: Yes, it was my first book. Which of my books did you read?

Jay: Well, I didn't read any, but my teacher says you are a good writer. Do you think I could be a good writer?

You can probably tell that Jay is in trouble. He called Mr. Solomon by the wrong name. He didn't ask ahead of time for permission to tape. His first question was too general. Also he hasn't read any of Mr. Solomon's books!

Surveys

A **survey** is a method of gathering information and opinions from a large number of people. In doing research through a survey, you ask many people the same question. You can ask about their experiences or about their opinions on a specific topic. For example, you could ask, "What is your favorite vacation spot?" or "What changes, if any, should be made in the current school dress code?" People who call you at home and ask you what TV shows you watch or what magazines you read are taking a survey.

JOURNAL ENTRY

Instead of always doing library research, my friend and I decided to do a survey. We created a list of questions about how people our age get and spend money. We asked questions such as "Do you get an allowance?" "If so, how much do you get?" "What things are you expected to buy with your own money?" We surveyed forty students and did a big report with charts. It was a lot of work but we had a good time doing it, and I learned enough to convince my grandmother to raise my allowance.

Use these guidelines for your survey questions:

1. *Ask only a few questions and talk briefly.*
   More people will be willing to respond if you ask for only a few minutes of their time.

2. *Ask questions that can be answered simply.*
   Use questions that require either *yes* or *no* answers or short statements.

3. *Ask everyone the same questions in the same order.*
   In order to compare answers, you need to be sure everyone heard the same message from you.

4. *Record your answers carefully.*
   Don't try to remember what people tell you. Check boxes or write down the suggestions so you are able to count and organize the responses.

The sample survey on the following page shows how one student arranged her survey questions.

SAMPLE SURVEY QUESTIONS

1.   What kinds of foods do you buy at most meals?

_____ Drink

_____ Dessert

_____ Salad

_____ Sandwich

_____ Chips/snacks

_____ Hot main dish

2.   How often do you buy more than a drink and dessert?

_____ Every day   _____ 1–2 times a week   _____ Never

3.   Given this week's menu, rate the food. Use 1 for the meal you enjoyed most and 4 for the meal you enjoyed least.

_____ Cheeseburger

_____ Taco plate

_____ Spaghetti

_____ Hot dog

4.   How would you rate the cafeteria food? (Check one.)

_____ Very good

_____ Good

_____ Average

_____ Bad

_____ Very bad

Apply

Look at the following topics and pick out those you might use in a survey of students and teachers in your school.

- How to Start a Coin Collection
- The Need for Computers in All Classrooms
- Favorite Movie Stars
- Language Requirements for Honor Students

Unless you are at an unusual school, it would be hard to do a survey on coin collecting. Few people know a great deal about this topic.

The following is an example of survey research collected by a student for her speech.

After taking a survey of forty-five classmates, I found that seventeen like to dress in the latest style. Fourteen like to dress in a traditional fashion. Thirteen said they don't care about fashion, as long as they are comfortable. One person said he hates to think about clothes. My survey showed the average student changes clothes 782 times a year.

PRINT MATERIALS

When you research print materials, you are doing library research. There are many kinds of printed library materials that you can use. They include books, magazines and journals, pamphlets, newspapers, and general information sources such as encyclopedias and dictionaries. You can locate these materials through computer searches or in a card catalog.

Books

To do research in books, you must know how to use the card catalog and the library computer system. These filing systems list every book in three different ways: according to the subject or topic area, according to the title, and according to the author's last name. The filing system will tell you the book's library number, which will help you locate the book on the shelves. A computer system may also tell you if the book has been checked out recently.

Magazines and Journals

Magazines and journals are types of periodical literature. Periodicals are published at regularly scheduled times. These include publications ranging from popular magazines to specialized journals on unusual topics.

If you are looking for general magazine articles, you can use the *Readers' Guide to Periodical Literature* (*Readers' Guide* for short). This guide lists articles in 180 of the most popular magazines in the United States. The articles are listed alphabetically according to subject, title, and author. When you locate an article in the *Readers' Guide*, you will also find the date and volume of the magazine and the page numbers of the article you wish to read.

INTERACT

Working with a partner, pick a speech topic that interests you both. In the *Readers' Guide*, find the titles of ten articles that might relate to your topic. Look up at least five of them. List the title of each article and give a short description of it.

Sample entries from the *Readers' Guide to Periodical Literature*

subject heading → **COMPUTER GAMES**
> *See also*
> Carmen Sandiego (Games) ——————————— reference
> CD-ROM—Games
> Computer sports games
> DinoWars (Game)
> Heart of China (Game)
> Information systems—Games
> Lemmings (Game)
> Lexi-Cross (Game)
> Lightspeed (Game)
> Martian Memorandum (Game)
> Police Quest (Game)
> Video games
> Violence in computer games ——— title enhancement

title of article → World of electronic games [special section] il *Omni (New*
York, N.Y.) 14:93-4+ N '91 ——————————— date of periodical

volume and
page number → The world of electronic games [special section] il *Compute*
13:95-6+ N '91 ——— title of periodical

Design
Games are us [interview with W.M. Hawkins] P. Scisco.
pr *Compute* 13:144 S '91
Grand illusions. K. Ferrell. il *Omni (New York, N.Y.)*
14:94 N '91 ——————————— author

Educational use
> *See also*
> Reader Rabbit (Computer program)
> Treehouse (Computer program)
BushBuck Charms, Viking Ships, & Dodo Eggs/
GeoJigsaw. J. Sides. il *Compute* 12:126-7 O '91
Headline Harry and the Great Paper Race. C. Olgshc-
illustrated
article → laeger. il *Compute* 13:110+ O '91

Exhibitions ——————————— center heading
Special report [computer games at CES] T. Netsel and
P. Scisco. il *Compute* 13:110+ O '91

Political use
The electric body politic G. Keizer. il *Omni (New York,*
N.Y.) 14:100 N '91

Psychological aspects
Anecdotes, facetiae, satire, etc.
Games addiction: the troubles I've seen. D.P. Mckeeman.
il *Compute* 13:116 N '91

Testing
Arachnophobia. C. S. Holzberg. il Compute 13:133-4
S '91
Big Business. A. Giovetti. il *Compute* 13:130 N '91
Castles. D. T. Sears. il *Compute* 13:123 D '91
Champions. D. T. Sears. il Compute 13:121 D '91

Many current articles are found in magazines such as *Time, Newsweek,* or *U.S. News and World Report.* These weekly news magazines cover the major news events of the past week.

To find magazines on very specific topics, ask your librarian for help. Another way to locate special articles is by finding an index that lists articles on certain topics. Examples of such indexes are the following:

- *Social Sciences Index* (sociology, psychology, criminology, and so forth)
- *Humanities Index* (English and American literature, history, music, speech, theater, and so forth)
- *Education Index* (elementary, secondary, special education, and so forth)

Pamphlets

Pamphlets and public documents are also valuable sources of information. For example, government pamphlets on health may tell the kinds of medicines to use for different illnesses. In most libraries pamphlets are kept in a vertical file index. Your library may also have a *Monthly Catalog of U.S. Government Publications;* the *United Nations Documents Index,* which lists what the U.N. prints; and the *Public Affairs Information Service,* which names special books and articles on different topics.

Newspapers

Daily newspapers are good sources of information when you are studying your local government or a famous person in your town or city.

Sometimes you need to use old newspapers or a major out-of-town paper to research your topic. Some of these newspapers have their own indexes. By using a microfiche reader, you can see what the *New York Times* headlines were on your date of birth or how the paper covered the Persian Gulf War or the breakup of the Soviet Union. Some libraries subscribe to current newspapers from major cities.

General Information Sources

Suppose you want to know something about songbirds, World War II, or the human skeleton. To get this information, you could turn to sources that give you factual information on a wide range of topics. These sources include various encyclopedias, *Facts on File,* and the *Information Please Almanac.*

Dictionaries of the English language can give you background on words you want to use. The most commonly used dictionaries are *Webster's* and the *Random House Dictionary.*

If you need information that deals with numbers, you can check the *World Almanac.* It contains good statistical information. It includes, for example, how many people are born each year in India, how much beef the United States sells to Japan, how many cars are made in Detroit factories, and other similar types of information.

You can also contact government offices and local or national organizations. For example, on the subject of prospecting for gold or exploring caves, you can get free literature from the U.S. Department of the Interior. To get information on how to help accident victims, you could write to the Red Cross. In addition, you may find pamphlets on health-related issues at the local pharmacy.

Suppose your teacher asks you to give a speech on Stephen Hawking, Oprah Winfrey, Abraham Lincoln, Winston Churchill, or Harriet Tubman. Where would you start? There may be books on each person in your library. But you could also turn to the following indexes of famous people:

- *Who's Who in America*
- *Dictionary of American Biography*
- *Webster's Biographical Dictionary*

ELECTRONIC MEDIA

The electronic media can be an important source of information. To use information from radio or television, you need to include the name of the program, the name of the speaker, and the date on which you heard it. For example: "Newscaster Linda McClennan said on June 4, 1992. 'The unmistakable wail of an ambulance siren....'"

Electronic media information cannot be rechecked easily unless you can replay the program. Therefore you have to take careful notes. Because electronic media information usually cannot be rechecked, many speakers use the media for stories, examples, and background information only. They turn to other sources for direct quotes, facts, and figures. Occasionally printed copies of transcripts of radio and television programs are made available on written request. If you tape shows, you must follow the legal guidelines for such copies.

INTERACT

With a group of three classmates, decide the source or sources you might use to find information on:

- The increase in the U.S. population since 1970
- Last year's major forest fire in California
- The early life of President John F. Kennedy
- Guidelines for CPR
- The length of the Mississippi River
- Student opinion about the new cafeteria program
- The author of *All Quiet on the Western Front*

RECORDING YOUR INFORMATION

Perhaps you've been in the library for an hour and found an encyclopedia article and two books on your topic. What do you do next? After finding the information, you must record it. Take your notes carefully. This requires time and effort, but doing it correctly can save you a repeat trip to the library.

If you are using information based on observations, you also need to keep records. For example, if you are growing plants from seeds, write down how many grow and how tall they are every three days. You will need this exact information for your speech.

RESEARCH CARDS

Use 3×5 or 4×6 index cards to record information. Cards are easy to sort, file, and organize. Keep your cards in a file box with dividers for organizing your information. Arrange your cards according to areas of information. Put stories, problems, solutions, quotations, and so forth into separate categories.

The more cards you have, the better informed you will be on your topic, and the more choices you will have when selecting the information most appropriate for your occasion and audience. For example, to give a two- to three-minute speech, you should have at least twenty cards and as many as thirty or thirty-five. For a four- to five-minute speech, you should have no less than thirty research cards and as many as sixty-five to one hundred.

WHAT TO RECORD

Each research card should contain only one quotation, fact, or example. It should have a heading of one or two words that states the card's content. In addition, it should include the source of the information, complete with the production date and page number. If you are going to have many cards with information from the same source, put the source information on a numbered key card, and then place the key card number on all your cards with quotes or information.

Key Card

"The High Frontier of the Rain Forest Canopy."
by Edward O. Wilson
National Geographic
December 1991 (vol 180 #6)
pp. 78-101

Source 2

Content Card

Source 2
p. 102
Life is piled upon life in the tropical rain forest. "But this great edifice is all a house of cards. Most of the millions of species are so highly specialized that they can be quickly driven to extinction by the disturbance of their forest homes."

Content Card

Source 2
p. 104
1979 — rain forest and monsoon forest were destroyed at a rate of 29,000 square miles a year.

1990 — figure doubled to 55,000 square miles (larger than the state of Florida).

Most research cards fall into three types: information summary, direct quotes, or specific facts or examples. Information summary cards contain a short summary, in your own words, of the main ideas of an article or section of material. Direct quote cards give the exact words of an author. The author's words are put in quotation marks. Cards that contain specific facts or examples may simply list the important facts that will help you make your points in your speech. Look at the examples to see what kind of information is contained on each type of research card.

Information Summary

heading

information summary

complete source information

> Coast Guard Work
>
> The Coast Guard Service employs cutters, ice breakers, patrol buoy tenders, helicopter pilots, and many more who can work in air stations and navigation stations that circle the globe. About 5,000 officers are needed to command vessels and stations.
>
> "always Prepared"
> Boy's Life May 1986 p. 22

Direct Quote

heading

direct quote

complete source information

> Gettysburg Address
>
> "... That this nation, under God, shall have a new birth of freedom; and that government of the people, by the people, and for the people, shall not perish from the earth."
>
> Dedication of the National Cemetery Gettysburg, Nov. 19. 1863

Specific Facts

heading

specifics

complete source information

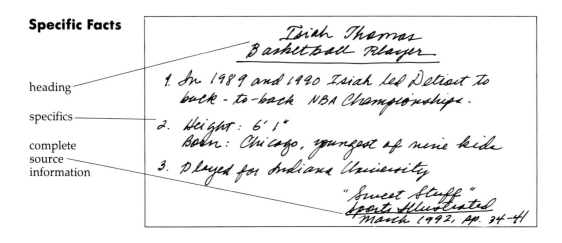

> Isiah Thomas
> Basketball Player
>
> 1. In 1989 and 1990 Isiah led Detroit to back-to-back NBA Championships.
> 2. Height: 6' 1"
>   Born: Chicago, youngest of nine kids
> 3. Played for Indiana University
>
> "Sweet Stuff"
> Sports Illustrated
> March 1992, pp. 34-41

Apply

Using the following news article, write three cards; one on which you summarize the entire article, one with a quote, and one with a single fact.

CHA KIDS FOLLOW A PATH OF SAFETY

by Jerry Thornton

Gang activity isn't as prevalent, fighting is down, and the word "safety" has a real meaning for pupils whose parents belong to a volunteer tenant patrol in the Chicago Housing Authority's Ida B. Wells development.

A hundred men and women at the Darrow Homes extension of the Wells complex have taken to ensuring safe passage for their children to and from Einstein Elementary School by posting themselves at the school and along the way. They take turns patrolling the area.

"It's safer to come to school now," said LaShanda Beal, 12, a 6th grader at the school at 3830 S. Cottage Grove Ave. "There used to be a lot of fighting. Now there's not as much, and the patrol breaks them up."

LaShanda's words were backed Thursday when raucous play and a few scrimmages were quickly stopped by parents, who identify themselves by dark blue jackets and caps with the words "Tenant Patrol" in bright yellow letters.

"The patrol was started last June because of rumors of a child molester being in the area," said Robert Byas, captain of the patrol.

"We started out with just the kids in my building," added Byas, a resident of the Wells project for 25 years.

Soon, other children were meeting at Byas' building at 706 E. Pershing Rd., and the tenant patrol started placing members at various points along the routes to school, he said.

"We try to set a positive image in front of the kids," Byas said. "We respect them, and they give us that respect back."

Patrol members concede that the children known for fighting haven't turned into angels, but things are quieter.

"A lot of the fighting has died down since we've been on patrol," said member Dwayne Al-Amin. "Kids come to us if there is a problem, and we escort them home."

To keep older gang members away, the patrol got help from the Chicago police, who have patrol cars at the school two days a week, and from CHA police, who are there the rest of the week.

So far, there has been no problem with gangs, patrol members said. "But we are letting them know we are not going to tolerate that kind of activity around our school, and when they gather we are going to report them," Byas said.

The morning patrols begin at 8:30 a.m. and last until 9:15 a.m. "for stragglers," Byas said.

Patrollers are back at the school when classes let out at 2:30 p.m. and remain until 3 p.m. They return at 4:30 p.m. Tuesday, Wednesday and Thursday, when late classes are held.

"Tenant patrols were formed by the CHA and are in operation at CHA sites through the city, but the school patrol was an initiative of the parents at Wells," said CHA spokesman Andre Garner. "They are the eyes and ears of the community."

Those eyes and ears belong to members like Betty Reynolds, who volunteered six months ago "because I wanted a safe environment for my kids and grandkids."

"We have our eyes on everything for the protection of the children," Byas added.

The CHA provided members of its tenant patrol with walkietalkies and space in buildings from which to operate, Garner said.

"It has been very effective," said Phyllis Tate, principal of Einstein School, which has an enrollment of 551 pupils.

"Before the patrol, there were more incidents and problems," Tate said. "In fact, one of the children was raped in a building after school.

"Before, there was a higher incidence of fighting. When that happened, the confrontations outside the building would be brought inside, disrupting the whole class. The patrol has helped to stop that, and in turn create a more conducive climate for learning."

Some members of the patrol are members of the local school council, Byas said.

"Since the patrol formed, the kids seem to want to go to school," Byas said. "They feel safe that the gangs won't bother them, and the gangs have shied away."

USING INFORMATION TO SUPPORT YOUR SPEECH

Effective speeches are built on a foundation of solid ideas and information. Main points in a speech must be explained or defended with additional information. This information is called supporting material. **Supporting material** develops the main point. As you prepare your speech, you will use the information you find through your research as supporting material.

Apply

One student used the following statement as the main idea of a speech: Drunk drivers must be kept off the road. What might the speaker say next to prove the point?

1. An average of 50,000 persons are killed by drunk drivers each year.
2. My best friend's aunt was killed by a drunk driver last winter.
3. Police Chief McMasters says, "Drunk drivers claim more lives than any other type of criminal."
4. Another national problem is gang crime.
5. We must get drunk drivers off our roads.

The first three statements support the main idea. Number 4 does not relate to the topic of drunk driving. Number 5 should not be used because it just restates the previous sentence in different words.

TYPES OF SUPPORT

Effective speakers find a number of ways to make their points. They support ideas with different types of information in order to reach all their listeners and to keep their listeners involved. Materials that can be used to support speeches include description, examples, quotations, statistical information, personal experience, and visual aids.

Description

Description can be used to help listeners picture a person, place, or thing. It can also be used to illustrate how something works or how something is done. Here is how one student described a nursery-school classroom:

> The first thing you see is color—there are children's pictures hanging on every wall. Some are combinations of shapes in bright colors. Others show the trees and flowers the children saw on their nature walk. From the ceiling hang Halloween mobiles—ghosts, black cats, and skeletons. . . .

In another example, a speaker described how her classmates could put clown makeup on nursery-school children:

1. Cover face and eyebrows with white face paint.
2. With bright red lipstick, draw triangle shapes above each eye, at corner of each eye, and on chin.
3. With same lipstick, draw a circle around the nose and fill in with color.
4. For a laughing clown, draw mouth curving up at the ends. For a sad clown, draw mouth with ends pointing down.
5. With eyebrow pencil, draw brows following the shape of triangles. For the final touch, draw a teardrop on each cheek.

Examples

Examples help an audience remember the main point and make the speaker's point come alive for the listeners. They help listeners picture what the speaker is discussing. This makes the speech more interesting and memorable.

When you use examples you are telling a story or narrative about a person, place, or thing. The example may be based on facts or it may be fiction. One speaker used the following fictional example in a speech about rudeness:

> The scene is rush hour in a city train station. A woman is on her way home from work. As she enters the subway station, she is pushed against the stairway by three well-dressed businessmen running for a train.
>
> As she opens her purse to buy her token, the woman behind her snaps, "Hurry up, lady." When the train arrives people are packed together like sardines. She is thrown against a pole while someone steps on her foot.

Quotations

When you use quotations, you are presenting another person's words on a subject. Usually, you quote persons who are experts in the topic area. Sally Steenland, deputy director of the National Commission on Working Women said:

> Although more women than ever before are employed in the television entertainment industry, many of them in decision-making positions, it is still much more difficult for women than for men to get jobs and promotions in that business. Despite almost two decades of rising female employment in television networks and production studios, the top jobs remain largely male-dominated.

Sometimes a speaker has to select certain ideas from a direct quote to help the listeners understand. For example, a student speaking on crime used the following statement by a school security chief:

> Social and cultural deprivation also play a significant role in the individual's predisposition to violence. While poverty does not cause crime, poverty coupled with an

impoverished home life—unhappy family relations, lack of moral values and education, lack of opportunity—can lead a young person into crime.

The student paraphrased the chief's statement this way:

It is Chief Goggins's belief that poverty and home life without moral values, family support, and education, can lead young people into crime.

When you use quotations be sure to double-check your information. Be careful not to put your own words into someone else's mouth!

Statistical Information

Statistical information, or numbers, can be used to support a point. Often the numbers show the importance of a topic or the size of a problem.

In a speech on pollution, one student used the following statistical information to discuss how ordinary people must fight pollution:

In Houghton, Michigan, a park was named for Verna Mize who struggled for 13 years to prevent a mining company from dumping 67,000 tons of waste matter a day into Lake Superior.

It takes but one gallon of solvent to make 20 million gallons of groundwater unfit for drinking; it will take 10 years and $1 billion to clean up Chesapeake Bay.

Personal Experience

When you use personal experience in a speech, it can provide a special kind of support, because it shows a personal connection to a topic. For example, if you are talking about a hobby such as raising rabbits, you can talk about your own rabbits. If you are talking about pollution, you might describe the smog you saw when you visited Los Angeles. When you can give personal examples, you show that you have knowledge about a topic based on firsthand experience.

In the following statement a student describes her personal experience as a zoo volunteer:

I have volunteered at the Parkside Zoo for the last two summers. At first, I just worked on the line for the pony rides. Near the end of last summer I was asked to work in the small-animal section of the Children's Zoo. I hold mice and guinea pigs so the children can pet their fur.

Visual Aids

In addition to using verbal supporting material, a speaker can use nonverbal materials such as a picture or an object. For example, you can use a graph to show the increase in sports injuries over the past decade. If you were demonstrating how to make shell jewelry, you could show examples of pieces you made. If you were speaking about computer power, you might display some computer graphics.

All these types of supporting material explain or defend the speaker's points. They also make a speech more interesting and effective. Finally, they serve as evidence to prove a point.

EVALUATING SUPPORTING MATERIAL

As you collect your supporting materials, evaluate them to be sure they honestly support your points. Critical thinkers ask themselves the following questions when evaluating supporting evidence:

1. Is it fact or opinion?
2. Is it reliable?
3. Is it relevant?
4. Is it timely or up-to-date?
5. Is it representative?

Fact or Opinion

A **fact** is information based on evidence that can be proved or disproved. Facts are concerned with the truth or certainty of a statement. Some examples of facts are the following:

- Sharon Lytle has three red-headed brothers.
- The first A-bomb test occurred on July 16, 1945.
- The chairs were turned over and paint was splattered on the walls.

An **opinion** is a judgment based on belief or feelings. It cannot be proved. Some examples of opinions are the following:

- Sharon Lytle dislikes her brothers.
- The first A-bomb destroyed the world's hope for peace.
- The chairs were thrown by a very strong person.

Facts and opinions are necessary and helpful. Neither is better than the other. But problems arise when you confuse statements of opinion with statements of fact.

INTERACT

With a partner, discuss the following announcement and identify the sentences that contain facts and those that contain opinions.

The Northfield Soup Kitchen needs your help. We serve 140 to 160 people every Tuesday night. We only have a staff of 10 to 12 people. Therefore, the lines are long. People have to wait for tables. The staff begins cooking and setting up at 2 P.M. We need people to shop and clean up. If we don't get enough volunteers, we'll have to close down.

Reliability

Evidence should come from a reliable source. For example, if you are trying to persuade your audience to use seat belts, you could use an expert on traffic accidents or the chief of police as a reliable source. You would not want quotes from a fire inspector or a carpenter, because they are not experts on the subject of seat belts and auto safety.

Many magazines and newspapers give an author's name and experience at the end of an article or editorial. On a radio and television talk show, the host usually gives the background of the guests. This information should help you decide if a person is a reliable source on a subject.

Relevance

The evidence must relate, or connect, to the exact point you are making. If you are talking about the books Judy Blume writes for teenagers, you should not quote sections of her books for adults. If you are describing the causes of the Civil War, you should not discuss the history of railroads.

It's easy to get offtrack during a speech. For example, during a speech on athletic training, one student got so involved in describing how Kristi Yamaguchi skated in the Olympics that she really never talked much about the training process.

Timeliness

Your evidence must be up-to-date. If you are using statistics on drunk driving, you don't want to use figures from 1974. Figures on drunk-driving deaths are now much higher. If you are using a quote from an expert, be sure the person still holds the same opinion. A person who thought pollution was the nation's greatest problem in 1978 may not hold that view fifteen years later.

Representativeness

Don't describe a very unusual situation as if it is normal. If you use an example, a number, or a quote that is the exception to the normal pattern, you aren't being honest. If you speak on the major problems in your school and can only find one example of recent vandalism, the example is an exception. Perhaps vandalism is not one of the major problems in your school. Be sure your supporting material does not describe a once-in-a-while happening.

SUMMARY

This chapter provides the foundation for creating a speech. The research process is described, including using personal experience, interviews and surveys, and print and electronic media materials. Guidelines for recording information are included, as are samples of supporting material. Finally, the chapter discusses the five ways of evaluating supporting evidence.

CHAPTER REVIEW

THINK ABOUT IT

1. Describe four sources of research information.
2. If you had to help a friend prepare to interview someone, what guidelines for good interviewing would you share?
3. Give examples of each of the various types of supporting materials.
4. What five questions should you ask when evaluating supporting materials?
5. What is the difference between fact and opinion?

TRY IT OUT

1. Which research sources might you use to find out the following information?
   - The average annual rainfall in Ethiopia
   - The grain production in the United States over the past ten years
   - The structure of the British parliament
   - The best way to set up a darkroom
   - The average weekly allowance of American fourteen-year-olds
2. Choose a speech topic and a purpose for your speech. Interview a person who is an expert on this topic. Follow all the guidelines for good interviewing. Describe the information you obtained through the interview.
3. Choose a speech topic and a purpose for your speech. Write three survey questions. Conduct a survey using the guidelines outlined in this chapter. Share the results of your survey with your classmates.
4. Bring to class a recent editorial from your local newspaper. With a partner, analyze the supporting material in the editorial, using the criteria discussed in this chapter.

PUT IT IN WRITING

1. Choose a speech topic and a purpose for your speech. Assume your audience will be your class. Begin researching your topic by listing your own experience and observations concerning the topic, the people you should interview, possible print material and electronic media sources, and two questions you could ask in a survey.
2. Select a speech topic and find three written sources of evidence on that topic, such as a magazine article, a pamphlet, and a chapter in a book. Record two evidence cards for each source using the correct form.

SPEAK ABOUT IT

1. Choose a speech topic and a purpose for speech. Think of how you can use a personal example in the speech. Share the personal example with your classmates.
2. For the same speech topic, decide on two other types of support. Share these with your classmates.
3. Choose a school-related topic. With a partner, role-play an interview between an expert on that topic (for example, a principal, cafeteria worker, bus driver, or teacher) and a student reporter from another school. Ask for feedback from your classmates on the effectiveness of the questions used in the interview.

CONSTRUCTING THE SPEECH

After completing this chapter, you should be able to

- define *purpose statement* and give an example.
- describe the main speech organization patterns.
- create a sentence and a word outline.
- list the characteristics of language that help get the meaning across.
- identify and give examples of figures of speech.
- develop introductions and conclusions for your speeches.
- develop transitions to connect main ideas.

KEY WORDS

conclusion

hyperbole

introduction

metaphor

personification

purpose statement

simile

transition

The hardest part of preparing a speech is getting all the pieces to fit together and make sense.

When I try to write a speech, I can't figure out how to begin it or how to organize my points.

That speaker is jumping all over the place. I still don't know what his point is.

How often has a speaker made you feel frustrated because the speech was confusing or disorganized? What does a good speaker do to help you follow along? The outline and organization of a speech are very important, because the audience has only one chance to understand. A person reading a paper can go back to reread the parts that were unclear. But an audience doesn't get a second chance. When giving a speech, you have to present clear and organized ideas or your audience will get confused.

There are five major steps to organizing a speech. They are (1) creating a purpose statement, (2) finding the right organizational pattern, (3) outlining the speech, (4) choosing the language, and (5) creating introductions and conclusions.

PURPOSE STATEMENT

The first step in organizing the speech is to write a purpose statement. A **purpose statement** summarizes the main idea or purpose of your speech. The purpose statement in a speech is similar to the thesis statement in an essay. Some speakers use one carefully worded sentence as a purpose statement, while others use two or three sentences. These statements are given in the introduction to a speech.

A good purpose statement tells the audience the topic of the speech, provides a guide to the organization of the speech, and gives the audience goal for the speech.

The purpose statement should tell the listeners about the main points of the speech. For example, if you hear the following statement in a speech introduction, what do you think the speech will cover?

Soccer is a valuable experience because it teaches athletic skills, keeps you in condition, and gets you involved in extracurricular activities.

You can be almost certain that the speaker will give a three-point speech describing the values of soccer as (1) teaching athletic skills, (2) keeping you in shape, and (3) involving you in extracurricular activities. As you will probably guess, this speaker's audience goal is that listeners will be able to explain the three values of soccer.

INTERACT

With a partner, identify the three parts of the following purpose statements.

1. There are eight safety rules that careful bikers should follow.
2. There are three reasons why helping to resettle refugee families is a worthwhile use of your time.
3. To appreciate Hopi kachina dolls, you need to know their history and what types of kachinas there are.
4. Raising sheep can bring you fun and profit.
5. Open adoption has many advantages and should be legalized.

PATTERNS OF ORGANIZATION

Most formal speeches have a three-part structure—an introduction, a body, and a conclusion. This structure is similar to that of a composition. The introduction gains the audience's attention and tells the listeners about the topic and direction of the speech. The body contains the main points. The conclusion summarizes the message and ends the speech in an interesting way.

The body of the speech contains the structure, or organizational pattern. The purpose statement and the audience goal should help you choose the organizational structure.

There are a number of common organizational patterns that speakers can use. These include time order, space order, process order, topical order, and problem-solution order.

TIME ORDER

Time order refers to placing the points of the speech into a time, or chronological, pattern. The speaker may talk about time in terms of the past, present, and future. Time may refer to predicting the future or placing historical events in sequence. Time may also refer to smaller segments such as morning, noon, and night. This time-oriented pattern is easy to use because you are able to see the logical movement. Some topics that might be time oriented include the history of air travel, the past and future of the Olympics, and plans for building the community center.

The following is a sample purpose statement for a time-order speech:

> For the next few minutes I would like to describe the seven days of the Outward Bound program that you will attend.

Often a story or narrative follows a chronological pattern. One event or comment follows another in the telling. You can imagine the time order a speaker might use in telling stories about the following events:

- The Time I Almost Drowned
- Our Trip to the Grand Canyon
- My Brother's Big Car Wreck

SPACE ORDER

Space order refers to organizing a speech based on the physical relationship of people, places, or objects. A speaker may talk about experiences or people in one place and then move on to another place. Some topics that might be organized according to place include historical sites in New England, the neighborhoods of San Francisco, and the religions of China and India.

The following is a sample purpose statement for a space-order speech:

> As an exchange student I had the opportunity to live three months in three different cities—Munich, Hamburg, and Berlin. Let me tell you a little about each of them.

PROCESS ORDER

Process order refers to explaining the way something works. The speaker explains the steps in a process from beginning to end. A process speech describes the steps that the listener needs to understand in order to use the information. Some topics that might be organized in terms of process include screening your own T-shirts, making music videos, and creating homemade pizza.

Here is an example of a purpose statement for a process-order speech:

> There are five easy steps to taking great pictures with a 35mm camera.

TOPICAL ORDER

Topical order refers to dividing a whole speech topic into its natural parts. There is no specific sequence. Any point could be first or last. Yet together these points will tell the listeners a great deal about the entire topic. Some subjects that may be organized by topic are types of video games, the paintings of Picasso, and understanding the library.

Here is a sample purpose statement for a topical-order speech:

To fully appreciate your visit to historical Williamsburg, you need to experience the historical buildings, the craft demonstrations, the ceremonies, and the restaurants.

PROBLEM-SOLUTION ORDER

Problem-solution order refers to organizing information around two major areas—the problem or problems and the solution or solutions. This order is often used in a persuasion speech, when the speaker is trying to persuade the listener to believe or do something. The listener needs to understand the problem fully and to grasp the connection between the problem described and the suggested solutions. Examples of speech topics that could use the problem-solution order are world hunger, school cliques, and acid rain and pollution.

The following is a sample purpose statement for a problem-solving speech:

In order to reverse the pollution from acid rain, we need to understand the extent of the damage and to mount a three-pronged attack to prevent more extensive pollution.

INTERACT

With three or four classmates, decide which patterns of organization might work for the following topics:

- Fashion in the Twentieth-Century
- Sections of the Orchestra
- Tap Dancing
- Card Tricks
- Violence on Kids' TV
- The Bermuda Triangle
- Teenage Alcoholism
- Lincoln's Gettysburg Address

Select one topic and create a sample outline using the organizational pattern you have chosen.

OUTLINING

A very important step in speech preparation is outlining. The purpose of an outline is to help you organize your speech. Besides helping you order the material, it helps you identify major points and supporting points. An outline is useful both in preparing and presenting a speech.

A good outline provides you with a map. If you follow the map, you won't get lost during the speech and—of equal importance—your listeners won't get lost either.

Creating an outline is a lot of work, but when you are delivering the speech, you will be able to keep your points straight. You will be more relaxed and sure of yourself. Your audience will be able to follow your points easily, and your speech will be more effective.

TYPES OF OUTLINES

There are two basic types of outlines:

1. A *sentence outline* shows the relationship of information and development of arguments or ideas.
2. A *word outline* lists only key words and divisions.

If you are a beginning public speaker, you should use the sentence outline. A sentence outline lets you use more detail and forces you to think about each main point and supporting point carefully. This gives you more confidence while learning the topic.

Once you have practiced and gained confidence, you may wish to use a word outline while actually delivering the speech. Word outlines permit you to have greater eye contact with your audience.

Following are examples of the first point in both a full sentence outline and a word outline for a speech titled "Our Dying Planet":

Sentence Outline

Our Dying Planet

I. The Problem of Pollution
   A. Sulfur emissions from power plants return to earth in acid rain.
      1. It deadens lakes.
      2. It kills fish.
      3. Humans are poisoned by eating fish.
   B. Carbon dioxide builds up from the use of coal, oil, gasoline, and from a warm atmosphere.
      1. New deserts are forming in Africa.
      2. Floods are created.
      3. Farmland is diminishing.

Word Outline

Our Dying Planet

I. Pollution Problem
   A. Sulfur/acid rain
      1. Lakes
      2. Fish
      3. Poison
   B. Carbon monoxide/warmth
      1. Deserts
      2. Floods
      3. Farms

GUIDELINES FOR OUTLINING

Most outlines follow a detailed form. They use numbers and letters to show the importance of each idea. Roman numerals (I, II, III) show the main points. Capital letters (A, B, C) show subpoints. Arabic numerals (1, 2, 3) show specific details about, or support for, the subpoints; and small letters indicate support for, or information about, those specific details.

I. _____
   A. _____
      1. _____
      2. _____
         a. _____
         b. _____
   B. _____
      1. _____
      2. _____

You need to remember that the type of symbol you use shows the level of importance of an idea. I, for example, is more important than A, because A is included under I. The numeral 1 is included under A since it is a subpoint to A, and so on throughout the outline.

All roman numerals should be lined up under one another, as should all capital letters, and so on. The symbols should be used consistently to indicate main points, subpoints, and supporting statements. When a new roman numeral is used, begin the subpoints with a capital A. Whenever a new capital letter is used, begin subpoints with the numeral 1, and so on.

Every point must be divided into two or more subpoints. No point should have just one subpoint.

LANGUAGE

Competent communicators take pride in their use of language. They work to create a message that is meaningful and memorable. Speakers are concerned with getting the meaning across, using figures of speech, and linking ideas through transitions.

For example, in his speech at a political convention, Senator Bill Bradley said:

People are angry, and so am I.

For twelve years, I've seen kids kill kids in our cities and people sleep in the streets.

For twelve years, I've watched workers lose their jobs, our land further poisoned, and government yield again and again to the special interests.

For twelve years, I've heard our leaders say, "Nothing can be done."

For too long, American leadership has waffled and wiggled and wavered.

These words were more effective than if he had simply said, "Everyone is angry about the lack of leadership in this country for the past twelve years."

GETTING THE MEANING ACROSS

To make sure the audience understands the message, speakers try to use language that is accurate, clear, appropriate, and original.

Accuracy

As you learned earlier, people interpret messages differently. Words such as *liberal, expensive, friendly, large,* and *attractive* have different meanings to different people. Your meaning will be more accurate if you use words that are concrete and specific, rather than abstract and general. Define any words that might be unusual or unfamiliar to your audience.

If you talk about karate training, be sure your audience understands the terms *kata, kumite,* and *khihon.* If you talk about attending a *quinceanera,* be sure you explain this traditional Latin American custom if your audience is not familiar with it.

JOURNAL ENTRY

When I gave my first demonstration speech I was pretty confident. I am a brown belt in karate, and I knew the class would be interested in my demonstration of karate moves. What I did not realize was how many technical terms I used that confused them. I talked about *kata* and *kumite* and synchronized *kata* without explaining the names. I mentioned a roundhouse kick and a block. Unfortunately, even though the class liked the karate moves, I didn't do well on the speech, because no one really knew what I was referring to.

Appropriateness

The statement "Hi, y'all. I sure am glad you could stop by to see us in our fancy threads" may not be the best way for a speaker to address an audience at a graduation. Speakers must use language that is appropriate to the topic, the listen-

ers, and the occasion. Your language should be formal and dignified when the occasion is formal (such as a graduation ceremony). It should be informal when the occasion or topic is casual, for example, if you are telling the Scout troop about the upcoming campout.

Whether your language is formal or informal, your speech gives you an opportunity to practice both correct grammar and articulation.

Originality

How do your friends say something is good? Do they use *sweet, dope, cool, excellent, awesome,* or other "in" words? Some of these terms are overused and trite. Competent communicators work to find original ways to say something familiar.

A good speaker is creative without being unclear. One student decided the sentence "I had to feed the cat" sounded dull. Instead, she said, "I could no longer ignore the outraged cry. It was time to fill the stomach of the gray beast." The more effort you put into finding the best language for your speech, the greater your chance of reaching your audience goal.

USING FIGURES OF SPEECH

Figures of speech help a speech come alive. They appeal to listeners' imaginations and help them remember what you say.

Apply

Choose the sentence from each of the following pairs that would be more likely to get your listeners' attention.

The sky was dark and the stars were out as we rode our bikes home.

The sky was black velvet sprinkled with stars. Our bikes flew across the bridge when we saw the lights of home.

You can use your computer to do your book reports.

That computer saved my life! My book report was done in one-third the normal time.

In each pair, the second sentence contains figures of speech and would be more likely to gain attention.

Figures of speech are ways of making your language more imaginative and more easily remembered. There are many different kinds of figures of speech. Four of the most commonly used are simile, metaphor, personification, and hyperbole.

Similes

A **simile** is a comparison of two unlike things. A simile includes the words *like* or *as*. For example, a speaker might say: "The frozen hiker was *shaking like a leaf* when the safety patrol reached him." Or, "I entered the subway *as cautiously as a jungle fighter,* watching every shadow." One student speaker used a simile to describe her time in a foreign country.

> Living in the Spanish countryside was like going through a time warp. People still used horses to pull their ploughs. The teenagers met at special parties chaperoned by older community members....

Metaphors

A **metaphor** is a comparison of two things that are not alike. The comparison is implied. The words *like* and *as* are not used. For example, a speaker might say, "My family is a rock. It makes me feel secure" or "Rivers of ice cream flowed from the cone, splashing to the sidewalk." One student effectively used metaphors to describe a city cleanup campaign:

> We are the urban pioneers. We circle our wagons around the city lot. We reclaim the wilderness, clearing away the jungle. We sow new seeds of life. At harvest we see green grass and flowers.

Personification

Personification gives human characteristics to nonhuman things. For example, a speaker might say, "The graffiti laughs at me as I turn the corner" or "The tree comforted the child in its branches."

Often speakers use talking animals or talking objects as a humorous part of their speeches. Comments such as "Did you hear what the apple said to the banana?" let you know objects are being given human characteristics.

Hyperbole

Hyperbole is an intentional exaggeration. For example, a speaker might say, "This computer saved my life!" or "The fish I caught would have fed an army." One student used hyperbole to describe a baseball hit:

> The bases were loaded. It was the bottom of the ninth. Simmons came to bat. I was on second base ready to go. The pitcher wound up, let go, and Simmons swung. He hit that ball to the moon!

Apply

Identify the following statements according to the figures of speech. Some of the statements may fit more than one category.

- Alone my life is just a sketch. With friends my life becomes a masterpiece.
- That puppy took off like a rocket when the cat snarled back.
- The elevator sagged under the weight of its load.
- Life is a shoe. Friendships are the laces.
- Life is like a swamp filled with dark and dangerous critters.

INTRODUCTIONS, CONCLUSIONS, AND TRANSITIONS

There is a piece of metaphorical advice that says, "If you haven't struck oil in two minutes, you'd better stop boring." For the speaker this means that if you don't grab the audience in the introduction, you might as well make it your conclusion!

The effect of a speech depends heavily on how you greet the audience, how you leave the audience, and how your speech hangs together. Therefore you must put time and effort into introductions, conclusions, and transitions.

INTRODUCTIONS

An **introduction** should serve three general purposes:

1. *Gain attention.* This is your big moment! You need to get the group interested. Find a way to make people say "This is going to be good!"
2. *Present your topic and purpose.* Before your introduction is completed, your audience should know your topic and the purpose of your speech. Your introduction should preview your main points.
3. *Connect with your audience.* You must come across as a person who is interested in the topic and your listeners. Show your listeners you recognize any connection they might have to the topic. Your ideas and your delivery will help you connect to your listeners.

Types of Introductions

There are many ways to introduce a speech. Here are some of the most common:

1. *Startling statement.* A startling statement presents information that surprises the audience. For example:

   Jessie is a normal three-year-old child except for one thing—she is the victim of child abuse. She has already been hospitalized with broken bones four times in her short life.

2. *Rhetorical question.* A rhetorical question requires no answer from the audience. It challenges the audience to think. It should not be answered by a simple *yes* or *no.* For example:

   What do Albert Einstein, Nelson Rockefeller, Cher, and Tom Cruise have in common? They all have overcome dyslexia, a learning disability that interferes with the ability to read.

3. *Humor.* A joke or funny statement serves to relax an audience. Yet humor should relate to the topic. For example:

What ten-letter word starts with *G-A-S?* It's *automobile.*
And this year we may run short again.

4. *Quotation.* A quotation from a famous person can interest
an audience. For example:
Abraham Lincoln once said, "You can fool all of the
people some of the time; you can even fool some of the
people all of the time; but you can't fool all of the people
all the time." We can no longer be fooled by the
newspapers in this city.

5. *Story.* A story involves the audience in the topic. For
example:
Many years ago, a stranger arrived in our town. He wore
ragged clothes and carried a walking stick.

6. *Personal experience.* A personal experience gets the
listeners' attention and helps the audience connect with
the speaker. For example:
Who would want to spend hours in the blazing sun
digging carefully in the dirt with a small spoon? I did.
Last summer I spent two weeks at the Kampsville dig
doing archeological research. And I have the calluses to
prove it.

7. *Example.* An example gives a vivid picture of the topic.
For example:
Anne Graves, age four, died from a gunshot wound to
the chest. Her killer was shocked and heartbroken. He
was her six-year-old brother who found a loaded gun.

8. *Reference to occasion, audience, or topic.* A reference to the
reason for the speech lets the listeners know what is
going on. For example:
I am very pleased to present this award for the
Outstanding Student of West High School. Rhonda
Washington has maintained an almost perfect record in
math and science while also taking part in many school
activities.

INTERACT

Listen carefully to the beginning of three presentations, such as political speeches on TV, class lectures, or sermons. Record the way each speaker opens the presentation. If the speaker does not use a method to gain your attention, write a sample introduction the speaker might have used to interest the listeners. Share your introductions with your classmates.

CONCLUSIONS

During the conclusion of your speech, you need to remind your listeners of what you told them and give them a final thought. A **conclusion** has three purposes:

1. *Summarize your main points.* Listeners can forget your main points because they cannot go over them again. Therefore, you need to remind them. Summarize the main points so they stay in your listeners' minds.

2. *Repeat your main goal.* Get your audience set to reach the audience goal.
3. *Provide a clear ending.* Don't leave the listeners wondering if the speech is over. Give a final statement.

Types of Conclusions

There are many types of conclusions. Following are some of the main points of your speech.

1. *Summary.* A summary should consist of a restatement of the main points of your speech.
2. *Quotation.* The quotation should summarize your speech or suggest the action or attitude you want your audience to have.
3. *Appeal.* An appeal asks the audience to do something for themselves or someone else. For example:

   Please remember that seat belts save lives. Seat belts prevent serious injury. Wear seat belts!

4. *Challenge.* A challenge serves to motivate an audience to action. It is a bit like a dare. For example:

   If we ignore the problem, it won't go away. Vandalism will end in this school only when you and I work to end it. I'm willing to stop vandalism. Are you?

5. *Story.* Just as a story can be used to introduce your speech, it can also be used to end it.

CONNECTING THE INTRODUCTION AND CONCLUSION

When possible, tie your introduction and conclusion together by referring back to your introduction in your conclusion. This is sometimes called a turnaround. It reinforces your purpose and gives your speech closure and balance.

For example, suppose you introduce your speech with the startling statement, "Jessie is a normal three-year-old child, except for one thing—she is the victim of child abuse." You might conclude your speech with a sentence such as, "We must keep children like Jessie safe."

Whatever form of introduction and conclusion you choose, make sure each is appropriate to your audience, purpose, and topic. Some topics don't lend themselves to humor. Some audiences will enjoy humor, others will not. Persuasive speeches often use a startling statistic or startling statement. Speeches of social ritual sometimes use a reference to the occasion as an introduction.

LINKING IDEAS THROUGH TRANSITIONS

The key sentences that move you from your introduction to your conclusion are called transitions. For example:

> *Now* that you've seen the problem, *let's*
> *move on* to a solution.

> My *second point* is that underdeveloped
> nations need help.

These statements link, or connect, parts of your speech and help the listeners follow your ideas. **Transitions** are words or phrases that form links between ideas. After a speaker has made a point, he or she usually indicates that a new idea is coming along and that it is connected to the earlier idea.

In the next example, a speaker concludes a point on the recent growth of radio and moves into discussing cable television:

> Radio has found a place in the sun again. In addition,
> we are witnessing the tremendous growth of cable
> television, which. . . .

In this case, the phrase *in addition* indicates a shift, linking the previous idea of radio to the new discussion of television. Here are some other examples of transitions:

> The third dance company I wish to discuss is the
> Joseph Holmes dance company.

> We've looked at ratting and roping.
> Now let's look at rappelling.

> Jessie is only one case. Let me now summarize
> several others.

The following words are simple transition words or phrases. They may serve as verbal clues showing that the speaker is moving from one point to another.

meanwhile	moving to	in contrast
first, second	but	in conclusion
also	on the contrary	in the second place
next	to sum up	another point
as a result	another point	finally
in addition to	on the other hand	therefore

Transitions are important because they help your listeners stay with you. Transition words tell the audience that you are linking parts of the speech together as you move to a new idea. If you plan your introduction, conclusion, and transitions carefully, they will become the structure that helps the audience follow your speech.

SUMMARY

Constructing a speech requires planning and following organizational patterns. It takes time and effort. This chapter discusses purpose statements, organizational patterns, outlining, language, and introductions, conclusions, and transitions. All of these are necessary in building a speech. Taking the time to construct your speeches carefully will help to make you a successful speaker.

CHAPTER REVIEW

THINK ABOUT IT

1. What is a purpose statement?
2. Describe the five patterns of speech organization.
3. Describe two types of outlines and give reasons for the use of each one.
4. What are the characteristics of language that help get meaning across?
5. What are the three purposes of an introduction? Of a conclusion?

TRY IT OUT

1. Choose a speech topic and write a purpose statement. Develop an introduction and conclusion and choose an outline structure for the speech. Possible topics include:
   - space travel
   - today's fashion
   - adoption
   - patriotism
   - missing children
   - teenage life
   - skateboarding
   - sports in schools
2. Choose a different speech topic and write a purpose statement. Explain which organizational pattern should be used for the topic. Provide reasons for your decision.
3. Find two examples of each of the following figures of speech: simile, metaphor, personification, and hyperbole. Include these in your communication journal.
4. Select two main points in the body of a speech you plan to give. Develop a sentence outline and a word outline for these points.

PUT IT IN WRITING

1. Using what you know about introductions and language, rewrite the following introduction to make it interesting and more effective.

   I'm going to talk to you today about something I find interesting. I've been interested in this for a long time. Most of you find fish interesting, too. You may have goldfish or you may look at aquariums in pet stores. My topic will be on communication with dolphins.

2. Using one of the topics you chose in the Try It Out activities, write two transitions of two to three sentences each, to link the three main points in the body of your speech.

SPEAK ABOUT IT

1. Present the purpose statement, introduction, and conclusion you wrote for activity 1 in Try It Out to your class, and ask for feedback.
2. Choose four topics. Write a purpose statement for each. After presenting all four purpose statements to your classmates, find out which topic they'd like to hear more about.

DELIVERING THE SPEECH

KEY WORDS

audiovisual aids

clarity

delivery

extemporaneous method

gestures

impromptu method

manuscript method

memorized method

pitch

rate

stage fright

vocal quality

volume

After completing this chapter, you should be able to

- define *stage fright* and describe ways of developing speech confidence.
- describe the four methods of delivery and explain when each might be used.
- list the nonverbal factors in delivery and explain their importance.
- explain how to rehearse a speech.
- describe guidelines for making and using audiovisual aids.

Mr. Anderson gave a great lecture on his trip to China. He showed slides of Chinese classrooms.

I could listen to Meagan talk about gospel music for hours. She gets so excited about it.

Last week we had a guest speaker who told folktales from around the world. She told some scary stories and made them sound so real.

The success of each speech depends on what you say and how you say it. The last chapter discussed constructing the speech. Now you need to find out about delivery. **Delivery** is the way you use your voice and body to present a speech. Delivery includes (1) speaker confidence, (2) methods of delivery, (3) personal delivery, (4) rehearsing the speech, and (5) use of audiovisual aids.

SPEAKER CONFIDENCE

When I get up to give a speech, I wait until people are looking at me before I start. I try to stand balanced on both feet so I don't sway. I try to remember why I am there and tell myself the listeners will be interested in what I am saying.

When I get up to talk to a group of people I feel really nervous. I get really very shaky. My hands shake and get sweaty. I also sway and shift my feet.

Most people worry about delivering their speeches. Some people worry about giving speeches because they experience stage fright. **Stage fright** is nervousness when talking to an audience. Being nervous, or having stage fright, is very common. Even the best speakers experience it sometimes.

What happens when you have stage fright? People have various experiences with stage fright. Some signs of nervousness while speaking include:

- dry mouth
- tense voice
- sweating palms
- shaky legs
- eyes looking down

- fast breathing
- "butterflies" in the stomach
- hands in pockets
- pounding heart
- shifting from foot to foot

Although you may not like the way you feel when you are nervous, stage fright can have an advantage. If you can turn the nervous energy into speaking energy, you can make the speech better. You can make your nervousness work for you. Having stage fright shows you care enough about speaking in public to want to do a good job.

Most speakers feel more confident about their ability to handle stage fright when they keep in mind that stage fright becomes easier to control with practice and that nervous people usually look much better than they feel. One student dealt with her stage fright in this way:

Every time I get up to speak my knees knock against each other. I was sure everyone could see my legs shaking. Now I wear a longer skirt when I have to speak. It makes me feel more comfortable and more confident.

GUIDELINES FOR DEVELOPING CONFIDENCE

Here are some guidelines for helping you develop speaker confidence. These guidelines will help you to use stage fright to your advantage.

1. Prepare thoroughly. The more prepared you are, the more poised or self-confident you will feel.
2. Take a few deep breaths before you begin to speak. Deep breathing helps you relax.
3. Remind yourself of your audience goal. You are not there to perform. You are there to make a change in your audience.
4. Start well. Have your first two or three sentences memorized so you can say them without mumbling or stumbling over your words. There is nothing like making a good start to build your confidence.
5. Reduce signs of nervousness, such as playing with a pencil or with your hair. Plan ahead so you will not have those distractions. For example, leave the pencil on your desk and push your hair back.
6. If a visual aid such as a chart is helpful, use it. The energy you need to display your visual aid will help use up some of your nervous energy.
7. Pay attention to your listeners' nonverbal feedback. If you try to respond to the listeners, you will not pay as much attention to yourself.

THINKING ON YOUR FEET

Confident speakers are able to think on their feet. Most confident speakers have high self-esteem and know that if something goes wrong they will adjust and make the best of it. If they recognize a problem, they find a way to cope with it. Some speakers worry that a problem will happen during their speech and they won't know what to do. If you are prepared, even if a problem occurs during your speech, you will be able to cope with whatever happens.

Apply

Look at the following situations. What would you do if one of them happened to you?

1. You are in the middle of your speech when an announcement comes over the loudspeaker into the room.

2. You stumble and nearly fall down on your way to the front of the room.

3. Halfway through your speech, you realize your remaining note cards are out of order.

4. The audiovisual equipment breaks during the speech.

5. Your audience bursts out laughing because you have said "hoppimess" instead of "happiness."

6. You forget your next idea.

If any of these situations ever happens to you, you must, above all else, remain calm. In situation 1, stop, wait for the announcer to finish, and then continue your speech. In situation 2, you should stand up and continue walking to the podium. In situation 3, you could stop for a few seconds to put your note cards back in order. In situation 4, you might say, "My audiovisual equipment is broken, so I'll explain the process as clearly as I can," or you could draw a basic diagram on the board. Situation 5 could be a good chance to use humor. You might say, "Let me untie my tongue and try that again." In situation 6, you might admit you forgot and pause until you remember, or you could check your notes and then continue.

A key to handling all problems is to deal with them and move on. The less upset you are, the less your audience will notice the problem. Don't make a face, roll your eyes, or do anything that calls attention to your problem. Keep your audience goal in mind and move ahead.

METHODS OF DELIVERY

Whenever I give a classroom speech, I speak from note cards. I memorize the ideas but never say the speech exactly the same way each time.

When I introduced the speakers at the sports banquet, I wrote out each introduction and read from my paper. I had practiced enough so I could look up at the audience.

When I go to a speech contest, I have to deliver a speech I memorized. I may give the exact same speech three or four times in one day.

At Scout meetings we practice giving speeches without real preparation. We draw topics from a hat and get one minute to think before we have to talk. My last speech was on bowling balls.

Public speakers use four methods for delivering a speech: extemporaneous, manuscript, memorized, and impromptu. Each has different strengths and weaknesses. Each works better in certain situations. In this section you will look at each of the four methods.

EXTEMPORANEOUS

When using the **extemporaneous method,** speakers use a prepared outline but do not plan each word or sentence. Therefore, the *ideas* remain the same each time the speech is delivered, but the *words* change. For an extemporaneous speech, the speaker usually puts the speech outline on note cards, using key words or phrases. The cards contain names of people or statistics, or a descriptive word to help the speaker remember an example or story. Most speakers print their information on a card or single sheet of paper held in the vertical position. That way, when they are talking they can carry the card in one hand and read it easily. The example on page 289 shows notes for an extemporaneous speech on stepfamilies.

Good extemporaneous speakers prepare their introductions and conclusions carefully so they are very strong. Extemporaneous speakers also practice aloud to rehearse key phrases and ideas.

Extemporaneous delivery can be very effective because it leaves you free to respond to audience feedback. You can rephrase or repeat ideas if necessary. In addition, your tone will be more conversational, since you must think about your ideas as you phrase them.

One disadvantage of the extemporaneous method is that it may give you false confidence. Many beginning speakers think that by using this method they will not have to prepare very carefully. If you have this idea, you may be in for an unpleasant surprise when you get up to give your first speech!

MANUSCRIPT

When using the **manuscript method,** a speaker writes out the entire speech and delivers the speech from this paper. Effective speakers know the content of their speeches so well that they can look at the audience often enough to establish effective eye contact.

It is important to use this method of delivery when you must be sure to say *exactly* what you mean or when you have very detailed information to present. Politicians use this method when they want to make very specific points. Reading

Sample Notes for Extemporaneous Speech

<u>Communicating in Stepfamilies</u>

Intro: "No small child ever pushed a doll carriage and dreamed
of being a stepparent."
— surprise for many
— 1/3 of families in this school
— year 2000 — most common family type in America

Purpose: Describe the steps of blending families, the problems
and the advantages.

I. Steps
  A. Try it Out
    1. Hopes
      a. solve old problems
      b. get great brothers or sisters (Alice and Tamara)
    2. Differences
      a. Way people fight (Dad and Liz)
      b. Habits and ways to do things (eating, bed times)
  B. Confronting Problems
    1. Admitting them (summer vacations)
    2. Negotiating time together, discipline
  C. Resolving Problems
    1. Trusting each other
    2. Being open (Dad and fishing trip)

II. Problems and Advantages
  A. Problems
    1. Holidays
      a. mixing traditions
      b. travel schedules
    2. School Events
      a. who to invite
      b. names and introductions
  B. Advantages
    1. New sisters or brothers (Reggie)
    2. Part of big family (stepgrandparents, parties)
Conclusion: Pretty soon everyone will be a step-relative!

the manuscript keeps them from saying something they might regret later.

You may want to use the manuscript method when you introduce a guest speaker, because you may need a manuscript to make sure you have the correct information. One student described her experience introducing a speaker this way:

JOURNAL ENTRY

The senior-high group at our church took responsibility for all church activities on one Sunday. I had to introduce the guest speaker for education hour. I had to write it all out because I had to give her title, the schools she attended, and the organization where she worked. I never could have remembered all the correct names.

Most manuscript speeches go through two or three drafts as speakers write their ideas, read them out loud, and then revise their language. The example shows the stages of development for a manuscript speech about football.

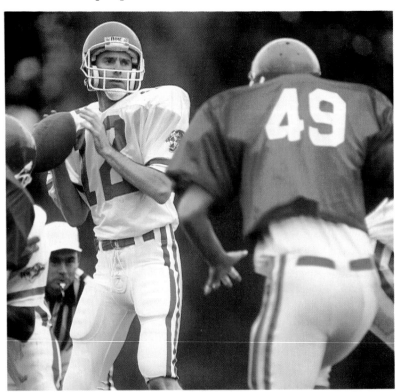

STAGES OF MANUSCRIPT DEVELOPMENT

DRAFT 1

The quarterback sends the football in my direction. I'm open and dragged out of bounds after a gain of 40 yards. This is the best part of the game for me. I love catching passes. I wish there was a pass machine that would throw passes all day so I could practice. Catching a pass takes all my troubles away.

DRAFT 2

The quarterback drops back to pass and I'm open down the sidelines. "Wilkinson catches the ball and he's dragged out of bounds after a gain of 40 yards." Catching a ball is like hitting a home run. I love to catch passes. I wish there was some kind of a machine that could throw passes to me all day. Every time I catch a pass my troubles are all gone.

FINAL DRAFT

"...the ball is snapped. Reeder drops back to pass. There's Wilkinson down the sidelines; he has his man beat. The ball is caught by Wilkinson and he's dragged out of bounds after a gain of 40 yards."

To me, catching a pass is like hitting a home run and trotting around the bases; it's my time to shine. I love to catch passes. I want some kind of machine that could throw passes to me every day, but I have to wait until the football season starts to do it. Every time I catch a ball all the bad things that happened are all gone. I get high catching passes.

Often people who give a speech on radio or television use a manuscript to be sure they stay within certain time limits. For example, an editorial may run thirty seconds. If the speaker's speech is not fully written and timed, he or she may get cut off before finishing.

Manuscript delivery has two possible problems. First, you may read the whole speech and never look at the audience. Second, you may never move because you can't leave the manuscript. You cannot adapt to audience feedback or maintain eye contact if you just read to your audience.

MEMORIZED

When using the **memorized method** speakers write out a manuscript and memorize it word for word. This takes a lot of work, but it leaves the speaker free to move and look directly at the audience because there is no need for notes. Often speech contest rules state that contestants must deliver memorized speeches. You may wish to memorize your speech for a formal occasion such as a school assembly or a religious program.

Speaking completely from memory can be a problem. You might end up memorizing the exact words but not the ideas. If your words are not attached to the main ideas you'll have a difficult time thinking on your feet if you forget even one word. Good speakers memorize the order of ideas *and* the words. Then, if they forget the next word, they can use an extemporaneous method to talk about the idea. Usually after a moment or two, they will remember where they were in the speech.

IMPROMPTU

When using the **impromptu method** of delivery, speakers talk without notes and with very little preparation. An impromptu speech is a spur-of-the-moment presentation. The speaker may have a few seconds or a minute to prepare a short talk. The time it takes the speaker to rise from a seat and walk to the front of the room may be his or her preparation time.

Generally, the best way to organize an impromptu speech is to look at the audience and

- Tell them what you're going to tell them.
- Tell them.
- Tell them what you've told them.

In real-life situations people often are called on to say a few words. A teacher may ask you to say a few words about how the soccer tournament went on Saturday or about an upcoming event. For example, your English teacher might say, "Tim, why don't you take a minute and tell us about this year's freshman play?" If Tim is not able to think on his feet, he might say, "Um, well, this weekend there'll be a play about a stepfamily. It's, um, funny and you should see it." However, if Tim has had practice giving impromptu speeches, he might say, "This weekend the freshman class will present the play *Step On a Crack*. It's about a young girl's life in a stepfamily. It's very funny but very realistic. Audrey Jackson will play the part of the girl. I play her father. The curtain goes up on Friday and Saturday night at eight. It's free. I think you'll all enjoy *Step On a Crack*."

As you might guess, the impromptu method is a difficult type of delivery to use. However, it is useful to practice it, since you will be asked frequently to speak on the spur of the moment at a meeting or before a small group of people. The more you practice giving impromptu speeches, the more comfortable you will be when you have to think on your feet.

INTERACT

In small groups of six or eight, divide into pairs. Each pair should submit three topics for an impromptu speech. Place the topics facedown on a desk. Have each pair pick

a topic. One person in each pair will have only 30 seconds to prepare an impromptu speech on the topic. The other person will have five minutes to write notes for an extemporaneous speech. Do this for each pair. Each pair should give its speeches to the others in the group. Compare the differences in the speeches on the same topic.

PERSONAL DELIVERY

Personal delivery involves your nonverbal messages, or how you use your appearance, voice, facial expression, eye contact, gestures, and body movements during your speech. Your nonverbal messages may support your spoken message, or they may prevent your listeners from getting your message.

APPEARANCE

I kept getting distracted by all her shiny, sparkling jewelry.

Wearing shorts and a ripped T-shirt to talk to the school board did not make a good impression.

You are communicating with your audience from the moment you rise from your seat to give a speech. The audience looks at your clothes, hair, posture, and mannerisms and creates an impression of you. Listeners expect you to be dressed appropriately for the occasion. You may dress differently for a classroom speech, a speech contest, and an assembly speech. Your appearance needs to support your message and not distract the listeners.

A speaker needs to appear confident. If you project an image of confidence and enthusiasm as you walk to the front of the room, your listeners will think, "This speaker will be interesting." Don't let your appearance keep your listeners from getting the message!

VOICE

I can't listen to him for more than two minutes before I fall asleep.

She gets nervous and talks so fast I cannot understand what she is saying.

How often have you left a speech feeling frustrated because you couldn't hear the speaker or because the speaker's voice was annoying? The vocal characteristics of volume, rate, pitch, quality, and clarity all affect a speaker's delivery.

Volume

Volume refers to the loudness or softness of a speaker's voice. Very often beginning speakers whisper or shout at their listeners. Competent speakers change their volume as their content changes. For example, when you are talking about something that excites or angers you, your voice may get louder. When you are describing something sad, scary, or peaceful, you may use a soft voice. You will adjust your voice to the feedback you receive from your listeners. If you see people in the back straining to hear, it's time to speak louder.

Rate

Rate refers to the speed at which you speak. Frequently beginning speakers talk as quickly as possible in order to finish and sit down. When this happens they leave their listeners confused or frustrated. Remember, a normal speaker talks at a rate of 120 to 180 words a minute. If you speak too slowly, your audience's attention will wander. If you speak too quickly, the audience will get confused. Experienced speakers vary their rate of speech. They adapt their rate to the topic, the feedback, and the occasion.

When you are making an important point, you may slow down in order to emphasize each word. This allows your listeners to understand your main points. If your listeners look bored, you may speed up your rate to get their attention. If they appear confused, you may wish to slow down to give them time to use their "thought speed" properly.

Pauses must be silent. A voiced pause, such as "ah," "um," or "you know," is distracting to listeners. When too many vocal pauses are used, listeners stop paying attention to the speaker's message.

Pitch

Pitch refers to the highness or lowness of the voice. Nervous speakers frequently tense their vocal cords and speak in a high voice. This may distract the audience or make the speaker sound boring. In everyday conversation, you change your pitch naturally. If you can think of public speaking as a type of conversation, your pitch will change naturally.

A speaker's pitch should help support the meaning of the message. For example, when speakers express pleasure or excitement, their pitch rises. When speakers express sadness or seriousness, their pitch tends to get lower.

Vocal Quality

Vocal quality refers to the sound of a voice. Poor vocal quality can distract from the speaker's message. For example, if a speaker has a nasal voice that sounds like a whine, the listeners may become annoyed. If the speaker's voice is raspy or throaty, it will distract from the message. The best way to know how your voice sounds to others is to record yourself on tape. You may be surprised by what you hear.

Clarity

Clarity refers to the clearness of a speaker's words. A competent speaker tries to say words carefully and correctly. Slurred words in a speech may give listeners the impression that the speaker is careless. For example, *gode* for *gold, candate* for *candidate,* or *eatin'* for *eating* give a careless image.

A speaker who mispronounces words does not appear to know the topic well. For example, a speaker who says *nucular power* instead of *nuclear power* sounds unprepared. If you know you have difficulty remembering how to pronounce a certain word, write its pronunciation on your note card. Then you can refer to it when you need it.

The following words are ones that are frequently mispronounced. People say:

yutes	for	youths
natcherl	for	natural
eggsept	for	accept
axed	for	asked
acshul	for	actual
tree	for	three
Settemba	for	September

If you practice your speech out loud for someone before your actual presentation, that listener can give you feedback about words that you may be mispronouncing.

OBSERVE

Listen very carefully to speakers for a week. Record the words that they mispronounce. Make a list of the six most commonly mispronounced words.

FACIAL EXPRESSION

If speakers are interested in their topics, they show this in their facial expressions. A deadpan face, or a face without expression, sends a message that the speaker thinks the topic is boring. An excited or animated face sends a message the speaker thinks the topic is important and interesting.

INTERACT

Say the following sentences first with facial expressions that match the idea and then with facial expressions that contradict the idea. Have listeners describe their reactions to each.

- I promise you the best summer of your life if you work at Adventureland.
- It is a great honor to speak to this group today.
- I want to talk about one of our country's most serious problems—the future of the farmer.
- It is time to welcome our winning basketball coach, Leslie Mannix.

EYE CONTACT

The eyes have been called the windows of the soul. People use eye contact to indicate their involvement with others. If the speaker looks over your head or at the floor, you may not feel connected to the person or the topic. The speaker who looks *at* you makes you feel recognized and important. After hearing a speaker talk about the need for students to tutor in an elementary reading program, one student wrote, "I signed up to work as a reading tutor because when he asked for volunteers, I felt like Mr. Horshak was talking just to me."

Good speakers use eye contact to get feedback. Confused looks, angry glances, or friendly smiles from the audience tell you how you are doing. As a speaker, you use your eyes to find the answer to the question "What do you think of what I'm saying?"

When you are speaking, concentrate on your audience members. Look at them and read the feedback they give you. Try to look at each audience member during the talk. Do not rush from one face to the next. Be careful not to look only at one side of the room or only at the people in the front or back. Don't just look at your audience, really concentrate on what they are telling you through their feedback.

GESTURE

Gestures are movements of the head, shoulders, hands, or arms that speakers use to describe or emphasize a point. A speaker may describe how to shoot a basketball by going through the motions. A speaker may place emphasis on an idea by pointing a finger at the audience or pounding a fist on the podium.

Apply

What do you predict a speaker would do while saying the following statements?

- There are three—only three—major issues in this campaign.
- When the pond was stocked with fish, most of them were about six inches long. Now we are catching two-foot-long trout.
- As the earth moves around the sun, we experience night and day.
- The center crouched, and then exploded with a winning three-point basket.

When you talk to your friends or family, you use gestures naturally. Don't change when you speak to an audience. It's easy to say gestures should appear natural, but what does this mean for the public speaker? Gestures must be large enough to be seen and understood by the audience. Gestures must be made above the waist, and they must move out and away from the body.

Beginning speakers often wonder what to do with their hands. Remember that the things that feel like watermelons at

the end of your arms do not look as large and awkward to your audience as they feel to you! Let your hands hang easily at your sides or hold your note cards in one hand and let the other stay near your side until you gesture.

Good speakers adapt their gestures to the audience. If you are talking to ten people, your gestures can be quite subtle. If you are talking to a group of sixty, you will need to use larger gestures.

MOVEMENT

Good speakers do not move constantly, nor do they stand perfectly still. They use movement to make their message clearer to the audience. Here are some simple do's and don'ts for movement and gestures:

Do

1. Take a few steps during the major transitions in the speech.
2. When you move, face in the same direction you are moving.
3. Stand balanced on both feet, with your weight forward.

Don't

1. Pace back and forth. Stay in one place when discussing a main point.
2. Gesture all the time. It is fine to stand with your hands at your sides.
3. Rest your weight on one foot. You can lose your balance.
4. Play with keys or loose change in your pocket.

 **Apply**

Assume you are watching a speaker. What might the following body movements signal to you?

1. The speaker pauses, takes two steps forward, and starts to speak again.

2. The speaker shrinks back and then returns to a normal speaking position.

In both examples a speaker is using movements to send a message. In example 1, the speaker may be telling the listener, "This is a transition" or "I'm moving on to a new point." Good speakers often use movements to get their listeners' attention. In example 2, the speaker may be acting out a story. Perhaps it is the story of a child afraid of a circus clown. Perhaps it is someone hiding until other people pass. The body movements support the speaker's message.

REHEARSING THE SPEECH

Just as in basketball, tennis, skating, or any other activity that involves skill development, speech-making requires practice. Rehearsing your speech is one of the most important parts of speech preparation. As you rehearse, you can try out different delivery techniques just as you try out various ways to do a jump shot or play a jazz piece.

In this section, you will examine ways to rehearse an extemporaneous speech. You can use many of the same techniques for other delivery methods. You will find that your words will change each time you practice, but your ideas should remain in the same order. Rehearsing involves ordering the ideas in your mind and polishing the delivery of your speech.

ORDERING THE SPEECH IN YOUR MIND

As you prepare to speak, you must be sure to fix in your mind the main ideas in the correct order. The following simple steps will help you do this:

1. Read over your entire outline silently two or three times. Go straight through without going back over any section.
2. Do the same as in step 1, but this time aloud.
3. Try to give your speech without looking at your outline or note cards. Stand up and practice gestures and movements. Even if you can't remember certain points, go on and try to complete the entire speech. Remember, this is a rehearsal, so it doesn't matter if you make mistakes. It is important to go through the entire speech without stopping.

4. Reread your outline silently as in step 1.
5. Reread your outline aloud as in step 2.
6. Try again to give the complete speech.
7. Continue steps 4 through 6 until you can complete your speech without any errors. Remember, in this part of your rehearsal, you are working on getting a grasp of the order of ideas in your speech.
8. Practice the visualization technique you learned in Chapter 4. This technique allows you to rehearse anywhere you can concentrate.

This work is well worth the effort. When the ideas are fixed in your mind, you will not get confused during the actual speech.

POLISHING YOUR DELIVERY

After you are able to deliver your speech aloud in the correct order, you can pay attention to your delivery. Following these steps can help you with the delivery:

1. Imagine your audience in your mind. Set chairs up in front of you, talk to a mirror, or have one or two friends listen to you. If you are using visual aids, be sure to practice with them.
2. Try to communicate with your real or imaginary audience. Be enthusiastic both verbally and nonverbally. If you are not excited about your topic, how can you expect anyone else to be?
3. If your audience is real rather than imaginary, adapt to your listeners. Watch for cues indicating that you need to change your delivery. Ask your audience for feedback.
4. Give special practice to the introduction, conclusion, and any stories, examples, or jokes. You may wish to memorize these parts so that they will sound exactly as you imagine them.
5. Spread your rehearsal time over three or four days. If you wait until the last minute, you will only increase your nervousness. Allow enough practice time so you will be able to rehearse your speech until you are comfortable with it. You may want to rehearse six to eight times.
6. Don't let your speech become stale.

OBSERVE

As you give two or three speeches, try to rehearse in a slightly different way. Work in front of a mirror one time. Try the speech out on your family or friends another time. Practice while moving around gesturing. Describe the ways that work best for you.

AUDIOVISUAL AIDS

On the graph you can see the number of teenagers who smoked in 1970 compared to 1990.

Here you can see the four chambers on the model of a human heart.

Listen to this tape of the last two minutes of Martin Luther King's "I Have a Dream" speech. This speech changed the lives of many Americans.

Audiovisual aids are supporting materials, such as graphs, diagrams, and tapes. In many speeches to inform or to persuade, speakers use audiovisual aids to make their points more clearly and to interest the audience. Think about speeches you have heard and try to remember what audiovisual aids the speakers used.

PREPARING AUDIOVISUAL AIDS

Audiovisual aids can ruin a speech if used improperly. They can distract the audience. Competent speakers think carefully about preparing and using audiovisual aids. These guidelines will help you prepare audiovisual aids for your speeches:

1. *Create audiovisual aids that can be seen or heard by all audience members.* People who have to strain to see a chart or to hear a tape might get frustrated and tune out.
2. *Make visual aids clear and readable.* Use dark heavy lines on white paper. Don't draw complicated, hard-to-interpret designs. Use colors to emphasize words.

COMMON AUDIOVISUAL AIDS

Examples

Actual Objects	a musical instrument, a completed needlepoint project, a lacrosse stick
Pictures	photographs or drawings of an object, event, or person
Models	miniatures of an actual object, scale models of houses, railroads, the human heart.
Diagrams	simplified representations of an area, a process, or a situation
Graphs and Charts	visual comparisons of information, such as bar graphs or pie charts
Visual Materials	filmstrips, slides, videotapes, overhead transparencies
Audio Materials	records, cassette tapes, sound effects

3. *Be sure your visual aids are simple to use.* The easier they are to hold, tape up, or prop up, the easier they will be to handle.
4. *Practice using your audiovisual aid.* Be sure you know how to operate any equipment. Don't hope a video expert will be sitting in your audience.
5. *Check out the equipment* before *the speech.* If you need a stand to display charts or posters, be sure you have one. You may discover you need a special plug or a new light bulb for an overhead projector.

USING AUDIOVISUAL AIDS

Remember that audiovisual aids should support you, not replace you. Visual aids should never become more important than your content. One student, who was giving a demonstra-

tion speech on caring for snakes brought his boa constrictor to class. His audience members were so frightened, they could not concentrate on what he was saying. Be sure the audience remembers the message, not the audiovisual aid. The following guidelines will help you make sure your audiovisual aids work for you, rather than against you:

1. *Speak to the audience, not to your audiovisual aid.* Sometimes beginning speakers talk to their visual aid. This makes it difficult for an audience to hear the speaker. Also, when you focus on your audiovisual aid and not on the audience, you cannot read the feedback your audience sends.

2. *Don't show visual aids until you are ready to use them.* When a visual aid is visible, your audience will focus its attention on the visual aid rather than on what you say. Once you have used the visual aid, remove or cover it.

3. *Don't play with the visual aid.* Pick it up or point out the various parts of it while you are talking about it. Otherwise, don't touch it.

4. *Do not pass the visual aid around.* This is distracting. When audience members take time out to examine the aid, they lose what you are saying at that moment.

5. *Don't hide behind your audiovisual aid.* Stand next to your aid, not behind it or in front of it. You are giving the speech, not your tape recorder or your graph. Don't hold charts in front of your face or allow tapes to run for long periods during your speech.

MICROPHONES

If you are going to use a microphone, check to see that it is working properly before you give your speech. If, while you are speaking, you don't think the speaker system is working, stop speaking until it has been fixed. There is little sense in continuing to speak when perhaps 50 percent of the audience cannot hear what you are saying.

If the group is small and you have a loud voice, don't use the microphone.

Guidelines for Microphone Users

1. Don't tap on the microphone to test it. Say, "Test one, two, three." Tapping is harmful to a microphone and annoying to audiences.
2. Don't stand too close to the microphone.
3. Don't yell or raise your voice when using a microphone. Check the volume of the microphone while you are testing it, and then decide how close you need to stand in order to be heard clearly.
4. Don't look at the microphone while speaking. Speak to your audience.
5. Don't let the microphone block your face as you speak.
6. Don't swing the microphone on its cord. This can break the cord.

SUMMARY

This chapter provides the important points in presenting a speech. Every speaker needs to have self-confidence. This can be gained by avoiding stage fright and thinking on your feet. As a speaker you may use one of four methods for delivery: extemporaneous, manuscript, memorized, or impromptu. Speakers need to control the nonverbal aspects, or personal delivery, of their speaking. As a final step in speech preparation, speakers must rehearse their presentation. If the speech requires audiovisual aids, a competent speaker plans ahead to create and use these aids effectively.

CHAPTER REVIEW

THINK ABOUT IT

1. Define *stage fright* and describe ways to develop speech confidence.
2. List the four methods of delivery and explain the use of each.
3. What are the nonverbal elements of personal delivery?
4. Describe ways to rehearse your speech.
5. What are the guidelines for preparing and using audiovisual aids?

TRY IT OUT

1. In order to get comfortable with gestures, practice your speech and exaggerate the gestures you plan to use. Make them much bigger and stronger than you would in a real speech. Then work to tone the gestures down and make them presentable. This may help you to become more comfortable with gesturing.
2. Listen to a recording of a famous public speaker (Martin Luther King, Jr., John F. Kennedy), a comedian (Lily Tomlin, Robin Williams), or a great storyteller (Orson Welles, Jackie Torrence), and pay attention to the way the person changes volume, rate, pitch, and vocal quality to keep the delivery interesting. Report your observations to the class.

PUT IT IN WRITING

1. Observe a cooking demonstration in a department store or on television. Write a paragraph that describes how the speaker used gestures, eye contact, and vocal variety to hold audience interest. If the speaker used an audiovisual aid, describe how it was used.

2. In your journal, write about your own speech confidence. How confident do you feel when speaking in public? What signs of nervousness do you have? Do you use the guidelines for overcoming stage fright? Do you have other techniques for reducing nervousness?

SPEAK ABOUT IT

1. Create an introduction for a speech and practice giving it using a variety of delivery methods. Write out the full introduction and deliver it to the class twice—once using the memorized method and once using the manuscript method. Ask for feedback on the effectiveness of each method.
2. To practice using audiovisual aids, make a collage about yourself and present it to the class. The collage should contain at least three things that are part of your life or your personality that most people do not know about.
3. Practice developing your extemporaneous style. Choose one of the following topics and take fifteen minutes to prepare an outline with an introduction, at least two main points, some supporting material, and a conclusion.

   - Something that should be invented (and why)
   - The person I would most like to meet (and why)
   - If I have children some day, I will be sure to...
   - When people get angry they should...
   - I feel happy when...
   - The best things about school
   - If I could change the world...
   - I would like to learn how to...
   - If I were invisible...
   - School would be better if...
   - If I were older...
   - Some day I would like to help solve the problem of...
   - The famous person I'd most like to be (and why)
   - The most pressing problem America is facing today

CHAPTER

13

CREATING THE INFORMATIVE SPEECH

KEY WORDS

connected information

constructive criticism

critic

critique

formal feedback

informal feedback

informative speech

social ritual speech

After completing this chapter, you should be able to

- list the six principles for making a speech memorable.
- create an informative speech.
- create a number of social ritual speeches.
- define *constructive criticism*.
- list guidelines for constructive criticism.
- critique a speech to inform.

Every day you listen to speeches to inform. Your history teacher may describe the Middle Ages, your minister or rabbi may talk about famous religious people, or your Scout leader may explain how to cook a one-pot meal. Each day you also hear social ritual speeches, such as school announcements or the introductions of speakers. Social ritual speeches are informative speeches that follow a formula or pattern. You might evaluate these speeches by saying "This is boring" or "That sounds terrific." This chapter discusses how to give informative speeches, including social ritual speeches, and how to evaluate these speeches effectively.

SPEAKING TO INFORM

Speaking to inform is the most familiar type of public speaking. An **informative speech** is a speech that presents or describes information. Your days are filled with informative speeches—those that you give and those that you receive. You listen to teachers' lectures, which are a type of informative speaking. You might announce to your classmates the date and time of the music department's winter concert. You might give an oral book report in English class. You might teach your Spanish club a dance you learned in Mexico.

PRINCIPLES FOR INFORMING

The main purpose of a speech to inform is to share information. When you speak to inform, you need to remember certain principles about sharing information. Audiences are more attentive and receive information better when: (1) they have a need to know; (2) the information is connected; (3) the information is well-organized; (4) the information is repeated; (5) the information is tied to feelings; and (6) the information is focused.

Need to Know

People who feel a "need to know" receive information more easily. When your teacher tells you what to study for an important test, you listen closely. Your audience, too, will listen closely if it has a need to know. Thus, one of your first duties as an informative speaker is to analyze your listeners' needs and create a need to know.

Connections

Connected information is more easily received than unconnected information. **Connected information** is new information that is related to information an audience already knows. If your teacher speaks to your class about persuasion, you may simply tune out. On the other hand, if your teacher connects that information to television advertisements and explains how you are personally affected by persuasion in advertisements, you will become more interested in the information. Competent speakers use information that connects to what the listeners already know.

Organization

Well-organized information is more easily understood. If you are describing a process, for example, you must start at the beginning and discuss each step in sequence until you reach the end of the process. If you skip around instead of presenting the steps in order, your audience will become confused and may not understand you. Process, time, space, and topic order are organizational patterns that work well in informative speeches. You learned about them in Chapter 11.

Repetition

Repeated information is more easily understood and remembered. Choose two or three of the most important ideas in your speech and use repetition to emphasize those points. But be careful not to overuse repetition. Too much repetition in a speech can become as tiresome as too many reruns of a television show.

Feelings

Information tied to feelings is more easily remembered. Think about the past week. What event stands out in your memory? Was it when you tripped and were embarrassed because you felt half the school was watching you? Perhaps it was a difficult exam or a compliment paid to you by a classmate. No doubt it was an event that involved your feelings. When giving an informative speech, use memorable examples, illustrations, and stories to help your audience remember your main ideas.

Focus

Too much information reduces understanding. You need to focus your speech so that you cover only a few main points. When your teacher lectures and covers too much material you will probably remember very little because of information overload. Information overload should be avoided in all types of speaking, because most people can understand and remember only five to nine pieces of information at one time.

INTERACT

With a partner, share information about each other's hobbies. Be sure to use a visual aid if necessary. Take turns with your partner to do what the other has demonstrated.

INFORMATIVE SPEECHES

There are many forms of informative speeches. The following are the most common ones.

Description

A speaker attempts to describe a person, place, thing, or experience. One person may describe what happens at a weekend forensics tournament, another may describe the experience of rollerblading, while a third may describe his feelings for his grandfather. These speakers attempt to create mental pictures for audience members.

Sample titles
ALS: A Progressive Destroyer
The Festival of Kwanza
The Grand Canyon Sunrise

Definitions

A speaker may use this type of speech to explain a word or concept in great detail. For example a speaker may attempt to define what the terms *family* or friendship mean to him or her. Civic groups often sponsor contests that require speakers to define terms such as *freedom* or *democracy*. Most speakers talk about dictionary meanings, general understanding, and personal meanings of words or concepts.

Sample titles
Grounded: The World's Worst Word
What *Liberty* Means to My Family
Swamp Is Not a Dirty Word

Demonstration

A speaker uses a visual aid to explain or demonstrate a particular concept or thing. You may use a large poster of a motorcycle to explain Harley Davidson's parts, their names, and how they work. You may demonstrate through gestures the correct form for various sports activities, such as swimming the butterfly stroke, pitching a fastball, or serving a tennis ball.

Sample titles
How to Pack a Duffelbag
How to Find Carmen Sandiego
Basic Tae Kwon Do Moves

Process

A speaker explains the step-by-step process by which something is created or operated. The speaker may or may not use a visual aid. For example, you may show how to create buttons with slogans by using the button-punch machine in class. You may explain the process of making double chocolate–nut brownies by writing each step on the board and sharing an example of the final product with the class. Or you may talk about the steps in conducting an interview or running a meeting according to parliamentary procedure.

Sample titles

How to Wrap a Present
How to Pitch a Curve Ball
How to Play the Trombone

Apply

Read the following example of an informative speech. Try to identify the outline pattern. Find examples of definition and description.

Stardust: The Adopted Wild Horse

We adopted a new family member last summer. No, the latest member is not a brother or sister. It's a wild horse named Stardust. Stardust came to us through the U.S. government Adopt-a-Horse Program. The U.S. government is giving away wild horses to people who prove they can take care of the animals. I'd like to tell you about the American wild horses and how we went about getting Stardust.

In the western part of the United States wild horses roam free on the open ranges. Spanish explorers brought the horses to America hundreds of years ago. For centuries they ran wild in large herds. By the 1960s most of the horses were gone because ranchers killed them to keep the horses from grazing on their land.

In 1971 Congress passed a law to protect these horses. Now there are so many wild horses that the government must take some off the range each year. Since 1973 the government has used helicopters to round up 64,000 horses. Cowboys rope the horses or helicopters drive them into corrals. These horses are sent across the United States to families who will provide them good homes.

How did our family get Stardust? My sister, Gretchen, has always loved horses. She has ridden since she was four and always helps out at the Crossroads Stables. My parents said she could have a horse, but they could not afford to buy one. When Gretchen heard about this program from a friend at the stables, she begged my parents to get a horse and keep it in the old barn.

My father called the Bureau of Land Management and found out that anyone can adopt a horse if the person has enough land for the horse to live on and pays the $125 adoption fee. We all went to the adoption center and helped Gretchen pick out Stardust. She liked Stardust because of her black and white color. She has a race, or a narrow white stripe down the center of her face, and a star, or a white patch, on her forehead. When we got Stardust she was undernourished and sad. Now she is fattened up and friendly.

Everyone in our family enjoys our new member. Now I want to adopt a wild horse of my own!

SOCIAL RITUAL SPEECHES

It's a pleasure to see you all here tonight....

I am here to nominate....

Thank you for this award, which....

The social ritual speech is a common speaking-listening experience. A **social ritual speech** is a special kind of speech to inform. It follows a set formula or pattern. Although you may never campaign for president of the United States or accept an Oscar for your movie roles, you will probably give some social ritual speeches and you will no doubt listen to many of them.

JOURNAL ENTRY

I am working toward becoming an Eagle Scout and, as part of my preparation, I must lead many meetings and act as the chairperson of many big troop events. I am often called upon to announce upcoming events, introduce a Court of Honor, thank a speaker, or tell a story about our camping trip. I used to be very nervous, but after you have to keep repeating these short speeches you become much more comfortable. It also helped that I earned the public speaking badge.

Some of the common social ritual speeches are introducing a speaker, welcoming the audience, presenting awards, accepting awards, nominating a person, making announcements, and relating stories. Success in giving each of these speeches depends on your ability to be brief, clear, and enthusiastic. A discussion of each type of social ritual speech follows.

INTRODUCTIONS

The goals of an introduction speech are to give the audience information about the speaker and to create a positive attitude about the speaker among the listeners. When introducing a speaker you need to give the speaker's name and title, tell something about the speaker's experience, and describe why the listeners will find the speech interesting or valuable. The following is an example of an introduction:

Today we have with us one of the most outstanding doctors in our community, Dr. Jerry Wilson. Dr. Wilson has practiced medicine in Riverdale for fourteen years. He has a special interest in nutrition, and he volunteers at a drop-in center for teenagers. He is here to discuss with us the problem of starvation diets—a problem that is increasing among young people. It is with a great deal of pleasure that I present to you Dr. Jerry Wilson.

WELCOMES

The goal of a welcoming speech is to make audience members feel comfortable and prepared for what is to follow. When giving this speech you need to express pleasure at seeing the listeners, and briefly describe the event to come. The following is an example of a welcoming speech:

> Good evening. I am happy to see you here this evening. I would like to welcome you to this year's student variety show. We students have enjoyed preparing this show for you and hope you will enjoy it also.

AWARD PRESENTATIONS

The goal of an award presentation speech is to honor someone who has done something special. When giving an award you must describe the award, tell why the winner deserves it, name the winner, and hand out the award.

If the audience knows who is going to receive the award, you can name the winner early in your speech. If the winner is a surprise, name the person at the end of the speech. The following is an example of a surprise award presentation speech:

> It seems right that we should be presenting the Outstanding Speech-Student-of-the-Year Award today on the birthday of John F. Kennedy, one of the greatest speakers in our country's history. The speech club presents this award every year to the student who has contributed the most to the speech team in terms of team spirit and rank at tournaments. Our award this year goes to Eduardo Romero.

If you hand out the award, shake the winner's hand with your right hand and present the award with your left.

ACCEPTANCE SPEECHES

Expressing appreciation at receiving an award or honor is the goal of an acceptance speech. When giving this speech you need to thank the person or organization who gave the award, tell why the award is important to you, and express how you feel about receiving the award. You also should thank anyone who helped you attain the award and then receive the award; that is, pick up the trophy or certificate. The following is an example of an acceptance speech:

> It is an honor to receive the Liberty Essay Award. I wish to thank the members of the Kiwanis Club and my English teacher, Mrs. Evelyn Klein. My grandfather came here as an immigrant from Hungary in 1943. I am pleased to have the chance to share his life through this essay. Thank you.

NOMINATIONS

The goal of a nominating speech is to support someone running for office and to convince the listeners to vote for this person. The person may be running for an office in school, in a club, or in a social organization. When making a nomination you must name the candidate and the office, describe the candidate's qualifications for the office, and express your hope that the listeners will vote for this person. The following is an example of a nominating speech:

> It is my pleasure to nominate Megan Murray for class treasurer. Megan has worked on the school athletic committee. She was in charge of the money for the Haywood School Car Wash last spring. She is also a good math student. I know Megan Murray is honest and will be accurate in keeping accounts. I hope you will support Megan at election time on Tuesday.

ANNOUNCEMENTS

When making announcements, the goal is to give important information or directions to the audience. When you make an announcement you usually give information about who, what, where, or why. The following is an example of an effective announcement:

> Hungry? Come to the Wallace School student council bake sale on Saturday, February 16, from 9:00 A.M. to noon, in the Commons. We will use the money we raise for the Homecoming Dance.

RELATING STORIES

A speaker may be asked to relate a story in order to give the audience background on a certain occasion or to capture a funny, moving, or important moment from a larger experience. A speaker may be asked to tell the story of the founding of an organization or program, or to tell the story of something funny or important that happened during a school trip or an event. When telling a story, you need to describe the background of the event, relate the main points in order, and create a clear and memorable ending. The following is an example of a story that relates background:

> In 1954 this land was cornfields, but there was a vision in the eyes of Elinor and Asher Levinson that said this land could be a special place for families to come together for fun and for growth. This couple began a community campaign to build a recreational and educational center that would house athletics, theatre, and classes. By 1956 a gymnasium was built and the first basketball games were played. My father was on that first team. Every few years a new wing was added to this building, which has become the heart of our community. Tonight we honor the Levinsons who have contributed so much to all of our lives. And I wish to add that in this gym, last week, I beat my father at basketball for the first time. Great things have happened in this building!

Sometimes a person is called upon to entertain an audience by telling original or fictional stories. This type of storytelling is discussed in Chapter 17.

Although social ritual speeches are brief, they are important speaking experiences because they are a part of everyday life.

INTERACT

In a small group, prepare imaginary social ritual speeches for three of the following. Share them with your classmates.

- Nominate someone for president of the French club.
- Accept an award for outstanding speech student.
- Introduce the mayor at a school assembly.
- Announce the school musical, *Oklahoma!*
- Welcome parents and community members to the school talent show.

EVALUATING INFORMATIVE SPEECHES

Public speaking is two-way communication. Although you may not talk much, as a listener you do affect the speaker. Have you ever watched a performer respond to the audience? When the audience claps or laughs, the performer seems to get more energy. When the audience does not respond, the performer seems to have less energy. Listener feedback can change a speech.

A listener may give informal or formal feedback to a speaker. **Informal feedback** consists of verbal and nonverbal messages given spontaneously to the speaker. The listener is giving the speaker a personal response. **Formal feedback** consists of planned written or oral comments. They are intended to affect the speaker's next speech.

INFORMAL FEEDBACK

How does a teacher in a large class know whether the students are bored or interested? How does someone speaking to a group of ten know how the audience members feel? Audience feedback tells speakers how they are doing. This feedback may come during or after the speech. There are various kinds of positive and negative feedback a speaker may receive from groups of different sizes.

Speakers try to read the audience's feedback during the speech. In a small group, they may be able to see all the faces clearly. When speaking to a large group, they may see only blurred faces in row after row of seats. The size of the audience affects the kinds of positive and negative feedback a speaker receives.

Your feedback during a speech affects what speakers do next. If you look bored, yawn, or squirm around, a good speaker will make a change. He or she may speak more loudly, ask a question, or start to use more gestures. A poor speaker will not change anything. If the poor speaker gets nervous, he or she may use more "ums" and "ahs" and try to finish the speech quickly.

If the members of an audience look interested, smile, or nod, a good speaker will respond by becoming more relaxed. He or she may look directly at the audience members more often or tell an extra joke or story. On the other hand, a poor speaker will not use the feedback.

Sometimes the feedback after a speech affects the speaker's next speech. A comment such as "I enjoyed the poetry you in-

cluded in the speech" may encourage a speaker to use poetry again. If someone said, "You used so many statistics I thought I was in math class," the speaker may try to cut down on the use of numbers in future speeches.

Sometimes feedback comes in the form of questions or comments about the topic. For example, a question like "Where can I learn more about magic?" tells the speaker the audience member was interested in the speech. Some comments will tell a speaker that the audience goal was reached. For example, the speaker's goal might be for listeners to learn the three things to look for when buying sport shoes. If a listener says, "My new shoes fit your three requirements of cost, support, and strength," the speaker knows the goal has been reached.

Competent speakers pay close attention to the feedback they receive during and after a speech. They use the feedback to become even better speakers.

OBSERVE

Watch someone for fifteen minutes giving a talk or lecture. Record in detail the verbal and nonverbal feedback the audience gives the speaker. Note yawns, smiles, and groans. Describe what changes the speaker made as a result of the feedback.

FORMAL FEEDBACK

I enjoyed your stories but I had trouble finding your main points.

You looked directly at the audience, so I felt as if you were talking to me.

There were times when I got lost because I did not understand some words you used.

What does the word *critic* mean to you? Many people think a critic is someone who finds fault. They see a critic as someone who only looks for problems or negative things. Actually a **critic** is a person who judges or evaluates. As a critic you make judgments of both strengths and weaknesses and look for ways to improve a speech. In other words, you give speakers feedback on their speeches.

The formal feedback given by a critic is called a **critique.** A competent critic gives helpful, useful critiques of speeches.

Learning to Critique

There are four reasons for learning to be a competent critic. As you learn how to be a competent critic you will (1) develop appreciation for speech making, (2) become a better listener, (3) improve your own speaking, and (4) help others become better speakers.

A competent critic develops appreciation for speech making and knows there is a difference between just talking and talking with a purpose. It takes skill to gather information, organize it, analyze an audience, and adapt the materials to fit that audience. It also takes skill to deliver the speech and adapt to audience feedback.

A competent critic becomes a better listener. As you develop your ability to analyze and critique speeches, you will become a smarter consumer of speeches. You will listen to public speeches more carefully in your everyday life.

You can improve your own speaking by observing the strengths and weaknesses of other speakers as well as your own. Suppose you say to a classmate, "You never looked at us." This reminds you to work on eye contact in your own public speaking.

As you give feedback to speakers, you can help them improve their performances. You may make comments such as, "I could not tell when you moved to the third point" or "I thought your gestures helped show what you thought was important." Your feedback tells the speaker what could be improved and what worked well.

Guidelines for Constructive Criticism

Constructive criticism tells the speaker what worked well, what could be improved, and how to improve. The following are some guidelines for giving constructive criticism:

1. *Be specific.* Don't say, "Your speech was good." Instead, tell the speaker exactly what was good—the evidence, the organization, the visual aids, or the speaker's delivery. Use specific examples from the speech.

2. *Establish some criteria.* Consider the speaker's purpose. That will help you focus your comments. If the speech is a type of social ritual speech, you can begin by asking if the speech contained the necessary parts.

3. *Describe what you saw and heard.* Don't jump in with comments such as "Your eye contact was great." Say instead, "You looked at everyone in the audience. It made me feel like you were talking to me." Don't say, "The ending was bad." Say instead, "There was no conclusion. The speech stopped at the last point. You need to remind us of the main points at the end."

4. *Limit your points.* Don't tell the speaker five things you liked, eight things you did not like, and six ways to improve. Select only the most important things.

5. *Discuss both strengths and weaknesses.* Critics too often focus on the negative. You need to point out what worked. This tells the speaker to continue doing what worked. In giving a balanced critique of the speaker's voice, you could say, "I could hear you easily in the back of the room. Keep up the good volume. However, you did not use pauses when you moved from one point to another. Stop at the end of an idea to let the audience think about it before you move on." Avoid making someone feel bad.

6. *Suggest improvements.* Suggest what the speaker could do to make the next speech better. Remember to be specific. You might say, "In your next speech, use more variety in

your voice. Changing your rate or pitch might help us stay interested" or "Try not to lean on the desk. It's distracting to the audience."

A critic's feedback is intended to help the speaker. As a critic, you should be supportive and note the strong as well as the weak points in a speech. Always discuss the weak points in a constructive way. Some critics like to follow this pattern: (1) describe what worked well, (2) describe one or two problem areas, and (3) make a suggestion for improvement of the next speech.

Apply

Read the following feedback comments and decide which one a speaker would not find helpful.

1. I liked your speech a lot.
2. I could not hear you when you described the painting. Be sure to talk loudly enough.
3. It was boring.
4. You looked at everyone in the audience, so it felt like you were talking to us.
5. You were really great.

As you might guess, comments 1, 3, and 5 really do not help a speaker. Although number 1 and number 5 are positive, they are not specific. The speaker might ask, "What did you like?" or "What was great?" A comment such as "It was boring" leaves a speaker feeling bad. If you could give some suggestions to make the speech more interesting, these might help the speaker.

Accepting Constructive Criticism

In addition to giving feedback, competent communicators accept and use feedback from others. Accepting constructive criticism is not easy. Speakers need to think about what was said, decide if the comments are valid or useful, and then reply. Frequently speakers just defend what they said or did and do not hear the suggestions for improvement. These guidelines can help speakers benefit from constructive criticism:

1. *Listen carefully.* Find out what specific points of your performance the other person is criticizing. Don't start planning your reply while the other person is talking.
2. *Get tips.* Ask the other person for specific suggestions for improvement.
3. *Think before defending yourself.* Do not immediately defend your actions. You do not need to make excuses. It is all right to make mistakes, because mistakes help you learn. If you have been acting according to certain rules or standards, you should explain those. Otherwise, stay silent for a moment and think about whether the criticism is true. You may say you will take time to think about an idea or suggestion.
4. *Try it out.* Try to correct your performance according to the other person's suggestions. Then ask in a friendly way whether you are doing what he or she suggested. For example, ask "Is this closer to what you had in mind?"
5. *Double-check the criticism.* If you have real doubts about whether a person's criticism is justified, check it with someone else. This second person should understand the problem and be objective. Don't ask a friend who will tell you only what you want to hear.
6. *Work on it.* Try out some of the suggestions in your practice sessions. Ask for feedback on changes.

JOURNAL ENTRY

I used to practice my speeches in front of a mirror, but I never really finished the speech and I never saw many problems. Now I do my speech in front of my mother. She is able to give me some helpful suggestions and point out places where I am not clear. You really need feedback from an audience member to know how you are coming across.

The feedback process is a critical part of communication. If you want to reach your audience goals, you have to know how you are doing. Formal and informal constructive feedback helps you reach these goals.

FEEDBACK FORMS

Sometimes it's hard to remember what you want to tell a speaker. At other times it is hard to remember what others tell you. During speeches many listeners use feedback forms, or critique forms, to give information to a speaker. The sample forms on pages 330–31 can help you give useful feedback to a speaker. Form A allows you to describe the parts of the speech that worked well, the parts that did not work as well, and an area for improvement. Form B allows you to rate each area of the speech on a scale of 1 to 3. One means excellent, 2 means good, and 3 means improvement is needed. Explanations for your ratings can be written in the Comments section.

When you evaluate a social ritual speech, you may use the same type of feedback form that you use for the speech to inform. You can add the very specific parts of the set pattern for the social ritual speech. For example, when evaluating a speech to introduce a speaker, include the following on your form: (1) the speaker's name and title, (2) a description of the speaker's experience, and (3) an explanation of why listeners should be interested in the speech.

Pay careful attention to the feedback process in public speaking. Responding to feedback can make the difference between a good speech and a great speech.

SAMPLE FEEDBACK FORM A

Speaker's Name _____

Speaker's Topic _____

The parts of your speech that worked well were:
Example: *The introduction got my attention.*

The parts of your speech that did not work as well were:
Example: *The speech ended with the last point. There was no conclusion.*

In your next speech, I'd like you to:
Example: *Tie your conclusion to the introduction.*

SAMPLE FEEDBACK FORM B

Speaker's Name _____

Speaker's Topic _____

Factors	Excellent	Good	Needs Improvement	Comments
1. Clear Purpose Statement	1	2	3	_____
2. Introduction				_____
Gained attention	1	2	3	_____
Appropriate to audience and occasion	1	2	3	_____
3. Body				_____
Main points well organized	1	2	3	_____
Supporting materials varied	1	2	3	_____
Transitions clear	1	2	3	_____
4. Delivery				_____
Eye contact with audience	1	2	3	_____
Movement, gestures supported ideas	1	2	3	_____
Voice clear and loud enough	1	2	3	_____
5. Language				_____
Difficult words explained	1	2	3	_____
Use of repetition/figures of speech	1	2	3	_____
6. Conclusion				_____
Summarized ideas	1	2	3	_____
7. Visual Aids				_____
Visual aids helpful to purpose	1	2	3	_____

SUMMARY

This chapter described the principles, presentation, and evaluation of speeches to inform, including social ritual speeches. Set patterns for seven social ritual speeches were presented: (1) speaker introductions, (2) welcoming an audience, (3) award presentations, (4) acceptance speeches, (5) nominations, (6) announcements, and (7) relating stories. Also discussed was the importance of giving and accepting feedback, including some specific ways to provide formal feedback by using critique forms.

CHAPTER REVIEW

THINK ABOUT IT

1. What are the six principles for informing?
2. Describe the steps of three social ritual speeches.
3. Distinguish between informal and formal feedback.
4. Describe constructive criticism and list guidelines for giving criticism.
5. List guidelines for accepting criticism.

TRY IT OUT

1. Bring a magazine advertisement to class. Explain how your advertisement uses principles of informing.
2. Critique a classmate's informative speech, using a feedback form. Also, give an oral evaluation following the guidelines for constructive criticism. Then ask for feedback on your critiquing skills.
3. Read the speech titled "533–12 Freeze" and answer the following questions:
   - How did the speaker attempt to get the listeners' attention?
   - How effective was his introduction?
   - What feelings were conveyed through this speech?
   - How do you imagine this speech was delivered in the classroom?
   - How did the speaker use his language to help create mental pictures in the listeners' minds?

533–12 Freeze
Matt Wilkinson

"...the ball is snapped. Reeder drops back to pass. There's Wilkinson down the sidelines; he has his man beat. The ball is caught by Wilkinson, and he's dragged out of bounds after a gain of forty yards."

To me catching a pass is like hitting a home run and trotting around the bases; it's my time to shine. I love to catch passes. I want some kind of machine that could throw passes to me every day, but I have to wait until the football season starts to do it. Every time I catch a ball all the bad things that happened are all gone. I get high catching passes.

When it comes game time, all I think about is catching passes. The pre-game routine points toward the next three hours of competition. Ten minutes of catching footballs gets me ready for my chance to get in the game. I try to get the fundamentals oiled, so right from the opening kickoff, I'm ready to do my part. Once the game starts I'm totally into it. After seemingly hours of anxious waiting the coach calls, "Wilkinson, get over here," and tells me to get ready to go in. The play: 533–12 Freeze. As I tell the quarterback, he smiles. He loves pass plays. When I run up to the line of scrimmage, I notice that the defense is playing perfectly to our advantage for this play. My confidence grows as our quarterback barks, "Set." The instant after the ball is hiked I begin my journey between the opposing jerseys that stand between me and my goal. I go around the outside linebacker and start upfield into the stretch of green grass between the cornerback and the free safety. There are no more opposing jerseys in my way, just me and the ultimate prize: six points. I turn my head but I see nothing but a little piece of leather on the horizon. As the ball comes over the skyline of linemen and into clear view, my legs shift into cruise-control. My eyes lock onto the perfectly spinning oval as it reaches the height of its flight, and my arms become hard driving pistons pushing me closer to where the tight spiral will make its floating descent out of the sky and into my hands. I lick my lips and smile as I watch the ball into my hands, right on stride! All I hear is myself repeating, "Yes, Yes, YES!" The ball feels warm to the touch. The words *WILSON PRO 2000* engraved in the cowhide and the eight white laces send a tingling to my fingers as I pull it in and tightly tuck it under my arm.

After I've got the ball where I want it, my body turns toward the majestic goalposts that sit in the middle of where I'd most like to be, the place on the field that will pay me back for all the time I've spent practicing. Getting there just once would make all that hard work, sweat, and pain worthwhile. Although I've caught many passes, I still haven't made it into the endzone. So, I will be working hard until that day comes when the perfect spiral will guide me into the center of where my dreams will become a reality. But until then, the night before every game will be spent dreaming about those few seconds of complete joy I will feel when I finally step across the goal line and hear the announcer bellow, "Touchdown, Evanston!"

PUT IT IN WRITING

1. Think of an occasion when you benefited from constructive criticism. This criticism may have been given to help you improve a sports skill, study habits, your performance in a group or your appearance. Write three paragraphs describing the criticism, your reaction to it, and the ways in which you changed your behavior in response to it.

2. In your journal, keep track of the informative speeches you hear during a week. Note the speaker's name, the topic of the speech and a brief description of the speech. Write a two-paragraph evaluation of one of the informative speeches, using the guidelines of constructive criticism.

SPEAK ABOUT IT

1. In a group of four students, have each person deliver a different social ritual speech. The specific parts of the speech should be distinct enough for listeners to recognize. Listeners should identify any missing parts and help that speaker develop information for those parts.

2. Prepare and deliver a presentation speech for one of the following:
   - The trophy for the varsity football team's most valuable player
   - A certificate for first prize in your school's science fair
   - A plaque for the best performer in your school's play
   - The student council award for Teacher of the Year

3. Prepare an informative speech using the six principles of informing. After delivering the speech, test your listeners on their ability to remember the key information you had in your audience goal.

CHAPTER

14

CREATING THE PERSUASIVE SPEECH

KEY WORDS

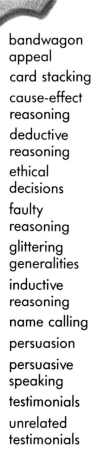

bandwagon appeal

card stacking

cause-effect reasoning

deductive reasoning

ethical decisions

faulty reasoning

glittering generalities

inductive reasoning

name calling

persuasion

persuasive speaking

testimonials

unrelated testimonials

After completing this chapter, you should be able to

- define *persuasion* and *persuasive speaking*.
- explain the difference between speaking to inform and speaking to persuade.
- list and describe Maslow's five human needs.
- describe ways to make yourself believable.
- identify various types of reasoning.
- recognize examples of faulty reasoning.
- create and evaluate a persuasive speech.

337

Ms. Garcia, may we have another day to study for the history test? We already had an English and math test today.

I ask all of you to avoid smoking. The life you save may be your own.

Both of the statements above involve persuasion. **Persuasion** is the process of changing a listener's beliefs or moving a listener to action. Every day, you send and receive persuasive messages in conversation and in speeches. You receive a large number of messages through the media. You may be trying to influence someone else, or someone may be trying to influence you. Persuasion is a complicated process. Some people are easily persuaded while others are not.

Whenever you try to convince others of certain beliefs or of the need for certain actions, you are using persuasion. Whenever you talk to an audience to convince the listeners of certain beliefs or of the need to take certain actions, you are involved in **persuasive speaking.**

Much of what you learned about how to create speeches to inform also applies to persuasive speeches. This chapter focuses on persuasive speaking and covers these subjects: (1) selecting a persuasive topic; (2) adapting to the audience; (3) making yourself believable; (4) using reasoning; (5) organizing a persuasive speech; and (6) evaluating persuasive speeches. Each of these subjects is part of a process of ethical decision making.

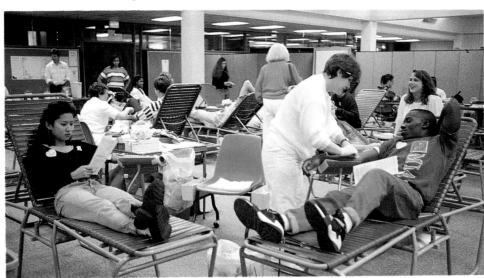

A persuasive speaker is often faced with decisions that have to do with questions of right and wrong. These are known as moral or **ethical decisions.** Persuasive speakers attempt to change the listeners' minds or move the listeners to action. A persuasive speaker may be tempted to talk about only one side of an issue in order to persuade the listeners to think or act in a certain way. In order to build a strong case, unethical persuaders ignore or avoid information that does not support their point of view. Ethical persuaders do not ignore one side of an issue. They consider both sides, acknowledge what might be important points on the opposing side, and then try to convince the listeners of why their position is stronger.

In every step of the persuasion process you will be faced with an ethical issue. You will have to ask yourself whether you have looked at all sides of the issue, whether you've given your listeners all the information they need to make a good decision, and whether you have been fair in your speech development and presentation.

SELECTING A PERSUASIVE TOPIC

When selecting a topic for a persuasive speech, you should find a topic that is personally important to you and about which there is disagreement. If you don't care about a topic, you will have a difficult time persuading other people that it is important.

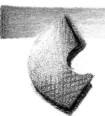

Apply

Look at the following titles and decide which are more likely to be used for speeches to inform and which for speeches to persuade.

1. Music Censorship: Who Is Behind It?
2. The Legal Rights of the Adopted Child
3. Adopted Children Should Be Able to See Their Birth Records
4. We Need to Rate Music Like We Do Movies
5. Children Must Be Fingerprinted for Their Safety
6. The Rise in Missing Children
7. Every Healthy Teen Should Donate Blood

You probably named items 3, 4, 5, and 7 as possible persuasive topics and items 1, 2, and 6 as possible informative topics that call for facts about the subject. The speaker on item 2 might inform the audience about the rights of an adopted child, without giving his or her opinion on the subject. The audience goal might be that listeners be able to explain the three main legal rights of an adopted child. The speaker on item 3, on the other hand, has taken a stand. This speaker is trying to persuade the listeners that adopted children should be able to see their birth records. This speaker is planning a persuasive speech.

OBSERVE

Consider the many persuasive messages you send and receive each day. Select a six-hour period of the day and record four to six persuasive messages you received. Note who was the receiver or sender of these messages.

Here are some sample topics you might consider for persuasive speeches:

- child abuse
- senior citizens' rights
- illiteracy
- teenage alcoholism
- drug abuse
- vandalism
- adoption
- animal rights

- school reforms
- nuclear weapons
- diets
- capital punishment
- missing children
- music censorship
- pollution
- voter registration

After you have chosen a topic for a speech, you may decide your position on the topic right away, or you may need to do research to decide what stand to take. No matter what topic you choose, be sure you and your listeners can get excited about it.

JOURNAL ENTRY

I believe kids are faced with many persuasive messages that are dangerous to their health. I believe it is unethical to try to persuade another person to smoke or do drugs. That's wrong.

INTERACT

Brainstorm as many speech topics as possible with your classmates. Then decide which topics on your list are controversial and therefore might make good persuasive speeches. Note any topics you see as presenting an ethical problem.

ADAPTING TO THE AUDIENCE

How do you persuade someone to accept your point of view or to agree with you? Look at the following situations and think of ways you would try to persuade the other person to act in a certain way:

1. The big party of the year is Friday night at a classmate's home. It will last long past your curfew. How can you persuade your parents to let you stay out late?
2. As chair of the social service club, you have to ask the student council for $16 a month to support a needy child in South America. How will you convince the council to provide the money?

After thinking about these situations, what strategies did you decide to use?

In the first situation, you probably have to convince your parents that you are responsible enough to stay out late. If you describe several instances when you were responsible and trustworthy, they may be persuaded. However, your parents may have valid reasons for not letting you stay out late. Therefore, they may try to persuade you to try things their way this time.

In the second situation, you would have to convince the group that supporting the South American child is a better social project than others the club has considered. You may have to explain how the money would help the child. You could explain that the money would go to one special child whom the school would sponsor for the year.

In both situations you have to figure out how to reach your listeners. The more you know about your listeners, the easier it is to find the right messages. To become a competent persuader, you must analyze your listeners and identify their needs.

LISTENERS' NEEDS

Persuaders try to learn about their audiences so they can appeal to needs the listeners find important. This helps speakers to plan audience goals. All human beings have similar needs.

Psychologist Abraham Maslow created a list of human needs ranging from the most basic to the least basic. According to Maslow, unless their most basic needs are met, people will not be interested in satisfying higher-level needs.

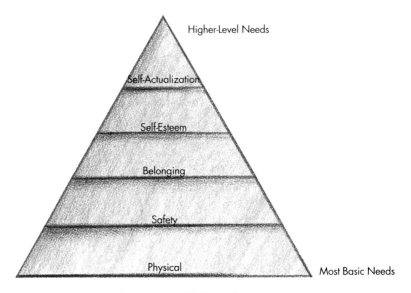

Maslow's Pyramid of Needs

Physical

Physical needs include basic things such as food, clothing, and housing. People need to satisfy these basic physical needs before they can worry about anything else. For example, if parents are worried about feeding their children, they probably won't be concerned about buying a large-screen TV or belonging to a certain social group. Physical needs are critical to basic survival.

Safety

Safety needs include security and a belief that one's friends and family will be safe from physical harm. People need to feel safe and able to protect themselves and those they love. Insurance companies often appeal to the parents' desire to protect their child's future when trying to sell insurance. A persuasive speaker may try to persuade you to take a self-defense course to protect yourself. Street gangs may try to persuade people to join for safety reasons.

Belonging

These include the human needs for affection and a feeling of belonging. Most people value having friends or being part of a group. Often persuaders will send the message that if you want to appear to be part of a certain group, you should dress or act like people in the group. A persuader may tell you that loyal friends never tell on each other. You may be persuaded to go to the amusement park instead of studying because you want to be part of a group.

Self-Esteem

Self-esteem needs refer to the desire to feel good about yourself. These needs are met by feeling worthwhile or feeling satisfied with your accomplishments. You may be persuaded to work on the Special Olympics for handicapped children because you feel good about yourself when you help other people. You may be persuaded to compete in a race or a dance contest to prove how fast or how graceful you really are. Persuaders try to discover what makes listeners feel good about themselves, and they appeal to those self-esteem needs.

Self-Actualization

The need to be creative and true to yourself is a self-actualization or self-fulfillment need. A self-actualization need is the need to be the best person you can be. Persuaders try to convince people to take risks in order to become the best they

can be. One may be persuaded to work at poetry, art, or sports. People may also reach self-fulfillment through their religious beliefs or by living according to certain values.

ORDER OF NEEDS

The needs at the base of Maslow's pyramid have to be met before people can worry about the needs higher in the triangle. It may be hard to persuade you to go to the mall with your friends (belonging need), if you are afraid of walking home in the dark (safety need). You may be persuaded to go, however, if you can ride home with a friend. When you create a persuasive message, choose the right listener need for your appeal.

JOURNAL ENTRY

In our community senior citizens are always trying to persuade the police chief to provide more police protection at night. People are not willing to take night classes, visit friends, or go to church activities until they can walk safely to these places. Their basic need is safety.

INTERACT

Divide into small groups. Match each persuasive statement to one of the needs on Maslow's pyramid. Each need is used once.

1. Always walk to and from school with other people. Do not go near strangers' cars if they try to talk to you.

2. If you join the band, you'll get to know all the people in the band and a lot of the athletes too.

3. Don't quit playing the piano. It's one of the things you do very well, and you can play better than most other pianists your age.

4. Since you lost your backpack, I'll give you half of my dried beef if you let me use your radio.

5. There's a light in you that can grow brighter. Help others and continue to grow into a stronger human being.

Now have each one in the group write statements appealing to three needs. Share the statements with the class.

MAKING YOURSELF BELIEVABLE

Why should anyone listen to you? What qualifies you to talk about homelessness, drunk driving, or animal rights? Why should someone be persuaded by you to attend a school play or donate to the community food drive?

The best persuaders are people who know a great deal about their subject and appear to care about it. In other words, persuaders must be believable. You can become believable by demonstrating your knowledge of the topic, connection to the topic, and interest in the topic.

KNOWLEDGE OF TOPIC

You can become an expert on a topic through firsthand experience or through study. For example, if you have gone camping with your family for several summers, you have firsthand experience about safe camping. If you have no camping experience, you could read books and government publications on safe camping. Or, you could interview a local Scoutmaster. If you give a persuasive speech on making your camping trip safe after becoming informed, you will demonstrate that you know your topic and you will be believable.

CONNECTION TO TOPIC

Tell your listeners why you are able to speak on a certain topic. You might say, "I became interested in this topic of poverty because of my volunteer work at the Haven House Soup Kitchen." If you do not have firsthand experience, explain how you obtained your information. You might say, "A recent article in *Newsweek* magazine estimates that 10 percent of Americans go to bed hungry each night."

INTEREST IN TOPIC

Persuasive speakers appear believable if they are excited or enthusiastic about their topic. This tells the listeners they really care. Use gestures and vary your voice to avoid appearing bored. If you are enthusiastic about your topic, you will have a greater effect on your listeners. As a persuader you are a type of living proof. Convince your listeners that your ideas are important.

INTERACT

In a group of three or four, list ways that teenagers can become believable experts on five of the following subjects:

- bicycle safety
- honesty
- care of animals
- support for cancer funds
- classical music

- air pollution
- space research
- stepfamilies
- individuality
- food labels

REASONING

There are thirty-two reasons why this school needs a swimming pool. I don't have time to list them, but I hope you will support the swimming pool campaign.

Senior citizens are lonely. We need to create a new senior citizens' center in town.

If you read these arguments carefully, you found that both contain problems in reasoning. In the first argument, the audience is not given any of the thirty-two reasons, only a general statement that there are numerous reasons. In the second argument, the problem-solving link is missing. No reason is given to show that a new senior citizens' center will help stop loneliness.

To make a strong argument, you will need to find information to use as evidence to support your ideas. You can use the suggestions given in Chapter 10 on how to research and find supporting materials for evidence. Remember that you can test your evidence and the evidence of other speakers with the following questions:

- Is it fact or opinion?
- Is it reliable?
- Is it relevant?
- Is it timely?
- Is it representative?

As you consider possible evidence, you must remember that an ethical persuader looks at *all* the evidence, not just the evidence that supports his or her idea. If you are trying to persuade your parents to let you have a party, you cannot just talk about how much fun the last party was. If someone broke a lamp at the last party and someone else dumped potato chips into the fish tank, this evidence must be considered, too, even if it does not support the idea of having another party.

TYPES OF REASONING

Once you have supporting materials, or supporting evidence, how do you use them? In most cases you use them to make your point clearer or to build your argument. You have to make all the supporting material fit together to help you reach your audience goal. In other words, supporting evidence is the raw material of your speech. A speaker uses reasoning to show listeners the logical connection between ideas. When you use reasoning, you develop arguments based on your evidence.

There are three major types of reasoning: inductive, deductive, and cause-effect.

Inductive Reasoning

Inductive reasoning involves using specific pieces of information to reach a general conclusion. When using inductive reasoning, a speaker lists many pieces of evidence to help listeners draw their conclusions. The following are examples of inductive reasoning:

Fourteen children in our community received state writing awards. Our schools train good writers.

In our class, Sandra, Pam, Dirk, and Rodney have the chicken pox. Chicken pox is running through the school.

It is important to test inductive reasoning by looking at the connection between the evidence and the conclusion. Look at the following example:

Evidence: I met five unfriendly people in the town of Lionsville.
Conclusion: Lionsville is a very unfriendly town.

What kinds of questions might you ask about the connection between the evidence (five unfriendly people) and the conclusion (the town is unfriendly)? First, you might ask whether there are enough examples. Have enough people been observed? Second, you might ask whether the examples are typical. Is there anything unusual about these people? Finally, you might ask if there are important exceptions or considerations. Would it make a difference in the conclusion if it turned out that all five unfriendly people had just come from the dentist's office?

When reasoning through induction, you need to ask the following questions:

1. Are there enough examples?
2. Are the examples typical?
3. Are there important exceptions or considerations?

Deductive Reasoning

Deductive reasoning involves using a general idea to reach conclusions about specific instances. When using deductive reasoning, a speaker lists a conclusion from which more facts are drawn. The following are examples of deductive reasoning:

People in Advanced Algebra are smart. Tom is in Advanced Algebra. Tom must be a great student.

Debaters like to argue. Carolyn is a debater. Get Carolyn to argue for permission to hold a class party.

Each of these examples represents three steps of reasoning. Although you may think through the three steps, most people actually talk in terms of two steps. For example, "Debaters like to argue. Let's get Carolyn to argue for permission for a class party."

As with inductive reasoning, it is important to test deductive reasoning. Look at the following example:

Evidence: Connie is a cheerleader. Cheerleaders are very popular.

Conclusion: Connie is very popular.

Questions: a. *Is the general statement true?* Are cheerleaders more popular than any other group?

b. *Is the specific example true?* Is Connie a cheerleader?

c. *Does the specific example apply to the general statement?* Is Connie very popular? Might Connie be popular for other reasons, such as friendliness?

After you answer these questions, you can decide if you agree with the conclusion that Connie is very popular.

When reasoning through deduction, ask yourself:

1. Is the general statement true?
2. Is the specific example true?
3. Does the specific example apply to the general statement?

Cause-Effect Reasoning

Cause-effect reasoning suggests that one event produces a second event. In other words, it suggests that an effect (what happens) can be tied to a specific cause. The following are examples of cause-effect reasoning:

The federal government has cut its contributions to local charities; therefore, people in our town are going hungry.

The 55-mph speed limit saved many people from dying in traffic accidents.

To test cause-effect reasoning, you need to look carefully at the relationship between the first and second events. Consider the following example:

Evidence: Jane studied for four hours.

Conclusion: She will get a good math grade.

Questions: a. *Is the cause connected to the effect?* Will studying for four hours result in a good math grade?

b. *Is the cause capable of producing the effect by itself?* Studying may not be enough. Jane also needs to attend school regularly and listen in class.

c. *Could some other cause produce the same effect?* Has Jane worked with a tutor outside of school?

When reasoning from cause to effect, you need to ask the following questions:

1. Is the cause connected to the effect?
2. Is the cause capable of producing the effect by itself?
3. Could some other cause produce the same effect?

FAULTY REASONING

Persuasive speakers must choose their evidence and types of reasoning carefully. Sometimes speakers use incorrect or false reasoning, called **faulty reasoning,** to try to persuade their audience members. Listeners must be prepared to recognize poor evidence and false reasoning so they are not misled by it. Examples of false reasoning include: glittering generalities, card stacking, bandwagon appeal, unrelated testimonials, and name calling.

Glittering Generalities

Glittering generalities are vague general statements. These generalities are not supported with specific information and are not linked to the main point. Below are some examples of generalities and questions that may be asked about them:

General Statement: Men make poor drivers.

Questions: Did the speaker see a male driver cut in front of another car this morning, or did the speaker look at accident reports to make this statement? What is the evidence for this general statement?

General Statement: Emily Bashnagel is a wonderful mother. Vote for her for PTA president.

Questions: Did the speaker link Emily Bashnagel's ability as a mother to her ability to run the PTA? What abilities does she need to lead the PTA? Does she have these talents?

Competent listeners check to see whether general statements are supported by specific information. They double-check to make sure the supporting material is linked to the main idea.

Card Stacking

Card stacking refers to piling up information in favor of an idea with very little backing. The speaker gives examples or reasons for one side of the issue without explaining them carefully. Look at the following example of card stacking:

Join the Urban Youth Corps. You will make friends, learn new skills, get to know the city, and make money. It's a great way to spend your summer. Sign up today in the counseling office!

What more would you like to hear about each of these points? So far you don't even know what kind of work teenagers do in the program, nor do you know how much you could earn. Each of these points needs to be explained.

As a listener you need to ask yourself these questions: Is the speaker just piling up points? Are the reasons that are given carefully explained? If the answer to either question is *no*, then you may be listening to the faulty reasoning of card stacking.

Bandwagon Appeal

A **bandwagon appeal** suggests that you should do something because everyone else is doing it. You may hear arguments with opening statements such as, "Everyone has one" or "We're all going to go. You don't want to be left out." Often you will hear commercials containing bandwagon appeals such as "People in the know buy their clothes at Bergoff's" or "Athletes who care about their feet buy Rabbit running shoes."

As a listener ask yourself: Am I getting pushed into something before I think about it? Going along with a crowd should be *your* choice; don't let someone else push you into it.

Unrelated Testimonials

Testimonials try to persuade listeners by linking positive feelings for one person, thing, idea, or event to another person, thing, idea, or event. The most common examples of this technique are advertisements that feature well-known entertainment or sports figures. They endorse products, programs, or activities. For example: "Mean Mike Matlock eats Great Grain Cereal before every football game."

Unrelated testimonials try to link things that are not related. As a listener, you must be concerned about connections and believability when you hear these testimonials. If there is no obvious connection between the person and the thing receiving the testimonial, you need to be careful. For example, what is the real connection between eating Great Grain Cereal and a football score? Not all testimonials involve faulty reasoning, but you need to recognize those that do.

Name Calling

Name calling attacks a person rather than the person's ideas by using unpopular names or labels. For example:

It is true that many people support a 75-mph speed limit, but these people are dangerous fools.

How can you listen to a guy who flunked math tell you how to use a computer?

I wouldn't pay attention to anything that airhead said.

Competent listeners are not fooled by the negative feelings created by name calling. Be sure to ask yourself: What evidence did the speaker present in addition to name calling? Can I check out this evidence? For example, did the person ac-

tually flunk math? How is flunking math related to describing computers?

All these types of faulty reasoning can be used to persuade listeners, especially listeners who are uninformed about the topic. An ethical persuader avoids using faulty reasoning.

INTERACT

With a partner, analyze the following appeals and identify the problems in reasoning. Then write two short sample paragraphs explaining the faulty reasoning.

There are some narrow-minded people who cannot look toward a better future. But I say to you that if I am elected president of this student council I will make changes. The halls will be cleaner, the cafeteria food will be better, there will be more sports events, and there will be a change in the homework policy.

This is going to be the best dance our school has seen. Our favorite assistant principal, Ms. Willer, says she has never seen such an organized group. Ms. Hong, the gym teacher, says the decorations are fantastic. Everyone is going to be there. You can wear whatever you want. Just come and have a good time.

ORGANIZING A PERSUASIVE SPEECH

Once you hear how serious the problem is, you will agree that we need to put a stoplight at Cook Avenue and Main Street.

You can't learn soccer in this community because there is no place to play. Once we build a new soccer field, eight teams will be able to play on Saturday, and many more kids can learn to play.

You can use many different organizational forms in a persuasive speech. The most commonly used form is the problem-solution method.

PROBLEM-SOLUTION

When using problem-solution organization, the speaker describes a problem and then describes ways to solve the problem. He or she tries to convince the listeners that the problem is serious and that the given solution is the best way to solve the problem. The following outline shows how one student prepared a persuasive speech on capital punishment:

I. **Introduction**
   A. Opening—Man and woman were murdered on Interstate 57
   B. Goal—Listeners will believe capital punishment is a deterrent to crime

II. **Problem**
   A. Criminals not afraid of consequences
   B. Homicide rates lower in other countries with capital punishment
   C. Executions decline in U.S.
      1. No fear of death
      2. Rates go down each year
   D. Value of life decreases
      1. Citizens are not protected
      2. Criminals do not have to respect life

III. **Solutions**
   A. Vote for candidates who support capital punishment
   B. Create commercials to show the truth
   C. Teach respect for human life

IV. **Conclusion**
   A. Summary of argument and ideas
   B. Don't let incident on Interstate 57 happen again

Notice that the speaker included everything necessary for good problem-solution organization. The outline includes four reasons why the problem is serious and presents solutions to solve the problem.

INTERACT

In a group, read the following short speech given by a junior high school student who addressed the problem of missing children. Identify the following:

1. The audience you think she addressed
2. Parts of the organizational pattern
3. Three pieces of evidence
4. One of the appeals to an audience need
5. The solution

I Think The Best—I Expect The Best
Kenyatta Wilson

On the morning after Christmas of 1974, thirteen-year-old Janna Hanson went to a friend's house. A short time later Janna's mother drove by to pick up her daughter; Janna wasn't there. On February 27, 1983, Jeana Rodriguez, an eleven-year-old sixth grade student in San Jose, California, got off her school bus and began her walk home, which was only one hundred yards away. Jeana never made it home. These are but two of thousands of children who are reported missing each year.

I think the best, I expect the best of society to help in the search for children who are missing. Missing children are a national problem that has to be solved. A missing child is defined as a child whose whereabouts are unknown. It is estimated that 1.8 million children are missing each year in the United States.

Many times the question is asked, Why are these children missing? About 1.3 million are runaways. Usually these children leave home because of social, school, or family problems. Runaways often end up in gangs and get involved in drugs, prostitution, and theft.

One hundred thousand children are abducted by strangers. Usually they will be taken while alone in places thought to be safe, such as parks and movie theatres. These children may be used in pornography, prostitution, and shoplifting.

Fifty thousand children are taken by divorced parents who did not receive custody of their child. Because there are so many reasons for missing children, the answer to why there are so many missing children remains complex.

There are agencies that aid in the search for missing children. These include the police, FBI, Missing Children Centers, and Child Find. However, these agencies are understaffed and lack the financial resources to be highly effective. For example, Missing Children Centers and Child Find send out flyers, posters, and pamphlets on missing children and take information from persons who think that they may have seen missing children. Yet the success rate is low when only five hundred children are located each year by the combined efforts of these agencies.

What then is the solution to this problem? I believe that the solution lies within you and me. Not only must we advocate that more governmental funds be made available to adequately finance our law enforcement agencies in the search for missing children, but we must volunteer our time and creative ideas to solve this problem. For example, we can get more media exposure to publicize missing children and establish a network system where pictures and information about missing children would be more visible. If you, the community, will give not only your money but your time as well, maybe this problem will be resolved.

Remember, missing children is a problem that causes many lives to be totally destroyed. The missing child is often faced with a life of cruelty and crime. The parents suffer many worries because of this. With the help of Missing Children organizations, parents, and you, perhaps this terrible problem will someday be just an awful memory of the past.

As for the two girls, Janna's body was found two days later in a trash can near an alley, and Jeana was safely returned home. But not all children are as lucky as Jeana.

EVALUATING PERSUASIVE SPEECHES

I believed you.

I don't care what you say; it's a dumb idea.

I couldn't agree with you. I'm a Democrat.

Critical reactions such as the above do not really help a persuasive speaker. The comments are not specific. They suggest that the critics made general responses or decided the speech could not apply to them and closed their minds.

As a critic you must remain open-minded and judge a speech on its merits. You should not make up your mind on the topic before you hear the speech on it. You should listen carefully for evidence, appeals, and speaker believability. Then you can decide how well the speech worked.

Feedback forms can help you to evaluate your own speeches and those of others. Chapter 13 contains examples of feedback forms for speeches to inform. Forms A and B in this chapter are examples of forms that are useful for evaluating persuasive speeches. Form A allows you to rate parts of a speech as poor, fair, good, very good, or excellent. Comments can be written on the bottom of the sheet. Form B allows you to describe the parts of the speech that worked well, the parts that did not work as well, and an area for improvement. You can create your own forms for persuasive speeches by adding certain sections to these forms.

FEEDBACK FORM A

Speaker's Name _____

Speaker's Topic _____

Rate each area on a five-point scale:

	Poor	Fair	Good	Very Good	Excellent
Clear audience goal	1	2	3	4	5
Use of material to support points	1	2	3	4	5
Valid reasoning	1	2	3	4	5
Topic appropriate to audience and occasion	1	2	3	4	5
Language appropriate to audience and occasion	1	2	3	4	5
Use of persuasive appeals	1	2	3	4	5
Speaker is believable	1	2	3	4	5

Comments: _____

_____

_____

FEEDBACK FORM B

Speaker's Name _____

Speaker's Topic _____

The parts of your speech that were most persuasive:

Example: *I was concerned by the description of the methods of capital punishment. You seemed excited about the topic. I thought you cared.*

The parts of your speech that were least persuasive:

Example: *You did not tell us the titles or qualifications of the people you quoted, so I questioned your evidence.*

To make the speech stronger you could:

Example: *Explain who you are quoting. Look up at the audience as you pause while reading the quotes.*

SUMMARY

Persuasion is a complicated process. To give a fine persuasive speech, you must select the topic carefully and adapt it to your audience in terms of listener needs and beliefs. You must make yourself believable by showing your interest in, and connection to, the topic. You need to use clear reasoning while avoiding faulty reasoning. Then you need to fit your evidence and reasoning into a workable organizational pattern. Finally, you need to know how to evaluate persuasive speeches given by yourself and by others. At each point, ask yourself if you are making ethical decisions as a communicator. Persuasion is a powerful tool. Competent communicators use it wisely.

CHAPTER REVIEW

THINK ABOUT IT

1. What is persuasion? What is persuasive speaking?
2. What is the difference between a speech to persuade and a speech to inform?
3. List Maslow's five levels of human needs and explain how a persuasive speaker could use these needs.
4. How can you make yourself believable for an audience?
5. List and describe the various types of faulty reasoning.

TRY IT OUT

1. During a trip to the grocery store, examine the various persuasive messages you find there. Check out promotional material, slogans, and information on boxes, store posters, and bulletin boards. List three different types of faulty reasoning used in this persuasive material. Note these in your journal.
2. In groups of five or six, brainstorm ways to handle certain persuasive situations. Some situations you might discuss include:
   - Getting a parent to raise your allowance
   - Asking a teacher for an extension on a late paper
   - Gaining votes for a student body president
   - Selling raffle tickets to raise money for sports team equipment
3. Analyze the persuasive speech titled "Meeting America's Challenge" and answer the following questions:
   - What is this speaker's goal?
   - What steps does she say our nation must take?
   - How does she support her argument about each step?
   - What does she say are the benefits of following her proposal?
   - What questions would you like to ask this speaker?

Meeting America's Challenge
Aliya Esmail

What are the challenges America faces as she moves toward the year 2000? What do we as Americans wish to stand for? Do we want to simply be a highly technological, intellectual society? Or do we wish to see America as a nation of cooperation, respect, motivation, diversity, culture, and encouragement? To create the latter, America faces a great challenge—that of creating a national unity. Recently in America, there has been emphasis on the power of the individual. America's power, her greatness, will originate within the power and the greatness of the individual, of course. However, we must never let the individual come before the family, and we must never let the family come before the American family.

To first create a powerful individual, we must educate. According to Vartan Gregorian, an educator, "Education has to teach us not only what we can know, but also what the limitations of our knowledge are—what we don't know." Once we have identified what we know, we must inspire our children—our future to forge forth. We must motivate them. We must make them *want* to learn. Education is simply an introduction to learning. Only by finding our own curiosity will we truly *seek* to learn. We must create this curiosity in every American.

Our next progressive challenge is to create strength within the family. Many members of the families in America have become too concerned with the individual. We must learn to strengthen our families. We must make an effort to not only live together and eat together, but to truly be together—to learn together and to grow together. By strengthening our individual families, we will create a powerful base upon which we must create an American family. And this, the creation of an *American* family, is our greatest challenge.

Ralph Waldo Emerson said, "What lies behind us and what lies before us are small matters compared to what lies within us." Our individual duties as Americans are to find that which lies within us and utilize it, make it grow, put it into our country. We are often worried about what we can extract from certain people, certain things—like a democratic nation. Now we must learn to concern ourselves with what we can put *into* our nation. We must be willing to come together with the other people of this country to unify. To become a true nation. To forget our minor differences and realize our similarities. Our diversity will not destroy the unity. It will but make us stronger and more powerful. People should be in America to create a better society. Not just a better living. America must find this American family. This is our challenge. The Founding Fathers did not create a land of opportunists. They created a land of opportunity.

America's challenge today is to strengthen the individuals of this nation with education. But it is also to use these strong individuals as a foundation for a stronger American community. Our challenge is to seek and to find national unity. To do this, we must show Americans that America's future is their future. It is their children's future; their grandchildren's future. America has graciously accepted challenges to help people, militarily or otherwise, in every corner of the world. Today we must not shy away from our own challenge. Just like previous goals, a goal of national unity may seem unattainable. Perhaps even impossible. However, as George Bernard Shaw once said, "Some men see things as they are and say 'Why?' I dream of things that never were and say 'Why not?' " Today, America's challenge, national unity, will begin to become a reality when each American looks inside himself or herself and asks, "Why not?"

PUT IT IN WRITING

1. Choose a topic for a persuasive speech. Write a one-paragraph introduction for each of three different audiences—an audience that agrees with you, an audience that disagrees with you, and an audience that holds a neutral position.
2. Select a problem you have with a friend, parent, brother or sister, or teacher. Using the problem-solution organizational pattern, write out two paragraphs that outline (a) what you see as the reasons for the problem, and (b) your ideas for solutions to the problem. Include the paragraphs in your journal.

SPEAK ABOUT IT

1. Prepare two possible introductions for a persuasive speech. Present each one to a small group. Ask for feedback about which introduction gains greater audience interest and why.

2. Create a three- to four-minute persuasive speech and present it to your class. Before you begin, research your topic and select your evidence carefully. Develop arguments based on your evidence using at least one of the following types of reasoning: inductive, deductive, cause-effect. As you listen to your classmates' speeches, try to identify the types of reasoning they included in their speeches.

3. Create a thirty- to sixty-second commercial to sell an idea, a product, or a service. Present the commercial orally in class. Be sure to
   - See that your introduction includes a device or gimmick for getting the audience's attention.
   - See that your conclusion includes a final appeal or sales pitch. (The body of the presentation is up to you.)
   - Have a specific purpose for your commercial and a specific goal for your audience.

LEARNING ABOUT DEBATE

KEY WORDS

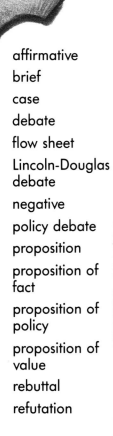

affirmative

brief

case

debate

flow sheet

Lincoln-Douglas debate

negative

policy debate

proposition

proposition of fact

proposition of policy

proposition of value

rebuttal

refutation

After completing this chapter, you should be able to

- define *debate, refutation,* and *rebuttal.*
- describe the values of debate.
- distinguish between the affirmative and negative sides.
- explain three types of debate propositions.
- describe ways to create arguments.
- describe two debate formats.

Chris: The science fair should be a competition. The best three exhibits should win the top prizes.

Jaime: No. It should be a time when everyone shows what they created. It should not be a competition.

Chris: How are you going to get people excited unless there are prizes for the best exhibits?

Jaime: A science fair should not be a contest. It should be a time for people to show what is interesting to them. Competition only makes it tense.

Chris: If you want people to do their best work, you have to....

The conversation above is an argument. Two people are expressing opposite points of view on the topic of running a science fair. Arguments begin when there is a difference of opinion between two or more persons and each person tries to persuade the other person to change his or her ideas. Arguments have no time limits or rules, and anyone may join in.

When arguments become formal and are run by an organized set of rules, they become debates. You may be part of a debate in an English or history class. You may be a member of the school debate team that competes with other schools. You may listen to politicians or lawyers holding formal debates.

This chapter describes the values of debate and how debate works. Debate involves creating a proposition, researching the topic, and arguing the issues. This chapter also discusses the two most common formats for school debates.

VALUES OF DEBATE

Why would people wish to learn to argue with each other? Debate helps people to develop valuable skills. The ability to do effective research, to organize well, to listen critically, and to speak with confidence can help you now and in the future. Many lawyers, businesspersons, and teachers say their debate training helped them in their careers.

RESEARCH SKILLS

The research skills you learn in debate will help you find information and evidence. You can use your research skills to do your English or history assignments. Your research skills could help you work on a community history project or study your family tree.

ORGANIZATIONAL SKILLS

The organizational skills you learn in debate will help you plan speeches or write papers. You will be able to decide quickly what are main points and what are supporting points. You will be able to organize a large amount of information quickly and clearly, using various organizational patterns.

CRITICAL LISTENING SKILLS

As a debater you will develop your critical listening skills. When another person presents an argument, you will be able to analyze it quickly. You will learn to examine the quality of the evidence and reasoning. You will develop questions to get more information.

SPEAKING SKILLS

As a debater you will also learn to create arguments for your case and to defend them aloud. The more you debate, the more confident you will become in presenting your ideas and standing up for your beliefs in front of a group. Debate is a valuable speaking experience.

JOURNAL ENTRY

Participating in a debate is like going to an auction. You have to listen very carefully, make decisions quickly, and then say something. Debates move quickly, so you had better be alert.

HOW DEBATE WORKS

Debate is a contest of spoken argument between individuals or teams. It is a contest that has rules, time limits, and a winner and loser. One side, the **affirmative,** speaks in favor of an issue or change. The other side, the **negative,** speaks against the issue or change.

Debates center around a problem or issue that is contained in a proposition. A **proposition** is a statement of a problem that is worded so that there are clearly two sides to the argument. For example, the proposition "Resolved: That the federal government should guarantee comprehensive medical care for all U.S. citizens" is debatable. The affirmative might argue that private insurance is too expensive, and that people who don't have full-time jobs are left without insurance coverage. The negative might argue that a federal insurance program would cost even more money than private insurance, and that the government already protects people who are unemployed. Each side would have to use evidence and reasoning to support its arguments.

A debate is won by the side that presents the best arguments and evidence in the opinion of the listeners or judges. There are time limits and rules that state which speaker can talk and what types of things the speaker can talk about. At the end of the debate, a judge names one side as the winner.

OBSERVE

Listen to examples of debates. Record the debate topic and the points made by each side. Decide which side won and which side lost the debate. Give reasons for your decision.

DEBATE IN ACTION

One of the best ways to understand debate is to look at a sample situation involving a debate. In some suburbs and cities, people are considering starting a twelve-month school year. This subject would lend itself to a formal debate for community members to hear. A proposition for this topic might be stated in the following way:

Resolved: That the Glenriver school system should establish a twelve-month school year.

Affirmative Position

The affirmative team would argue for a change in the current situation. They would try to point out the problems with the current nine-month school year. The affirmative team might

argue that students lose important learning time, and that during a three-month summer vacation, students forget much of what they learned. As proof, the affirmative team could show low test scores for students in nine-month programs compared to students in twelve-month programs. An affirmative speaker might say, "Summer vacations were started because farm families needed their children to help on the farm. Today children in this suburban community do not work on farms." An affirmative speaker might also describe the trouble students get into because of all the free time.

After describing the problems, the affirmative team might suggest a plan for a four-term school year with a ten-day vacation after each term. They might list some advantages of the twelve-month school year, such as higher test scores and better salaries for teachers.

Negative Position

The negative team would defend the present situation—the nine-month school year. The negative team would argue there is nothing seriously wrong with the nine-month school year. They would also argue that spending more months in school may not automatically result in higher test scores. The team would describe the benefits of summer vacations when students learn different skills, travel, and enjoy nature. The negative team could also show that it would be hard to find teachers willing to work twelve months of the year.

The negative team would attack the affirmative team's plan for change. The negative team might say, "Working parents could never get child care for ten-day periods every three months" or "Family life would be hurt because families spend more time together in the summer." In addition, the negative team might argue that the community would be hurt because camps and summer programs would have to close down.

During the Debate

The debaters for both sides would need good evidence and logical arguments to convince the audience and judges that they were right. They might quote famous experts on how people learn and use articles from education magazines that support their points. They could report the result of surveys of teachers' and parents' opinions.

In most debates there is time to build a case for each side and time to respond to what the other side said. Each speaker on a team knows the kinds of arguments or points that will be raised by other team members. Most teams follow an organizational pattern that helps divide up the responsibilities between the speakers on that side. In some formal debates, the members of each team may question, or cross-examine, speakers from the other team.

During the debate the judge usually takes notes. The judge tries to summarize the main points, the kinds of evidence used, and objections each team raises to the other side's ideas. These notes provide a map of what was said in the debate. The judge uses these notes about what was said and his or her judgment about each speaker's delivery to decide which side won. In a good debate the listeners should have heard strong arguments for both sides of the proposition.

In order to argue against opposing team members' ideas, you must have a good record of what they said. Most debaters take notes when their opponents are speaking. These notes are called a flow sheet. The **flow sheet** is a diagram of the arguments, listed in parallel columns across a page.

INTERACT

Good debaters begin their preparation by thinking of all the possible arguments, affirmative or negative, that could be raised on a topic. In groups of four, brainstorm as many affirmative and negative arguments as possible on two of the following broad topics:

- Censor ratings for records and tapes
- Required community-service hours for high school students
- Required B grade average for participation in extracurricular school activities
- School dress codes
- Required foreign language instruction in elementary grades

CREATING THE PROPOSITION

A good debate starts with a good proposition. A proposition should be worded so that there are two clear sides to the debate. Sample propositions include:

Resolved: That smoking in public places should be prohibited.

Resolved: That all elementary schools should provide time for daily prayer.

Resolved: That the Chicago Bulls are a better basketball team than the Boston Celtics.

TYPES OF PROPOSITIONS

Just as groups may discuss questions of fact, value, or policy, debaters may argue propositions of fact, value, or policy. Most formal debates center on propositions of value or policy. Propositions are introduced by the word *resolved*.

Propositions of Fact

A **proposition of fact** is a statement that something is or is not true. Propositions of fact center on statements with answers that can be discovered. You may debate with a friend over when the English assignment is due. You may argue over who directed the movie *Batman Returns.* You can check out a proposition of fact. You can ask your English teacher the correct date or do research to find the name of *Batman Returns'* director.

Often, propositions of fact are argued in courts of law. Lawyers may argue about whether Mark Jones cheated Lee Smith or about who stole money from the grocery store. The following are two examples of propositions of fact:

Resolved: That schools with vocational programs lower student dropout rates.

Resolved: That more than half of America's children are growing up in single-parent homes.

Propositions of Value

A **proposition of value** is a statement that something is good or bad, right or wrong, useful or useless. The teams debate which idea, thing, or person is better or more valuable. A good example of competing values may be seen in the clashes between those concerned with the environment and those concerned with the economy. There are struggles over which

is more important, the habitat of the spotted owl or the jobs in the local lumber industry. Many communities must face struggles between the value of protecting the environment and protecting the economy of the region.

The following are two examples of propositions of value:

Resolved: That one course in health education is adequate for high school students.

Resolved: That training in debate is valuable preparation for becoming a lawyer.

Propositions of Policy

Propositions of policy center on change. A **proposition of policy** is a statement that says something should or should not be done. The following are examples of propositions of policy:

Resolved: That all U.S. high school students should be required to take an environmental education class.

Resolved: That the Madison City Council should require all people under the age of eighteen to participate in the Safety Patrol's videotape/ fingerprint program.

INTERACT

In groups of three or four, read the following and identify which propositions are fact, value, or policy.

- Resolved: That smoking causes cancer.
- Resolved: That violent TV programs are harmful to children.
- Resolved: That students with a course grade of A should be excused from the final exam.
- Resolved: That millions die yearly from diabetes.
- Resolved: That the federal government should send aid to Oklahoma flood victims.

Most debate contests and many public debates center on propositions of policy. The success of such debates partly depends on the careful wording of the proposition. A carefully worded proposition sets the stage for a good debate.

QUALITIES OF A GOOD PROPOSITION

The following are four qualities of a good policy proposition:

1. *The proposition should be debatable.* It should have two sides, no more, no less. The proposition "Resolved: That piano training takes time," is poor. There may be disagreement as to how much time piano training takes, but everyone knows it takes time. There is only one side to this proposition.

2. *The proposition should be worded so that the affirmative supports the change.* The affirmative team must argue for a change. If the proposition is stated, "The federal government should not establish a required seat-belt law," the affirmative team would be supporting a negative proposition. This could make the debate very confusing.

3. *The proposition should be worded as a statement, not a question.* The proposition should be worded to call for a change in the present system. Do not ask a question such as "Should Congress establish a required seat-belt law?" or "How should a required seat-belt law be established?" These are not easily debated. The statement might be "Resolved: That Congress should enact a mandatory seat-belt law for all citizens."

4. *The proposition should contain only one problem.* The exact issue of difference should be clear. A statement such as "Resolved: That Hennepin County should start a free lunch program for senior citizens and a full-day kindergarten program" is actually a double proposition. The senior citizens' lunch program and the full-day kindergarten are totally separate issues.

Apply

Look at the following propositions and decide which does not fit the guidelines.

1. Resolved: That the Edgewater School District should adopt a student/faculty disciplinary board.
2. Resolved: That Kane County District 34 should provide free summer school for all students and care for children of working parents.
3. Resolved: That Kenmore High School students should be required to participate in one hundred hours of community service before graduation.

As you probably could tell, propositions 1 and 3 fit the guidelines for a good proposition. However proposition 2 contains more than one problem. "Summer school for all" and "care for children of working parents" are two separate issues.

It takes time to discuss and work out a carefully worded proposition, but the time is well spent. A well-worded proposition sets the groundwork for a good debate.

My partner, Cindy, and I are pleased to be here today to debate the proposition

Resolved: That the Edgewater School should adopt a student-faculty disciplinary board.

As students in Edgewater School, we believe there is a need for new ways to handle disciplinary cases. A student-faculty board would be able to solve some of the problems with the current disciplinary process. We believe students, faculty, and parents would be more satisfied with a program that would increase morale, attendance, and student responsibility.

Let us describe the problem with the disciplinary code as they exist today. They are (1) unequal treatment for the same offense (2) confusion in interpreting the ....

RESEARCHING THE TOPIC

Debate requires strong research skills. Debaters must be able to find evidence to support their positions and create arguments based on the evidence. Researching the topic takes time and effort but the research helps you develop your speech and respond to your opponent's speech. This section on the research process will be based on the following debate topic:

Resolved: That the Molina City Council should ban smoking in all restaurants.

FINDING EVIDENCE

What can we say about how smoking affects the bloodstream?

Can we find some doctors' opinions on the effects of secondary smoke?

Secondary smoke? What's that?

These and many other questions could be asked by debaters who are starting to learn about the above debate topic. Although debaters defend only one side of the argument, they need to know a great deal of information about the overall topic. A competent debater finds evidence, creates arguments, and is ethical in the use of evidence.

How much evidence is enough evidence? There is no easy way to answer that question, but remember that you are not working on a persuasive speech. When you give a persuasive speech, you decide which points you will make. In debate you also need to have evidence to refute, or attack, the argument or evidence used by the other team. For this reason, you need much more evidence for debate than you will actually use. You never know which ideas the other side will discuss.

To find information, you may follow the research guidelines and steps described in Chapter 10. You may need to use specialized kinds of periodicals or books. For example, to research the smoking topic, you may need to read medical books or city building codes for restaurants. Your reading will help you

learn a great deal about the subject. It will help you to learn the vocabulary words related to the topic. For example, *secondary smoke* refers to the smoke that affects a nonsmoker in a room with smokers. In your research, you will learn about the history of the subject, the main experts on the topic, and the important issues that could come up in a debate.

When you gather your information, record it on note cards. Because you will use the cards during the debate, you need to group the cards in certain topic areas. For example, when debating smoking in public places, your topic areas may be "Medical Effects," "Personal Rights," "Economic Effects," and "Other Cities' Bans."

CREATING YOUR ARGUMENTS

You create your arguments based on the evidence you find. In debate, an **argument** is created when you use your evidence to reach and defend a conclusion. As you build your arguments, be sure to test your evidence and types of reasoning as discussed in Chapters 10 and 14. You can build arguments by using examples, expert testimony, statistics, logic, and analogies.

Examples

You can give examples of similar situations to support your position. For example, you could use evidence based on medical studies of people who were exposed to secondary smoke. You could describe the effects on restaurants that banned smokers. You might say, "In a national survey of 100 restaurants, which banned smoking in all areas, only 12 percent indicated a drop in customers. Sixteen percent reported an increase."

The examples you choose must be typical. If only one of eight restaurants had increased business as a result of banning smoking, the example is not typical.

Experts

You can also support your position by using quotations from experts on the subject. You need to explain to the listeners why someone is considered an expert, why the person is qualified to speak on the subject, and why he or she is unbiased on the subject.

You might quote medical experts' opinions on the physical effects of secondary smoke. For example, you might say, "Dr. Alicia Chavez, a lung specialist, calls smoking by parents a form of child abuse because of the damage to the children's lungs."

A person such as the president of a cigarette company would be considered a biased source. You would not wish to quote this person saying that secondary smoke is harmless.

Statistics

You can use numerical information to show links between things. For example, you might discuss the link between the number of people who smoke and those who develop cancer. You might show a link between restaurants that banned smokers and an increase or decrease in their incomes. For example, a debater might say, "Over 50 percent of the Center City restaurants that banned smoking reported an increase in customers after three months. Many reported that new patrons stated a desire to eat in a smoke-free environment."

Logic

You can also use reasoning to argue that if x happens, y might follow. For example, one team might argue, "If one person at a table becomes uncomfortable because of smoke, the entire table of people will leave early and reduce the income of the restaurant owner." The other side may respond, "If you don't allow people to smoke, certain people will never come into the restaurant."

Analogies

You can create an argument by drawing an analogy, or describing likenesses between two things or ideas. A team might create a direct or literal analogy by suggesting eating in smoke-filled rooms is similar to eating in high-asbestos areas, and that no one would wish to do that. Another team may use a figurative analogy to highlight the problems of eating healthy food in a smoke-filled environment saying, "There is no use cleaning the house when rats are swimming in the basement." A debater might say, "Eating a vegetarian meal in a smoke-filled restaurant is like painting a house that has rotting walls."

INTERACT

Debaters need to find information on very specific topics. Specialized magazines or journals are those with a narrow content focus. These are not general-interest magazines that cover many different topics. In teams of two or three, find two specialized magazines or journals that could be used to find evidence on three of the following topics.

- Desktop Publishing
- Rifles
- Extraterrestrials
- Changing Roles of Women
- Medical Education
- Teenage Alcoholism
- Illiteracy

- Fishing Rights
- Water Pollution
- Animal Rights
- World Travel
- Native American History
- Child Abuse
- Pollution

ARGUING THE ISSUES

The affirmative believes there is a serious problem in our community that must be changed. We fear that in two years. . . .

The negative believes no serious harm will come to our community. In fact, our community is stronger. . . .

When arguing the issues, affirmative and negative debaters perform two major jobs:

1. They build their own cases using evidence and reasoning to support their position.
2. They respond to their opponent's case using refutation and rebuttal.

BUILDING A CASE

Each side in a debate must build a case. A **case** consists of all of the arguments that will be made to support the affirmative or negative position. The arguments should be logically organized and supported by evidence.

In debates based on propositions of policy, cases are built to answer the following questions:

1. Does a serious problem exist at present that makes a change necessary?
2. Will the suggested plan solve these problems?
3. Will the plan bring about new and greater benefits than those that exist at present?

The affirmative case tries to answer these questions with a *yes*, and the negative answers them with a *no*.

Debaters often organize their cases into outlines known as briefs. A brief contains arguments and evidence. Briefs are developed both to present cases and to defend against anticipated attacks from the opponent.

REFUTATION AND REBUTTAL

In addition to building a case, each side in the debate must argue against its opponent's case. Both the affirmative and the negative teams must also rebuild their own cases. This involves refutation and rebuttal.

Refutation

Refutation is the process of attacking the opposing side's case. When you refute the case, you try to find fault with the team's evidence or reasoning. For example, you might say:

My opponent said, "Secondary smoke does not cause serious harm." He quoted an unknown, Dr. Alvin Keefer, saying "Smoking only hurts the smoker." Well, we maintain secondary smoke causes serious harm. I will read the evidence from three medical researchers in the Surgeon General's office. Dr. Martin Wheeler says, "Secondary smoke presents great danger to people within fifteen feet of the smoker...."

Rebuttal

Rebuttal is the process of rebuilding your own case after it has been attacked by the other team. A speaker may say:

We told you there was no serious harm from secondary smoke. We cited Dr. Alvin Keefer. The affirmative said there is great harm and questioned Dr. Keefer's expertise. They quoted medical researchers. Well, Dr. Keefer is a director of a heart program at Boone Hospital. We have two other authorities who support his ideas. I will read the statement to you (the statements follow). Therefore our position still stands. Smoking harms only the smoker.

Effective debaters have enough evidence to rebuild their cases after their opponents have refuted them.

DEBATE FORMATS

There are two major types of debate formats. These are policy debate and Lincoln-Douglas debate. These formats may be used in the classroom, although classroom debaters also may create their own format. If you are a member of a school debate team, you will learn to debate using one or both of these formats.

POLICY DEBATE

The policy debate format is similar to the type of debate discussed in this chapter. In **policy debate,** two teams debate a proposition of policy. Each team member speaks two or three times. The first speeches are designed to build the case; the second speeches involve refutation and rebuttal. There is a question period, called cross-examination, during which the debaters may ask questions of the opposing team.

The following are topics that could be debated in the policy format:

Resolved: That the federal government should establish a computer network for identifying and locating missing children.

Resolved: That the federal government should establish national standards for the certification of elementary- and secondary-school teachers.

In the policy debate format, speeches are always given in the same order. Times vary, according to tournament rules. The usual speaker order and allotted times are as follows:

First affirmative speaker	8 minutes
Cross-examination	3 minutes
First negative speaker	8 minutes
Cross-examination	3 minutes
Second affirmative speaker	8 minutes
Cross-examination	3 minutes
Second negative speaker	8 minutes
Cross-examination	3 minutes
First negative rebuttal	5 minutes
First affirmative rebuttal	5 minutes
Second negative rebuttal	5 minutes
Second affirmative rebuttal	5 minutes

LINCOLN-DOUGLAS DEBATE

The Lincoln-Douglas format is named after the famous political campaign debates between Abraham Lincoln and Stephen Douglas. In **Lincoln-Douglas debate,** one speaker on each side debates a proposition of value. Each speaker delivers at least two speeches, building the case and supporting it. There is usually a chance for each speaker to cross-examine the other. The following are topics that could be debated in the Lincoln-Douglas format:

Resolved: That capital punishment is morally wrong.

Resolved: That school uniforms are desirable.

The usual speaker order and allotted times for Lincoln-Douglas debate are as follows:

Affirmative speaker   6 minutes
Negative speaker   7 minutes
Affirmative rebuttal   4 minutes
Negative rebuttal   6 minutes
Affirmative rebuttal   3 minutes

If cross-examination is used, there is a three-minute cross-examination period after the first two speeches.

SUMMARY

This chapter presented an overview of a special type of persuasive communication called debate. Debate is a contest of persuasive argument between individuals or teams with rules, time limits, and a declared winner and loser. This chapter discussed the values of debate, how debate works, and the three types of debate propositions. It stressed the importance of researching the topic and arguing the issues. Two major forms of debate are policy debate and Lincoln-Douglas debate.

CHAPTER REVIEW

THINK ABOUT IT

1. Define *debate* and describe three places debates take place in everyday life.
2. What are the values of debate?
3. What are the differences between the affirmative side and the negative side?
4. What are the differences between propositions of fact, value, and policy?
5. List various types of evidence you may use to build an argument.
6. Define *refutation* and *rebuttal.* How are they different from one another?
7. Describe two debate formats.

TRY IT OUT

1. Interview an adult who participated on a school debate team. Find out how that person's debate training helped him or her in a career. Report your findings to the class.
2. Write a debate proposition of fact, one of value, and one of policy. In a small group, discuss the propositions, using the criteria for good propositions discussed in class. Choose one of the propositions for a classroom debate.
3. Create arguments for each of the following situations and then, with a partner, role-play the situations in class:

   - You want a later curfew. Your parents say no.
   - You want an extension on your homework assignment. Your teacher says no.
   - Your brother or sister refuses to help you clean the room you share.

Class members should listen to the arguments you and your partner created; discuss how each person used examples, experts, statistics, and logic to create the arguments and decide whether the evidence supported the conclusions each person drew.

4. Listen to a debate. Identify the types of evidence used by each speaker. Decide which speaker won the debate, and explain your decision.

PUT IT IN WRITING

1. Analyze a letter to the editor in your local paper. Record the use of examples, expert testimony, statistics, logical analysis, or analogies used by the writer to build an argument. Analyze two pieces of evidence used by examining how well the evidence supports the writer's arguments.

2. Using the proposition "All public school students should be required to wear school uniforms" or another proposition of your choice, write one affirmative argument and one negative argument.

SPEAK ABOUT IT

1. Present to the class the affirmative and the negative argument you developed for activity 2 of the Put It in Writing.

2. As a class, choose a proposition of policy to debate. The proposition could be concerned with a school or community problem. Divide into affirmative and negative teams. Research the proposition and create arguments for your side. An affirmative speaker will present one argument, and a negative speaker will refute the argument. An affirmative and a negative speaker will then be given a chance for rebuttal. Discuss how your experience helped you understand the responsibilities of the affirmative and negative sides in a debate.

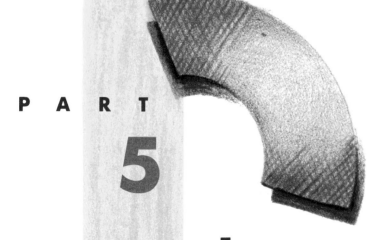

PART

5

INTERPRETIVE COMMUNICATION

CHAPTERS

Preparing for Oral Interpretation

Performing Oral Interpretation

Group Interpretation

CHAPTER 16

PREPARING FOR ORAL INTERPRETATION

KEY WORDS

conflict

dramatic speaker

mood

onomatopoeia

oral history

oral interpretation

plot

rhyme

setting

style

theme

After completing this chapter, you should be able to

- define *oral interpretation*.
- list various sources of material for oral interpretation.
- describe the four standards for selecting literature.
- select quality literature for performance.
- describe the four key points for analyzing literature for performance.

Every night my father reads *The Cat in the Hat* to my youngest sister.

I love to listen to my grandmother read from her mother's diary.

At the Thanksgiving show our class read three poems about the founding of our country.

Our school has a Writers' Showcase in which students perform material written by other students.

Although the term *oral interpretation* may be new to you, the experience of interpreting literature orally is part of everyday life. A lawyer may read a piece of evidence to the jury. A religious leader may read prayers as part of a service. Parents read to their young children, and teachers read to their classes.

You may remember how much you enjoyed being read to as a child. Or perhaps you heard stories told from memory around a campfire. Even now you probably find yourself enjoying another person's performance of some of your favorite authors' works.

In this chapter you will learn how to prepare for oral interpretation. You will learn the characteristics of oral interpretation, how to select material that is appropriate for oral interpretation, and how to analyze the material used in a performance.

CHARACTERISTICS OF ORAL INTERPRETATION

Oral interpretation is the reading of literature aloud to communicate meaning to an audience. An interpreter analyzes the literature and uses his or her voice and body to communicate the results of the analysis. The interpreter is the connection between the literature and the audience. He or she shares the meaning of the literature with the listeners.

An interpreter may use all kinds of writing for oral interpretation, including diaries, poems, stories, fables, essays, and plays. In addition to written literature, interpreters can use stories that have been handed down from generation to generation without being written down. This is called the oral tradition and is the source of much of our literature today.

You may be wondering how oral interpretation is different from public speaking. Is oral interpretation a type of acting? There are major differences between oral interpretation and public speaking or acting. Understanding these differences will help you imagine oral interpretation. When you prepare for an oral interpretation performance you must be aware of the following:

1. *You are not the author.* When you do oral interpretation, you are performing literature written by another person. Therefore you are not sharing your own personal thoughts or feelings with the audience, as you would in public speaking. At times you will perform something you have written yourself, but this does not happen often.

2. *You read the author's exact words.* As an interpreter you read and bring to life the exact words of another person. In public speaking you speak from an outline or note cards. Your speech may change slightly from performance to performance. However, oral interpretation requires you to perform the literature exactly as it is written.

3. *You interpret a piece of literature.* In oral interpretation, you are not trying to create a message to inform or persuade your listeners. Instead, you are trying to help the listeners "see" the situations and images you are creating orally. Your goal is to share the meaning of the literature as you interpret it.

4. *You remain yourself during the performance.* When you are acting, you take on the role of a character in the play. When you interpret literature, you share your understanding of the writing. You use your voice and body to suggest characters, but you do not become a character.

Oral interpretation helps you develop special connections to pieces of literature. As you work to bring literature to life through your analysis and performance, you will discover links between yourself and the author's writing. The connection will help you to recreate the literature for your listeners.

 OBSERVE

For one week record all the examples of oral interpretation you hear. You may hear literature read through the media, in school, at home, or in some other setting. Note the situation, the interpreter, and the kind of material read.

FINDING MATERIAL

Tamika read from a chapter of *Thirteen Ways to Sink a Sub*, a book about a substitute teacher in the classroom. I thought our substitute teacher would fall out of the chair, she laughed so hard.

Adam did a reading from the play *Step on a Crack*. It was about a girl getting a stepmother. It was very funny but it also had some sad parts.

KINDS OF LITERATURE

There are many pieces of good literature that are appropriate for oral interpretation. You can find lists of short stories, plays, and poetry in literary indexes in most library reference rooms. Indexes such as the *Short Story Index, Grainger Index to Poetry,* and *Play Index* are good sources for finding literature for oral interpretation. This section describes some of the many kinds of literature you could use for oral interpretation.

Favorite Authors

Maybe you like the poetry of Shel Silverstein, Robert Frost, or Nikki Giovanni. Maybe you are a fan of Ray Bradbury's or Robert Fulgham's short stories or of the novels of Judy Blume, Stephen King, or Madeleine L'Engle. If you have a favorite writer, you could choose his or her writings and share them with your listeners.

Literature Collections

You have probably read collections of literature, also called anthologies, in your English or reading classes. You can choose a short story, a poem, or an essay from one of these anthologies for your interpretation. You might also select from collections of folktales, particularly those from different cultures.

Biographies or Autobiographies

You may share the writing from a biography or autobiography of someone you admire. There are many biographies written about famous persons. You could read about Martin Luther King's civil rights march in Washington. You could describe Jackie Joyner-Kersee's Olympic performances or Dan Rather's career in journalism. You might read from Maya Angelou's autobiographical works.

Plays or Screenplays

You may enjoy dramatic literature, including plays or screenplays. For example, if you like Neil Simon's comedies, you may read a section from *Barefoot in the Park.* You could perform from a children's play for a young audience using *Amber Waves, Charlotte's Web,* or *Wiley and the Hairy Man.*

Oral Histories

Perhaps you have a grandparent who tells you stories of his or her childhood. These stories are part of your oral history. **Oral**

histories are stories that are told over and over and passed down through generations without being written down. With each retelling the details may change, but the central ideas remain the same. For example, refugees often tell their stories of leaving their country. Jewish refugees who lived through the concentration camps and Vietnamese refugees who escaped as boat people tell stories of how they survived.

Oral histories allow storytellers to make sense out of experiences and to pass on wisdom and ideas to the listeners. Often what the stories are about is not as important as why people tell them. Perhaps your grandparents like to tell you stories of their past because they enjoy reliving the experiences.

 OBSERVE

Listen carefully to the persons around you who are telling personal stories. Perhaps it is your uncle describing his first dance or your mother telling about her childhood adventures. Keep a log for a week of the stories you hear. List the name and age of the storyteller, the subject of the story, and why you think the speaker told it.

Your Own or a Friend's Writing

Sometimes you may choose to read something you wrote, such as a story or poem. Or you might interpret a story written by another student and share it with the class. To hear a poem you have written recited by someone else could be very interesting.

 **JOURNAL ENTRY**

I wrote a poem about the creation of colors, and my teacher chose it to be read at a school assembly. A girl read it, and I was surprised how she created moods for the colors. She did things I did not expect, like pausing between certain words. It almost became "our" poem by the time she was done.

The poem "Whatcha Gonna Do?" was written by a junior high school student and has been used for oral interpretation by other persons.

SELECTING MATERIAL

There are countless places to find material for oral interpretation. Enjoy yourself as you thumb through the literature to find some possible pieces. Once you find some material, you need to know how to select the best literature.

As you select your literature, think about these standards: the quality of the literature, audience analysis, the oral possibilities of the literature, and your feelings for the piece.

QUALITY OF LITERATURE

Good literature has certain characteristics. It has a **theme** that connects to common human experiences. Most people have experienced love, anger, joy, and pain. They have felt scared, sad, or happy. Good literature also has **conflict.** All people have experienced conflicts. They may have had conflicts within themselves, with other individuals, with nature, or

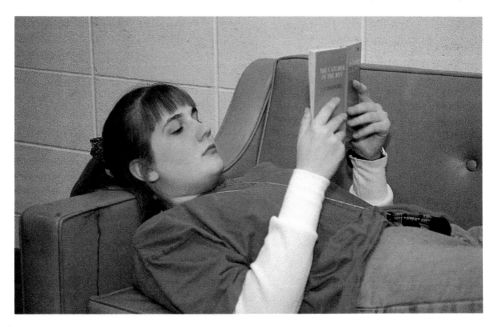

Whatcha Gonna Do?

Whatcha gonna do
when the world
breaks down,
child,
Whatcha gonna do
when we all pull
that great big plug
of existence
out of its socket?
Whatcha gonna do
when the earth
stops turning,
and the sun
stops shining,
and the rain
stops falling?
Whatcha gonna do
when they drop
the bomb
on all
that you live for,
child,
Whatcha gonna do
when they blow up
all your dreams?
Whatcha gonna do
when all your ideals
crash in around you,
along with all
that you ever thought
was right?
Whatcha gonna do
when a smile
becomes a rare thing
of the past,
child,
Whatcha gonna do
when the words *hope*
and *harmony*
and *endurance*
get erased
from the human
dictionary of life?
Whatcha gonna do,
Whatcha gonna do...

I know
whatcha gotta do,
child,
I know...

You gotta
hold on tightly
to the few
broken ideals
you're left with,
child,
you gotta
find new dreams
to dream
as soon as
the old ones die.
You gotta
always stop
to hug
the other soul
you meet,
and don't forget
to tell them
that you're praying
for them,
that you're fighting
for them.
You gotta
always remember
that someone,
somewhere
is pulling
for you too,
child,
you gotta
never forget
that courage
and determination
will forever fight
alongside you.
You gotta
understand
that there
are other forms
of sunshine

besides light,
that there
are other forms
of rain
besides water.
You gotta
push yourself always
as far
as you can go,
child,
and most of all,
you gotta
pick up
that great, big plug
of life
and pull it
along behind you,
until your muscles ache,
until your heart pains,
until your endurance
begins to wither away,
until your standstill hope
all together collapses.
Keep going,
keep dreaming,
'till
you reach
that lonely, empty socket,
and thrust
that dusty plug into it
with all
the fierce will
to live
you've built up
inside yourself.
Then,
child,
you gotta
get behind
this old, frail earth
and start pushing
it 'round
with all
your might...

—Kathleen (George) Kearney

within a hostile environment. Many fables contain a **moral** or lesson that is taught through the literature.

Readers should feel connected to the theme of their pieces. The theme in good literature is usually presented in a new and different way. The literature should help the reader see an ordinary idea in a new way. The literature should excite the reader's imagination.

The poem "Foul Shot," by Edwin Hoey, describes an ordinary scene in a special way. The poem gives a vivid picture of a young basketball player's struggle to sink a shot. Anyone who has tried to accomplish a goal under pressure can relate to this struggle. You may not play basketball, but you may have struggled to reach other goals. As you read the poem, you can imagine this scene and the tension of both the player and the spectators.

AUDIENCE ANALYSIS

You need to ask yourself how your listeners will respond to your selected literature. You want to use a piece of literature that will appeal to your listeners. To evaluate the audience, ask yourself whether the literature is appropriate to the age, concerns, and feelings of the audience members. Does the literature fit the occasion? A poem or essay that you like may not be the best piece for the senior citizens' evening or the Sunday school assembly.

Read the poem "Mean Maxine." Who would be the best audience for this poem? What might be an appropriate occasion?

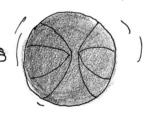

Foul Shot

With two 60's stuck on the scoreboard
And two seconds hanging on the clock,
The solemn boy in the center of eyes,
Squeezed by silence,
Seeks out the line with his feet,
Soothes his hands along his uniform,
Gently drums the ball against the floor,
Then measures the waiting net,
Raises the ball on his right hand,
Balances it with his left,
Calms it with fingertips,
Breathes,
Crouches,
Waits,
And then through a stretching of stillness,
Nudges it upward.

The ball
Slides up and out,
Lands,
Leans,
Wobbles,
Wavers,
Hesitates,
Exasperates,
Plays it coy
Until every face begs with unsounding screams—

And then

        And then

                And then,

Right before ROAR-UP,
Dives down and through.

                —Edwin A. Hoey

Mean Maxine

There's no one mean as mean Maxine,
she smells like old cigars,
her brain is smaller than a bean,
I wish she'd move to Mars.

Some day I'll list the things I hate,
and that is where I'll list her,
I'd like to pack her in a crate—
too bad Maxine's my sister.

—Jack Prelutsky

ORAL POSSIBILITIES

You also need to ask if your listeners can grasp the meaning of your piece in just one reading. In oral interpretation, as in public speaking, you get only one chance to reach your audience. Your listeners cannot hear a certain line again or ask what a strange word means. When the language is too difficult or the sentence structure is too involved, that literature is not appropriate for reading aloud.

As you select your literature, look for words and ideas that can be clearly communicated to your listeners. As poet Ted Hughes says in his book *Poetry Is*, look for words that "live":

Words that live are those which we hear, like "click" or "chuckle," or which we see, like "freckled" or "veined," or which we taste, like "vinegar" or "sugar," or touch, like "prickle" or "oily," or smell, like "tar" or "onion." Words which belong directly to one of the five senses. Or words which act and seem to use their muscles, like "flick" or "balance."

YOUR FEELINGS

If you are going to communicate a piece of literature to other people, you must feel a connection to the material. Ask yourself, Have I ever had a feeling or experience similar to the ones described by the author? What can I bring to the performance? As an oral interpreter you cannot expect the audience to get excited over something that has no meaning for you. If you don't feel connected to the literature, you will have a hard time communicating its meaning to your audience.

The essay "Forget-Me-Not" was written by a high school student. Another student chose to interpret it because it reminded her of feelings she had after her uncle's death.

Forget-Me-Not

It was the weekend and since I didn't have anything better to do, my mother had assigned me to clean the basement. I was glad to do it because my mom had this habit of keeping useless things: my old toys, outdated clothing, and various other old things. I, on the other hand, have to have everything in its proper place or I can't think straight. I had already cleaned away three shelves when I saw the box wedged between the toastmaster oven and my brother's old lava lamp. The memories of my father jumped back into my mind.

When it happened, I already knew that he was going to die. During those last weeks, I tore myself apart wondering whether I should still expect him to get well or whether to accept it. I remember feeling so helpless and depressed. I wondered when I could stop thinking about him, when my mind would clear of all the doctors and hospitals. Yet, my conscience wouldn't let him die. The inevitable call finally came. I thought that when I heard the news an incredible rush of emotions would flow out of me, but I just felt numb, cold, and very alone.

The next day, my mom and I went down to the hospital where my father had died. I didn't want to go, I never wanted to go near another hospital ever, but I could see that my mom needed me to help her, so I went. When we walked into the office, the first thing I noticed was the endless wall of white boxes. "These are the belongings of _____" was written in bold letters on each box. Each box represented a death. Each box represented a grieving man, woman, or child.

"Let me see," the nurse said as she groped in the corner for my father's box. "Watkiss, Watkiss, ah, here it is." She handed me the box. My mom finished the rest of the paper work and we went home.

I had forgotten all about the box. I didn't really want to know where it was or what was in it. I was angry that he was gone. I felt bitter towards him for leaving us.

Now here it was again: here he was again. I wondered what I would want to have with me when I died. I wondered what my box would contain. So, if nothing else, out of curiosity, I decided to open the box.

I gently pried the flaps of the box open. The first thing my eyes fell upon were his pajamas. They were his favorite pair. My mother had given them to him the last Christmas that he was well. They were made of flannel printed with little blue ducks. They were wrinkled from the years of wear. I folded them up and set them aside.

The next thing in the box was a brown paper bag filled with get well cards. I remembered how he had stood the cards up all around his room, so he could see them all at a glance. I started to look through them and then I came to the Snoopy card that my brother had given him. It was his favorite card. It had been right next to his bed in every hospital room that he had been in. I read some of the other cards and then I looked in the box for the next item.

It was a small plastic bag containing two objects. The first was his slateblack, square-framed glasses. It felt funny to look at them without seeing his face. They seemed so empty and ordinary. The other item was his wedding ring. I can't remember a time when it wasn't on his finger. His doctor wanted him to take it off for his operation, but he refused, so they had to sterilize it just before the surgery.

The next thing in the box was our family portrait. When I used to visit him, he would just sit and stare at it. I always wondered what he was thinking. Whatever it was, he would always be depressed after looking at it and he wouldn't talk for the rest of the visit.

The final item at the bottom of the box was his cup. He had had it from the first day he was in the hospital. I had brought it with me the first day I saw him there so that he would know that I was thinking about him. It was a light blue color with the words, "I LOVE DAD" in big bold letters. Part of the enamel on the handle had worn away from use. This was the one thing that I had given him that he had kept until his death.

I sat and looked at all of the things for a long time. I remembered all the things we had done together. I remembered his patience and his perseverance. I know now that he was only human, and that he didn't die on purpose. The pain I felt came from the destruction of his body, but no disease could destroy my memories of him and love for him.

I put everything back in the box except the cup, which I washed and filled with dirt. I planted the tiny seeds of the forget-me-not and watched it struggle and stretch its way into existence.

—Carol Watkiss

Selecting the right piece of literature is the first step toward giving a fine performance. If you apply these standards you just read, you will find a piece worth your time and the time of your listeners.

INTERACT

Select five of your favorite topic areas from the following list. Use the guidelines you just studied to find a piece of literature for each topic you chose.

With a group of four classmates, share your favorite reading topics and give each other examples of your favorite work under each topic.

- love stories
- baseball
- murder mysteries
- famous people
- historical tales
- mythology
- true-life adventure
- poetry
- scientific experiments
- movie stars

- automobiles
- science fiction
- history
- people of other lands
- how to make things
- football
- teenagers' problems
- basketball
- animal stories
- space travel

ANALYZING LITERATURE

Did you know that Katherine Paterson wrote *Bridge to Terabithia* as a way to help her own son understand the death of his friend? Did you know Anne Frank actually was between twelve and fourteen years old when she wrote in her diary?

As you prepare for a performance, you must become very familiar with the literature you have selected. The better you understand the piece, the easier it will be to communicate its meaning to your audience. You must therefore analyze the piece carefully to understand its full meaning.

If your performance piece is part of a larger piece of literature, such as a section of a novel or a play, you need to first read the entire piece of literature. You have to understand the larger piece to understand how your section, or cutting, fits into the whole. The cutting is the section you select or "cut" from the entire work. Cutting is discussed in Chapter 17.

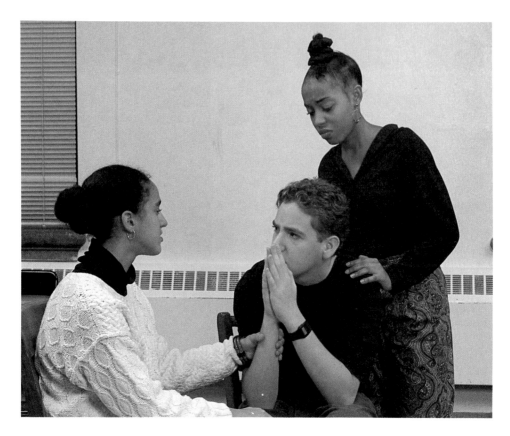

There are four keys to analyzing literature. When you analyze a piece of literature for performance, you need to look at the dramatic speaker, the elements of the literature, the language, and the author. Each key is examined in detail in the next pages.

THE DRAMATIC SPEAKER

The voice that is heard telling the story or poem as you read is the voice of the **dramatic speaker.** This is the person telling the story or describing the scene. It is not the author's voice but a voice created by the author. The voice may belong to a character in the literature or to someone looking at the scene from a distance. As an interpreter, you communicate with the audience as if you were the dramatic speaker.

Two cuttings follow. Cutting A is from *Dicey's Song,* and cutting B is from *Dear Mr. Henshaw.* Read each cutting and see if you can identify whose voice is speaking.

Cutting A

What a day, Dicey thought. What a summer, for that matter, but especially, What a day. She stood alone in the big old barn, in a patch of moonlight; stood looking at the sailboat resting on its sawhorse cradle, a darker patch among shadows. Behind her, the wind blew off the water, bringing the faint smell of salt and the rich, moist smell of the marshes....

So. So they were going to live here, on the rundown farm, with Gram—Dicey's heart danced again, inside her, to say it to herself like that. *Home.* Home with their momma's momma, who was also a Tillerman. Home: a home with plenty of room for the four children in the shabby farmhouse, room inside, room outside, and the kind of room within Gram too—Dicey had seen Gram and how she listened when Maybeth sang, how she talked with James, how her eyes smiled at the things Sammy said and did—the kind of room that was what they really needed. One of the lessons the long summer had taught Dicey was how to figure out what they really needed.

—Cynthia Voigt,
from *Dicey's Song*

Cutting B

Like I've been telling you, I am Leigh Botts. Leigh Marcus Botts. I don't like Leigh for a new name because some people don't know how to say it or think it's a girl's name. Mom says with a last name like Botts I need something fancy but not too fancy. My Dad's name is Bill and Mom's name is Bonnie. She says Bill and Bonnie Botts sounds like something out of a comic strip.

I am just a plain boy. This school doesn't say I am Gifted and Talented, and I don't like soccer very much the way everybody at this school is supposed to. I am not stupid either.

—Beverly Cleary,
from *Dear Mr. Henshaw*

In cutting A, it is clear Dicey is not the dramatic speaker because Dicey would not say "Dicey thought" about herself. If you read the book, you would find that the dramatic speaker is an adult who knows Dicey well and cares about her.

In the book *Dear Mr. Henshaw,* the main character tells the story through letters to Mr. Henshaw. For example, cutting B is from a letter dated November 20. The dramatic speaker is a "plain boy" named Leigh Marcus Botts, an average kid. It certainly is not the adult female author.

The search for the dramatic speaker is your first step, because you are going to behave as that speaker during your performance. If your speaker is a "plain boy," you will not want to sound like a highly educated adult. If your speaker is a wise old woman, you will not want to sound like a bored teenager.

ELEMENTS OF LITERATURE

As you analyze a piece of literature, you will need to look for elements such as setting, plot, mood, theme, conflict, and characters. Not every piece of literature will have all these elements, but when they exist they can help you create a better performance.

Setting

The time and place of the literature creates a **setting** for the performance. If the piece is set in a roller rink in 1992, the performance will be very different than if it is set in an English church in 1820. When you read *Anne Frank: The Diary of a Young Girl,* you can't understand Anne's desire for freedom during the twenty-five months her family hid from the Nazis unless you understand the setting. In the following excerpt, Anne brings that setting to life:

> I wander from one room to another, downstairs and up again, feeling like a songbird whose wings have been clipped and who is hurling himself in utter darkness against the bars of his cage. "Go outside, laugh, and take a breath of fresh air," a voice cries within me, but I don't even feel a response any more; I go and lie on the divan and sleep, to make the time pass more quickly, and the stillness and the terrible fear, because there is no way of killing them.
>
> —Anne Frank,
> from *The Diary of a Young Girl*

Plot

The **plot,** or story line of the piece, must be made clear to listeners. You must know the important events that move a story or play along. If you are doing a cutting, you need to know the entire plot and share the main points with the audience in your introduction. For example, if you are reading a cutting from Joseph Krumgold's *And Now Miguel,* you will need to tell your audience that the life of Miguel's family revolves around the life cycle of sheep. Thus, Miguel and his family must travel the mesa to the ranch to the mountains. Little of the story will make sense to your audience if they do not understand this. If you are reading the whole story, you need to decide which moments are most important so you can emphasize them for your listeners.

Mood

The interpreter creates the **mood,** or the emotional feeling, of the literature. This is done through nonverbal messages. A humorous piece, such as Ina Friedman's *How My Parent Learned to Eat,* may require a fast pace, quick movements, and many smiles. A cutting from a book like *Scorpions* by Walter Dean Meyers, in which a young boy faces problems with a gang, will need a slower pace and more serious facial expressions. Read the poem "Mending," and identify the mood you would create as its interpreter.

Mending

A giant hand inside my chest
Stretches out and takes
My heart within its mighty grasp
And squeezes till it breaks.

A gentle hand inside my chest,
With mending tape and glue,
Patches up my heart until
It's almost good as new.

I ought to know by now that
Broken hearts will heal again.
But while I wait for glue and tape,
The pain!
The pain!
The pain!

—Judith Viorst

Theme

Finding the **theme,** or main idea, helps you know what to emphasize in your performance. The theme may make a statement about society, human nature, or the meaning of life. It may be a theme of survival or of peace at any price. Here are some examples of themes in literature:

- *Charlotte's Web* by E.B. White—Friendship can be found in many places.

- *Dicey's Song* by Cynthia Voigt—Home is where one is loved.

- *Bridge to Terabithia* by Katherine Paterson—Death does not end the influence of someone in your life.

- *Mufaro's Beautiful Daughters: An African Tale* by John Steptoe—Greed and selfishness are harmful.

- *The Planet of Junior Brown* by Virginia Hamilton—Pride in individuality is important.

- *Dragonwings* by Lawrence Yep—Prejudice is dangerous.

Conflict

Conflict is at the heart of most literature. If no conflict existed in novels, stories, and plays, it would be hard to get involved in them. **Conflicts** can exist within individuals or between individuals. Conflicts also can exist between characters and the environment or nature.

Many stories about adolescents show internal conflict, as the teenagers struggle to find their identity and to fit into the world. Often the struggles also exist between characters.

In some literature, the forces of good and evil fight one another to rule the world, as in *The Lord of the Rings*, J.R.R. Tolkien's epic trilogy.

Individuals may be in conflict with society at large, as they are in *The Outsiders* by S.E. Hinton, or in *The Witch of Blackbird Pond* by Elizabeth George Speare, in which a young girl is accused of being a witch because she does not fit into the society around her.

Finally, characters may struggle against nature. In *Island of the Blue Dolphins* by Scott O'Dell, *Julie of the Wolves* by Jean Craighead George, or *Hatchet* by Gary Paulsen, the main characters try to survive in hostile environments.

Characters

The interpreter needs to understand the characters who exist in the literature. You need to study the characters carefully to get a sense of how to suggest them in your performance. Your study should include their appearance, words and language, actions, attitudes, and what others say about them.

For example, in the novel *Anne of Green Gables*, by Lucy Maud Montgomery, the heroine is described as follows:

> A child of about eleven, garbed in a very short, very tight, very ugly dress of yellowish gray wincey. She wore a faded brown sailor hat and beneath the hat, extending down her back, were two braids of very thick, decidedly red hair. Her face was small, white and thin, also much freckled; her mouth was large and so were her eyes, that looked green in some lights and moods and gray in others.

This pale young woman turns out to have quite a temper. It is described in the following scene from *Anne of Green Gables:*

Gilbert reached across the aisle, picked up the end of Anne's long red braid, held it out at arm's length, and said in a piercing whisper,

"Carrots! Carrots!"

Then Anne looked at him with a vengeance!

She did more than look back. She sprang to her feet, her bright fancies fallen into cureless ruin. She flashed one indignant glance at Gilbert from eyes whose angry sparkle was swiftly quenched in equally angry tears.

"You mean, hateful boy!" she exclaimed passionately. "How dare you!"

And then—Thwack! Anne had brought her slate down on Gilbert's head and cracked it—slate, not head—clear across.

The more you know about a character like Anne Shirley, the better you will interpret that character for an audience.

As you read a piece of literature several times, you will find new ways of thinking about it or looking at its characters. These deeper meanings, found through your analysis, will strengthen your performance.

LANGUAGE

Writers create art with their words. A poet, playwright, or novelist works and reworks each sentence, struggling to find just the right words. Interpreters must respect the author's efforts. As an interpreter you need to study the author's word choice, style, and rhyme. If you do not understand exactly what the author says or why something is expressed in a certain way, you cannot communicate the meaning of the literature to your listeners.

Word Choice

As an interpreter you must make every effort to say exactly what the author means in the selection. Remember that the author chose a particular word for a reason. The word is not *almost* what the author wanted but *exactly* what the author wanted. If you are unfamiliar with any of the author's words, look them up so you can understand their meaning.

As you probably remember from Chapter 2, words have two

types of meanings. One type is the *denotative* meaning, which is the literal meaning or the dictionary definition. The other is the *connotative* meaning, which is your emotional or personal response to a word.

For example, the definition of *rose* is "any type of shrub with prickly stems and five-parted, usually fragrant flowers of red, pink, white, or yellow." This is the denotative meaning of *rose.* It suggests no feeling or emotion. Roses may have a positive connotation to you because you think roses are beautiful. They may have a negative connotation if you are allergic to them.

Suppose you read the words "a blue rose." When you think about the word *blue,* you might realize that this color makes the rose unique and valuable. The choice to use *blue* in the description of a rose creates a connotative meaning because it suggests a unique or rare rose. You can see this in the following cutting from *The Blue Rose:*

> You see, Jenny is different.
> Different?
> Yes, different from most other girls
> But surely, all people don't
> Have to be alike,
> think alike,
> act alike
> or look alike.
> To me Jenny is a blue rose.
>
> —Gerda Klein,
> from *The Blue Rose*

An author's use of language is extremely important. For example, in Verna Aardema's *Who's in Rabbit's House?* each animal has a sound associated with it. The jackal trots off "kpata, kpata," the leopard jumps "pa, pa, pa," and the frog laughs, "dgung, dgung, dgung." Such language makes this African folktale come alive for your listeners.

Style

How the author says something may be as important as what the author says. The **style,** or the way a piece is written, helps you to create the mood or feeling for your listeners. Look at the following two descriptions of the same scene. The images created are very different. In version A, author Lloyd Alexander creates a setting and mood from another time and place. Version B has ordinary language and little sense of time and mood.

Version A

From the corridor, a faint sound grew louder. Taran hastened to press his ear against the slot in the portal. He heard the heavy tread of marching feet, the rattle of weapons. He straightened and stood with his back to the wall. The girl had betrayed him. He cast about for some means to defend himself, for he had determined they would not take him easily. For the sake of having something in his hands, Taran picked up the dirty straw and held it ready to fling; it was a pitiable defense, and he wished desperately for Gwydion's power to set it ablaze.

—Lloyd Alexander,
from *The Book of Three*

Version B

The noise grew louder down the hall. Taran listened through a hole in the door. He heard a soldier and knew the girl had lied. "How can I defend myself?" he wondered. All Taran could find was loose straw.

A fine writer uses figurative language to appeal to the listeners' eyes and ears. (See Chapter 11 for a discussion of figures of speech.) For example, many poets use *personification* as they describe how "trees worry" or "chairs cheer." They may use *hyperbole*, as in, "Mean old Sarah shook the street as she pounded with her boots." You will find countless comparisons using *metaphors* and *similes*. Some writers also use **onomatopoeia;** that is, words that sound like their meanings, such as *hiss, crash, clang, roar, growl, slink, kerplop,* and *boing.*

Rhyme

Authors may use **rhyme,** or words that sound alike, to give life to a piece of literature. As an interpreter, you must decide if you will need to read the rhyme in a patterned way or if you should break up the rhyme to catch your listeners' attention.

You can see the difference by reading the first lines of Robert Frost's poem "Stopping by Woods on a Snowy Evening." If you read the poem in a singsong rhyme, you will create a different message than if you break the rhyme to create meaning.

Whose woods these are I think I know,
His house is in the village, though;
He will not see me stopping here
To watch his woods fill up with snow.

Audience is an important consideration when you interpret rhyming poetry. When you read a poem in a singsong rhyme, adult listeners may tune you out because the rhythm will be boring. If you break the rhythm, your listeners will pay more attention. Yet if you are reading to children they will enjoy the rhymes, and the rhythm will help keep them involved.

INTERACT

Select a children's poem, such as "The Duel" by Eugene Field, "The Little Boy and the Old Man" by Shel Silverstein, "The Cremation of Sam McGee" by Robert Service, or some rhyming stories such as those written by Dr. Seuss. In small groups read them according to the strict rhyme. Then read them breaking the rhyme. Discuss the differences in listening to each type.

AUTHOR

Sometimes you can understand more about a piece of literature by learning about its author. When researching the author, try to find out at what point in his or her life the selection was written. Was there a significance to the place, time, or title? Does the author have a theme he or she generally writes about?

You may think about what reason an author would have for writing the selection. For example, Virginia Hamilton is an

African-American writer who writes about black culture and history. Her characters are generally very sensitive, and often troubled, loners. They search for patterns to give meaning and order to their lives. In Hamilton's novel *M.C. Higgins, the Great*, M.C. Higgins tries to come to terms with his past. He is in conflict with his father, and he wants to escape his Ohio home. If you were to interpret a section from this novel, you might find it valuable to know that the character and theme of the novel are typical of Hamilton's writing and that she has a strong belief in the importance of family relationships.

When you are interpreting an oral history you will need to know about the author because you will be speaking for him or her. The following are the actual words of a newspaper publisher, Steven Simonyi-Gindele, as recorded by Studs Terkel in his book *Working*. In this section he describes his early working experiences and what they meant to him. If you were to interpret this orally you would speak as if you were the publisher.

I went to work when I was nine years old. I used to get up at three-thirty in the morning and deliver four hundred newspapers. I was bored by school and left in the last year. I was never afraid of working. I always enjoyed the challenge and I always enjoyed the reward. I did all kinds of things.

I was a busboy when I was thirteen. It took me six weeks of steadily looking for a job. It was high unemployment at that time in Canada. I realized then the only security a person has is what he himself can do. There's little security in a job working for somebody else. I like to control my fate as much as possible.

I don't believe the answer lies in making money. It didn't for me. By the time I was twenty-one I was driving a Cadillac and I could afford a fifteen-hundred-dollar-a-month seashore apartment in Florida, go to shows, and spend two hundred dollars a night and take my mother out, my grandfather, and live like a king. But I was more frustrated than when I was making thirty-four cents an hour delivering for a drugstore in Toronto.

I couldn't understand why I wasn't happy. Happiness is not related to money. Being successful at what you're doing is the measure of a man.

PIECES FOR ORAL INTERPRETATION

This chapter suggests ways to find material for oral interpretation. The following pages include some good choices for oral interpretation and for storytelling, a type of interpretive performance that is discussed in the next chapter. Reading and enjoying the literature on the next pages may help you decide what kinds of literature you would like to interpret.

Dreams

Hold fast to dreams
For if dreams die
Life is a broken-winged bird
That cannot fly.

Hold fast to dreams
For when dreams go
Life is a barren field
Frozen with snow.

—Langston Hughes

The Day We Die

The day we die
the wind comes down
to take away
our footprints.

The wind makes dust
to cover up
the marks we left
while walking.

For otherwise
the thing would seem
as if we were
still living.

Therefore the wind
is he who comes
to blow away
our footprints.

—Kalahari origin (Africa),
Translated by Arthur Markowitz

Life Is So Full

Well, here I am! Seventeen years old today,
boy the clock's ticking fast.
Birthdays are a special time,
a day to celebrate your existence
and cherish the ones around you.

Life is so full,
abounding with wonders to be seen
and emotions to be experienced.
If we all just open our eyes and gaze
upon the subtleties and finer shadings of life
greater worlds unfold.
Worlds we rarely find time to look at.
But they're here and always will be
when we choose to find them.

I'm grateful to be a leaf
in the ever growing tree of life
and this leaf's not falling off
for nothing.

   —Paul Garver
   The author was terminally ill when he wrote this poem.

The Dog and the Shadow

A dog once walked across a bridge,
Carrying a cheese in his mouth.
When Dog was half-way over the bridge,
He saw another cheese down in the water.
Dog was greedy.
He resolved to have both cheeses—
His cheese and its shadow.
Dog leaped in.
          He opened his mouth.
               He dropped his cheese.
Dog then recognized the shadow as a shadow.
For that shadow he had lost his cheese!

(To want too much may mean one loses everything.)

**The Rice Puller of Chaohwa
A Chinese Tale**

Near the village of Chaohwa, it is said, there lived a farmer by the name of Liu. He was not very different from the other farmers of Chaohwa, except that he was known as an impatient man. Some of his neighbors referred to him as Liu Always-in-a-hurry. When there was work to be done, he was always urging his wife and sons to go faster. If his wife had to go to the village for something or other, Liu practically pushed her out the door to get her started, and when she returned, he demanded to know what had kept her so long. When he was on the road himself, he was always stepping on the heels of anyone in front of him. He had an uncontrollable desire to be first in everything he did.

One day when Liu was in Chaohwa, he heard a group of farmers talking about their rice fields.

"My rice is sprouting very well," one of them said. "It is nearly two inches high."

Another farmer said, "Yes, my rice is doing well also. It is perhaps a little more than two inches high. In fact, nearly three."

"It is a good year for me, too," a third man said. "In some parts of my field the rice is nearly four inches tall already."

As Liu listened, he became very impatient with his own rice, which certainly wasn't four inches tall, or even three. Probably it wasn't even two.

He hurried back to his fields, stepping on quite a few heels as he went. He even took a shortcut, trampling through the mud of a neighbor's rice field. When he saw the rice sprouts in his own fields, his heart fell. They were so short that he could hardly believe what he saw. Not one of them was more than two inches tall.

He hurried home thoughtfully and pondered rapidly

over his problem. When his wife and sons spoke to him, he hardly heard them. All night long he rolled and tossed sleeplessly. But just before dawn, he sat upright suddenly, shouting, "I will help them!"

He went to his fields, reached down, and took hold of one of the sprouts with his fingers. Then he pulled ever so gently. The sprout came up a little. "Aha, that's better!" Liu said. Then he pulled the next stalk up a little, then the next. He went through the field this way and that, pulling on the stalks as fast as he could. All day he did this, and in the evening he came home weary and worn.

The next day he rushed again to his fields and began again at the beginning. When he returned home at nightfall, he told his family, "Oh, I am tired! I worked so hard today! But the rice is much taller now, and I am happy!"

Liu's family was surprised at the news, for rice grows ever so slowly. So in the morning they went out together to see the results of Liu's hard work.

What they found was sad to see, for the rice stalks lay withered and dead in the morning sun.

"Alas, is this gratitude?" Liu cried out to the ruined field. "Is this my reward for giving you a helping hand?"

As for the people of Chaohwa, when the news got around, they had to laugh at the outcome of Liu's impatience. And although Liu himself was forgotten as new generations were born and died in Chaohwa, people still say to someone who is overly eager, "Don't be a rice puller."

Based on a translation by Hsin-Chih Lee and Cho-Feng L. Lee of a story recorded by Mencius (Meng-tse), who lived during the third and second centuries B.C.

Grasshopper Gumbo

Grasshopper gumbo
Iguana tail tarts
Toad à la mode
Pickled pelican parts
Elephant gelatin
Frog fricassee
Purée of platypus
Boiled bumblebee
Porcupine pudding
Steamed centipede skins
Squid sucker sundaes
Fried flying fish fins
Meadow mouse morsels
Cracked crocodile crunch

The school cafeteria
serves them for lunch.

—Jack Prelutsky

The Bad Kangaroo

There was a small Kangaroo who was bad in school. He put thumbtacks on the teacher's chair. He threw spitballs across the classroom. He set off firecrackers in the lavatory and spread glue on the doorknobs.

"Your behavior is impossible!" said the school principal. "I am going to see your parents. I will tell them what a problem you are!"

The principal went to visit Mr. and Mrs. Kangaroo. He sat down in a living-room chair.

"Ouch!" cried the principal. "There is a thumbtack in this chair!"

"Yes, I know," said Mr. Kangaroo. "I enjoy putting thumbtacks in chairs."

A spitball hit the principal on his nose.

"Forgive me," said Mrs. Kangaroo, "but I can never resist throwing those things."

There was a loud booming sound from the bathroom.

"Keep calm," said Mr. Kangaroo to the principal. "The firecrackers that we keep in the medicine chest have just exploded. We love the noise."

The principal rushed for the front door. In an instant he was stuck to the doorknob.

"Pull hard," said Mrs. Kangaroo. "There are little globs of glue on all of our doorknobs."

The principal pulled himself free. He dashed out of the house and ran off down the street.

"Such a nice person," said Mr. Kangaroo. "I wonder why he left so quickly."

"No doubt he had another appointment," said Mrs. Kangaroo. "Never mind, supper is ready."

Mr. and Mrs. Kangaroo and their son enjoyed their evening meal. After the dessert, they all threw spitballs at each other across the dining-room table.

—Arnold Lobel

(A child's conduct will reflect the ways of his parents.)

Two Haiku

On a leafless bough
    In the gathering autumn dusk:
        A solitary crow!

Listen! a frog
    Jumping into the stillness
        Of an ancient pond!

—Translated by Dorothy Britton

Jazz Fantasia

Drum on your drums, batter on your banjoes,
sob on the long cool winding saxophones.
Go to it, O jazzmen.

Sling your knuckles on the bottoms of the happy
tin pans, let your trombones ooze, and go husha-
husha-hush with the slippery sand-paper.

Moan like an autumn wind high in the lonesome
    treetops, moan soft like
you wanted somebody terrible, cry like a racing car
    slipping away from a
motorcycle cop, bang-bang! you jazzmen, bang altogether
    drums, traps,
banjoes, horns, tin cans—make two people fight on the
    top of a stairway
and scratch each other's eyes in a clinch tumbling down
    the stairs.
Can the rough stuff...now a Mississippi steamboat
    pushes up the night
river with a hoo-hoo-hoo-oo...and the green lanterns
    calling to the high
soft stars...a red moon rides on the humps of the low
    river hills...
go to it, O jazzmen.

—Carl Sandburg

SUMMARY

This chapter introduces oral interpretation, the art of reading
literature aloud to communicate meaning to an audience. The
chapter suggests a number of sources for finding literature for
interpretation. When selecting your material you need to consider four standards: the quality of the literature, audience
analysis, oral possibilities, and your feelings for the piece.
When analyzing material you need to examine four key points:
the dramatic speaker, the elements of literature, the language,
and the author.

CHAPTER REVIEW

THINK ABOUT IT

1. Define *oral interpretation* and describe three places you see it in everyday life.
2. List sources of material for oral interpretation.
3. What four standards are important when selecting material for oral interpretation?
4. Describe the four key points for analyzing literature for performance.
5. What are the elements of literature?

TRY IT OUT

1. Interview a teacher, TV or radio announcer, or a minister, priest, or rabbi. Ask any of them how they use oral interpretation in their work.
2. From an anthology of literature, select three pieces that meet the four standards for selecting material for oral interpretation. Share these with a partner and explain why each piece meets the standards.
3. Find a piece of literature that meets the standards for selecting material for oral interpretation and identify the characters, mood, setting, conflict, and plot.
4. With a partner, read "Foul Shot," "Mean Maxine," and "Mending." Identify the dramatic speaker in each piece.

PUT IT IN WRITING

1. List your three favorite authors and give an example of each person's work. Using a paragraph for each author, explain why you enjoy that person's writings and decide whether the writing has possibilities for oral performance.
2. Read the poem "Mending." Write a short paper in which you analyze the language used. Consider word choice, style, and rhyme. Explain how the language helps create a mood.

SPEAK ABOUT IT

1. Talk to a friend or neighbor who is at least seventy years old. With permission, record a story from the person's childhood. Play the tape to your class or retell the story.
2. Tell the class a fairytale from your childhood.

Performing Oral Interpretation

After completing this chapter, you should be able to

- prepare a script and cut literature for oral interpretation.
- write an introduction for a piece of literature.
- establish eye focus to support the literature.
- use vocal variety, gestures, and facial expressions to create mood and characters.
- mark a script for performance.
- use several rehearsal techniques.
- prepare and present a story.
- evaluate an oral interpretation or storytelling performance.

KEY WORDS

cutting the literature

eye focus

storytelling

marking the script

sense recall

When Mr. Cole read Charles Dickens' *A Christmas Carol* to the class, I could see the Ghosts of Christmas Past, Present, and Future so clearly. It was a really spooky story.

I saw a one-person show in which an actress created the life of Emily Dickinson through reading her poems and letters.

A well-performed oral interpretation can give listeners a different way of seeing the world. During a fine performance listeners become involved in the literature that the oral interpreter performs. The performance may lead listeners to understand the literature in a new way. Storytelling is closely related to oral interpretation. Like oral interpreters, storytellers weave magic for an audience out of the words of an author.

How do you create such moments for listeners? Good performance skills plus a good analysis equals a fine performance. As part of your preparation for an oral interpretation performance, you need to prepare your material, practice using your voice and body, mark and create a stage script, and rehearse. As part of your preparation for storytelling, you need to develop storytelling techniques. For both types of performance, you need to be able to critique your own performance and those of others.

Emily Dickinson

PREPARING THE MATERIAL

I found a great scene between the two main characters, but the maid comes into the scene for about four lines. This will get confusing. What should I do?

I think the audience will get tired of all the "he saids" and "she saids" in the story. What should I do?

Two important steps in the preparation of your material are cutting the literature and creating an introduction. Each of these tasks is a special process.

CUTTING THE LITERATURE

Sometimes you find a piece of literature that you wish to perform, but it is too long. If so, the material must be cut. **Cutting the literature** means shortening it by taking out parts without changing its meaning. As you cut you must try to save the sections that help the listeners understand the mood, the main conflict, and the characters. In shortening a piece, you can cut the following:

1. *Unnecessary descriptions.* A description of a house, mountains, or a dress, for example, may be interesting but unnecessary in presenting the main ideas or feelings.

2. *Descriptions of action or manner of speaking.* You can cut words such as "Lee looked up angrily" because you can create this feeling with your voice and body. You could cut a sentence such as "She shook her fist at the dog" because you can substitute a gesture for it.

3. *Statements of "he said" or "she said."* Since you are creating the characters through vocal tones and nonverbal actions, you can leave out words that tell who is speaking.

4. *Words that offend the listeners.* If a piece contains swear words or other words that could upset listeners, you can either substitute different words for them or leave out the offensive words.

5. *Unnecessary characters.* A minor character may enter the scene you are performing for only one or two lines. If so, you may wish to cut that person's lines. For example, a younger sibling may come into the scene to pester one of the main characters. Such an interruption can be cut if it does not change the meaning of the scene.

Look at the following example of cutting from the book *Johnny Tremain*. The reader wished to present the part in which Johnny learned to ride the skittish horse, Goblin. The reader was able to cut some of the landscape description and comments about the characters that did not relate to the riding lesson.

Rab had gone into one of the many stalls and backed out a tall, slender horse, so pale he was almost white, but flecked all over with tiny brown marks. The mane and tail were a rich, blackish mahogany. His eyes were glass blue.

~~Rab said: "I never saw a horse his color before. His sire was Yankee Hero, a white horse, fastest horse I ever saw run. Narragansett breed. We could no more afford to own one of Yankee Hero's sons than we could the Lytes' coach unless there was some little thing wrong with him. Eh, Goblin?"~~

The beautiful, wild, timid thing breathed softly, caressingly at Rab, but at the same time the queer, crystalline eyes watched Johnny as though sure that this was a boy who ate horses.

"Now you put on a bridle like this—see? And when winter comes, don't ever put a cold bit in a horse's mouth. Breathe on it first. The saddle blanket—steady, steady, Goblin—it won't hurt you. And then the saddle. Now you lead him out in the yard. You hold the reins like this—left hand *always* and the thumb on the upper side, but down on the reins. And you put your left foot in the stirrup. If you get on from the right side and get kicked, it serves you right. There, see how easy? On and off just like that. You hold him a second."

Rab went into the tavern, and when he came back he had permission to take out the landlady's genteel nag. With Johnny on the nag and Rab on Goblin, they went to the Common. ~~Here were acres upon acres of meadow and cow pasture, hard ground cleared for the drilling of militia. The sun and the wind swept through them. Trees were turned to scarlet, gold, beefy red, blueberry bushes to crimson. Through one patch a white cow was plodding, seemingly up to her belly in blood. The cold, wild air was like wine in the veins. And across the vast, blue sky, white clouds hurried before the wind like sheep before invisible wolves.~~

"Easy, easy," cried Rab. "Easy does it." Goblin had been cavorting, blowing through his nostrils, begging to be let out. Rab kept him at a close canter. The landlady's sorrel flung himself after him. Now and then Rab would glance behind to see how Johnny was making out.

CREATING AN INTRODUCTION

Which of these two introductions would get your attention?

This is a cutting from the play *Step On a Crack.*

Ellie Murphy's mother died when she was four. Since that time Ellie and her father, Max, have been best friends. Until now. Ellie's father just married Lucille and the three of them are figuring out how to be a stepfamily. Ellie finds great frustration in sharing her father; Max finds it hard to know how to react. In this scene from *Step On a Crack* by Suzan Zeder, Ellie and Lucille are struggling for Max's attention.

The second introduction is more likely to gain attention. You learned the importance of the introduction to a speech in Chapter 11. Introductions are equally important for oral interpretation. Through the introduction, an interpreter gets the listeners' attention and prepares them for the literature to come.

Successful introductions accomplish the following:

- Capture the audience's attention
- Tell the author and title
- Give any necessary background information about the author or literature
- Set the scene
- Tie the selection to the audience's experience, if possible

Apply

Read the following introduction for a children's performance and find each of the necessary parts of an introduction.

One of the most famous stuffed animals in the world is a bear named Winnie the Pooh. He belongs to a boy named Christopher Robin. In the following selection from *The House at Pooh Corner* by A.A. Milne, Pooh and Christopher tell each other good-bye because Christopher must go to school and won't be able to play with Pooh very often anymore. Pooh and Christopher express feelings most of us have felt when we must say good-bye to a very close friend.

As you can see, this introduction meets all of the requirements listed above. It is a successful introduction.

INTERACT

With a group of three or four classmates, select one of the following pieces: "Foul Shot," page 399, "Dreams," page 416, or "The Dog and the Shadow," page 417. Have each person prepare an introduction to the same piece. Share your introductions with one another. Combine the best parts of each introduction to create the final introduction to the piece.

USING YOUR VOICE AND BODY

When I perform "We Real Cool" by Gwendolyn Brooks, I use my voice to suggest different pool players saying the lines.

When I read "Foul Shot," I try to show the listeners the basketball hanging on the rim of the hoop by following an imaginary ball with my eyes.

After you have chosen, analyzed, and cut the selection, you are ready to decide how to use your voice and your body while presenting it. To begin, think of yourself as the dramatic speaker talking to an audience and ask yourself, "How would I feel? How would I react in this situation?" If the dramatic

speaker is an uninvolved observer, your voice and body should reflect this. If the dramatic speaker is a character in the middle of an argument, your voice and body need to show this anger.

Perhaps the most important thing to be aware of is that you will interpret the material, not act it out. You are sharing the story with your listeners. In order to look more carefully at the nonverbal part of your performance, you need to consider sense recall, use of voice, and use of body.

SENSE RECALL

As you begin to think about how to use your voice and body for oral interpretation, you can work with sense recall. **Sense recall,** or remembering experiences you have had, will help you suggest images to your audience. You may recall sounds, tastes, smells, touch, and sights.

Suppose you want to interpret a piece in which a character bites into the perfect peach and sighs. You can communicate the sensation and action to your listeners more easily if you can recall a similar experience, such as biting into a beautiful, juicy strawberry. Use your sense recall to remember experiences that can help you interpret the meaning of literature.

Apply

Think about the following in order to create your sense recall.

1. *Sounds.* Imagine the sound of a car horn, airplane overhead, marching band, an unfamiliar sound when you're in the house alone, or chalk scraping across the board in a silent classroom.
2. *Taste.* Recall the taste of a lemon, chocolate candy bar, or badtasting medicine.
3. *Touch.* Recall the touch of fur, hot sand under your bare feet, jumping into a cold swimming pool on a hot day, or the softness of a baby's hair.
4. *Smell.* Recall the smell of frying bacon, your favorite flower, skunk, mothballs, or the air after a spring shower.

5. *Sight.* Imagine the details of your room, your favorite vacation spot, a severe thunderstorm, or your sister's face.

Each person's responses will be slightly different because everyone has unique experiences.

You may have moved from one home to another and probably remember the experience well. Or you may have watched close friends or relatives move away. In the following poem a student describes a moving day in her life. Think about sense experiences in your life you could recall to help you interpret the following poem.

Moving Day

Crates
    full of my childhood
    stand by the door.
My mother's dishes are packed carefully;
    breaking them would mean losing part of our past.
The pale green curtains
    (the ones I picked out)
hang silently in the empty room.
Laughter—
    tears—
        talking—
the sounds of growing up
echo in the hallways.
Home.
New people will grow up here,
    will experience love and pain here;
this home will always be a home.
Our story will continue elsewhere;
We will still share laughter, tears, talking—
Love.
Boxes
    full of memories
    are being loaded into the car.
We will unpack these memories
    and use them to create
    a new Home.
But a part of me stays behind,
    watching my pale green curtains
    swaying in a warm breeze.

—Margaret Susan George

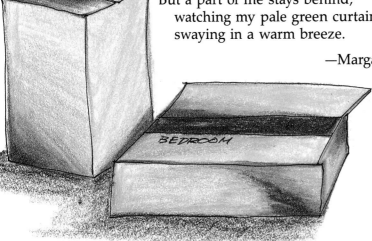

USE OF VOICE

How should your voice change to reflect the differences between the following two selections?

Selection A

Double, double, toil and trouble;
Fire burn, and cauldron bubble.
Fillet of a fenny snake,
In the cauldron boil and bake;
Eye of newt and toe of frog,
Wool of bat and tongue of dog,
Adder's fork and blindworm's sting,
Lizard's leg and howlet's wing,
For a charm of pow'rful trouble,
Like a hell-broth boil and bubble.
                           —William Shakespeare,
                                  from *Macbeth*

Selection B

The sun had never been brighter. This was the day Sheila had waited for, and even the skies were cooperating. The trip to the State Fair would take two hours, but she could spend that time just dreaming of the ferris wheel and the square dancing. It was a downright sparkling day!

Your voice should sound different as you perform these pieces. Selection A calls for a spooky, mysterious reading. Selection B calls for a brighter, lighter reading. To interpret these two pieces, you would change your volume, pitch, rate, and vocal quality.

Volume can have great effect on your performance. You may speak more softly while portraying a shy person than a confident one. Your angry character may be louder than your sad character. If you describe a snowfall in the woods, you would probably speak softly to create a peaceful scene.

Your *pitch* should vary as you read male or female characters. Women and children have higher pitched voices than adult men. An excited person's pitch will be higher than the pitch of someone who is depressed. The voice changes should suggest the difference but not exaggerate it.

If you are reading a playful poem, you can speak at a faster *rate* than if you are reading a sad story. Older characters may speak more slowly than younger ones. When you are shifting to a new character or changing the mood, you can use pauses to create the desired effect. Pauses also create suspense.

Your *vocal quality* should change to reflect different characters or different moods. For example, when telling a children's story you may use a raspy tone for the old queen and a nasal tone for the gnome.

There are many ways to create a vocal effect. Therefore, you have to experiment with vocal changes. Tape your reading as you try different vocal sounds. This will help you decide how you wish to sound.

Sometimes you may want to use an accent. If the dramatic speaker is an old Irish storyteller, you may want to use an Irish accent. If the main character is a Confederate soldier during the Civil War, you may want to use a southern accent. Performing with an accent requires extra time for practicing. Unless the accent is done well, it will distract or confuse listeners. People will pay attention to the accent rather than to the meaning of the literature. If you cannot speak easily with the accent, don't use it at all.

INTERACT

In groups of two or three, read the following selection from *Dicey's Song*. Try to create a voice for Gram, an old country woman. In this scene Gram tells Dicey about some regrets.

I didn't mind being alone, and I don't mind you living here. But that's not what I'm trying to say. I'm trying to say—I married John, and that wasn't a mistake. But the way we stayed married, the way we lived, there were lots of mistakes. He was a stiff and proud man, John—a hard man. . . .

I stuck by him. But I got to thinking, after he died—whether there weren't things I should have done, He wasn't happy, not a happy man. I knew that, I got to know it. He wasn't happy to be himself. And I just let him be, let him sit there, high and proud, in his life. I let the children go away from him. And from me. I got to thinking—when it was too late—you have to reach out to people. To your family too. You can't just let them sit there, you should put your hand out. If they slap it back, well you reach out again if you care enough. If you don't care enough, you forget about them, if you can. I don't know, girl.

—Cynthia Voigt,
from *Dicey's Song*

USE OF BODY

As a performer you use your body to bring characters to life and to convey the author's meaning. You must pay careful attention to movement, facial expression, and special ways to use your eyes, called eye focus.

Movement
Your gestures and posture help set the tone or create the characters for your listeners. As an interpreter you will remain in one place most of the time, so you cannot use movements

such as walking, falling, or touching others. There may be some performances when large movements are permitted in classrooms or contests. You will need to know what your listeners expect. Usually, you can suggest larger movements but you will not actually make them. Therefore, your gestures and posture take on great importance in communicating the meaning of the literature.

As an interpreter you may use gestures such as shrugging your shoulders, pointing your fingers, or scratching your head. You may throw a punch toward the audience to represent a fight, but you will not get into a fistfight with another character.

You can create a mood through your posture. For example, to suggest an embarrassed child, stand with your toes pointed in and your head turned toward your chest. Except when you are speaking as several characters, remember that you are taking on the role of the dramatic speaker. Try to imagine how this speaker would stand or move.

Facial Expression

Your facial expression should quickly communicate the mood of the piece to your audience. A joyous mood can be shown with a smile, and a scary mood can be shown by tension in

your face. If your character is frustrated, your face should show this. Because you do not use large body movements, you may wish to exaggerate your facial and eye expressions to communicate the meaning.

In the poem "It's All Right to Cry," Carol Hall creates many feelings. Try reading it and communicating the changes in mood to your audience.

It's All Right to Cry

It's all right to cry
Crying gets the sad out of you.
It's all right to cry
It might make you feel better.

Raindrops from your eyes
Washing all the mad out of you.
Raindrops from your eyes
It might make you feel better.

It's all right to feel things
Though the feelings may be strange.
Feelings are such real things
And they change and change
And change...
Sad and grumpy,
Down in the dumpy
Snuggly huggly,
Mean and ugly
Sloppy slappy,
Hoppy happy
Change and change and change...

It's all right to know
Feelings come and feelings go.
And it's all right to cry
It might make you feel better.

—Carol Hall

OBSERVE

Think about an experience you have had that made you feel angry, happy, sad, sorry, or determined. Let your body respond to the feeling. Concentrate on remembering the response of your body to the feeling so you can use the body movements and gestures in your oral interpretation performance.

Eye Focus

Although you usually look at the audience when performing, you may change this when you are portraying a character. **Eye focus** is where a performer looks while interpreting a piece of literature. Most interpreters show the difference between two or more characters by changing their eye focus. For example, you may look at one spot on the back wall when speaking as the first character, then shift your focus and look at a different spot when speaking as the second character. The audience should see your eyes and your head move slightly as you shift characters. You do not want to swing your head each time a new character speaks.

In the following figure you can see the way one interpreter places his characters from *Step On a Crack*. In figure A you see the placement when reading a scene with only the two women, Ellie and Lucille. In figure B you see the placement with the two women and Max. Because the two women are fighting for Max's attentions, Max is placed in the middle with the women on either side.

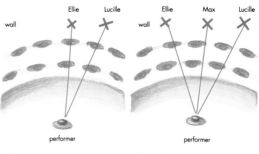

Figure A   Figure B

Apply

Pratice your eye focus using the two scenes.

Read aloud the following two short scenes from the play *No Problem* from Make It Live Productions. Melissa, a teenager from a wealthy family, struggles to gain attention from her parents. In the first scene she is talking with her mother; in the second scene she is shopping with her friend Meredith. If you wish to play male characters, you may write a similar set of situations from the male perspective.

Scene 1

Melissa: Shopping is a great way to relax and a great activity to do with friends. On a typical Saturday I go to the mall, have lunch, walk around, get a make-over, talk to friends, and try on the five-thousand-dollar dresses in the ritzy dress store on the top floor.

Mom: Melissa, remember, if you look good, you'll feel good!

Melissa: So, I started small...earrings. I have over two hundred pair. I try to pick up a new pair whenever I'm out.

Melissa, by this point, is out of her chair. Jennifer (as Melissa's mom) has moved into Melissa's chair and begins to apply makeup. Melissa gets her bag from the prop table and begins to exit.

Mom: Where are you going?

Melissa: Out!

Mom: You're not going anywhere. You're staying home with Max this afternoon. We discussed it last night.

Melissa: Mom...I told Meredith I'd meet her at the mall. I'll be home before dinner.

Mom: Well, you'll have to call her and tell her you can't make it.

Melissa: Why do I have to watch him?

Mom: Because I have an important meeting with a client and then your father and I have to be at that benefit downtown. (She turns to Melissa.) I thought I told you to throw those jeans away.

Melissa: They're my favorite pair.

Mom: Well, you look like a homeless person. What will people think?

Melissa: I don't care what people think!

Mom: Well, I do. Your father and I work too hard to have you traipsing around in ripped clothing.

Melissa: Fine Mom...I'll take them off!

Mom: Melissa, what has gotten into you lately? I don't know where you've picked up this attitude, but I will not tolerate it in my house. Do you understand?

Melissa: Fine.

Mom: Melissa, is there a problem?

(Pause.)

Melissa: Well. I just don't see why I have to watch Max all the time. I'm not his mother.

Mom: Because this is a family. You can order a pizza. I'll leave some money on the counter. (She freezes.)

Melissa: At the mall you can always get people to help you...to pay attention to you...They have to. It's their job....

Scene 2

(Melissa crosses to the prop table and picks up earrings.)

Melissa: Hey Mer', check out these earrings.

Meredith: Oh, Melissa, they're perfect. They're exactly what I need for my dress. Do you think they're real?

Melissa: Real? Let's see. (She bites them.)

Meredith: Melissa...

Melissa: What? This is how you figure out if they're real. You bite them.

Meredith: I don't think you're supposed to do that. You haven't paid for them.

Melissa: I have now. (She looks at imaginary sales clerk.)

Meredith: You can't buy a pair of $300 earrings.

Melissa: Who said anything about buying? (She puts them into Meredith's pocket.)

Meredith: Hey! Melissa!...

Melissa: Just act normal. Here he comes. (She speaks to imaginary salesclerk.) Oh, yes you can. Do you have those in silver? OK. We'll wait.

Meredith: If you want them, you take them!

Melissa: Fine. Whatever. You said you wanted to dress like me.

Meredith: I'll meet you outside.

Melissa: OK. (She watches Meredith leave, sit, and freeze. She puts the earrings into her pocket. To salesclerk.) No, I decided against that pair, they weren't what I wanted after all. I shop because in the mall I can be whatever I want, and that's very exciting.

PREPARING A PERFORMANCE SCRIPT

Several steps are necessary in the preparation of a performance script. First, you must arrange your literature pieces in the order in which you will perform them. Then you mark the pieces to reflect your thinking about how you plan to use your voice and body during performances. Finally, you create the actual script that you will use during your performance.

ORDERING THE PIECES

When performing several short pieces of literature, you need to put them in order to create the right mood or to keep your audience interested. For example, you could place a short story between two poems. Or you could shift moods by following up a sad piece with something funny. Take time to place your pieces in the order that will keep your listeners involved with the literature.

If you are preparing material for a class performance, you have great freedom in choosing, cutting, and arranging your pieces. If you are preparing for contest performance, you may have to follow stricter rules.

MARKING THE SCRIPT

After you have practiced various vocal and nonverbal techniques and have decided which are best for your selection, you will want to mark your script. **Marking the script** involves writing symbols that will help you to remember how to read the script. The following guidelines are just suggestions. You can devise your own system. The system itself is unimportant—what *is* important is that the marks you make on the script should help you remember how you want to read the selection.

SCRIPT MARKING GUIDELINES

PAUSES: Use one diagonal line (/) to show a pause; two diagonal lines (//) to show a longer pause.

EMPHASIS: Use solid underlining (___) to indicate words to be stressed; wavy line (∿) to underline words that need a special tone or special emphasis.

PRONUNCIATION: Write the letter x over a syllable that needs stress. (remember)

MOVEMENT: Write cue (*cue*) to show a special movement.

RATE: Use colors to show changes in pace.

In the following poem, a student has made oral interpretation markings on a poem written by a classmate.

Let's Go, Grandfather

impatient

Let's go, Grandfather!
I don't want to sit on the beach
anymore.
Do you hear me? //
Let's go back to the apartment
to see Grandma,

anticipation

so I can try on her false teeth
to see if they fit,

mischief

and so I can lock my jacket
in the bathroom, on purpose,
and make her pick the lock
with her hair pin.

move forward
bend over
stand up straight
read slower

Do you hear me grandfather?
Why don't you speak? //
Your silence scares me. /
And why did you fall over like that? //
And then the ambulance came,
but it was too late. /
He had been dead
for an hour.

—Carrie Kramer

INTERACT

Obtain a copy of Abraham Lincoln's Gettysburg Address. With a small group, mark it in two different ways and try out the effect of each performance.

CREATING THE STAGE SCRIPT

Once you know exactly what you are going to perform, type or write out the script. The script should be typed double-spaced or hand-written with a line of space between rows of words. The extra space will make the reading easier and help you later to mark the script.

Once the script is prepared, back it with dark construction paper or place it in a three-ring folder. Cut the script pages so you do not need to turn the page in the middle of a paragraph or verse of poetry. The end of a page should be where you pause in the script.

REHEARSING ORAL INTERPRETATION

I'll just read it over before I give it. It's not much work because all the words are there.

Often beginning interpreters believe the work stops after finding and analyzing the piece of literature. They think, "I can read. Why do I need any more preparation?" Just as in public speaking, rehearsal is a very important part of preparing a performance. Reading your script silently to yourself as you lie in bed the night before you give it is not an effective way to practice. You need to carefully order the ideas in your mind and polish your delivery. You also need to learn to relax. The more relaxed you are, the more confident your reading will be.

ORDERING THE PIECE IN YOUR MIND

As you prepare to perform, you must make sure you have the main ideas of the piece fixed in your mind. The following simple steps will help you do this:

1. Read your entire piece silently two or three times. Go straight through. Don't stop and start over, and don't go back over any section.
2. Repeat step 1, but this time read the piece aloud.
3. Now try to give your performance while looking up at regular times. Stand up. Practice gestures and movement. Work with your script. Follow your markings. Try to complete the entire piece. Remember, this is a rehearsal, so it doesn't matter if you make mistakes. It is important that you go through the entire piece without stopping.
4. Continue giving the entire performance until you can complete the piece with the planned vocal tones and body movements.

In this part of your rehearsal, you are working on getting a grasp of the meaning of the ideas in your material. You are also getting to know the piece well enough so that you can look at your listeners. When the ideas are fixed in your mind, you will not get confused during the actual performance.

POLISHING YOUR DELIVERY

Your preparation time will pay off in a fine performance. The following steps can help you polish your delivery. Be sure your first rehearsal is not also your actual performance.

1. Imagine your audience in your mind. Set up chairs in front of yourself, talk to a mirror, or have one or two friends listen to you.
2. Always practice aloud while standing to get used to gesturing and moving. Let your gestures flow from the literature—don't fake them.
3. Try to communicate with your real or imaginary audience. Look at your audience. Practice looking at each member.
4. If your practice audience is real rather than imaginary, adapt to your listeners. Watch for cues indicating a need to change your delivery. Ask your audience for feedback on points you can improve on and any movements you made that are effective.

5. Give special practice to the introduction and any words or dialogue that must be carefully performed. You may wish to memorize these sections so they sound exactly as you planned.
6. Try to record your performance on audiotape or videotape. That way you can hear or see exactly what your audience will hear or see.
7. Spread your rehearsal time over three or four days. If you wait until the last minute, you will only increase your nervousness. Leave yourself enough time so that you will be able to practice until you are comfortable.
8. Do not let your performance get stale. Vary your gestures, vocal tone, and facial expression. This will keep you thinking about the meaning of your piece.

PRACTICING RELAXATION

Before you perform your selections you may wish to use some relaxation techniques. These may help you feel less tense and more confident. Try some of the following to see which work for you.

1. Clench your fists tightly for a count of ten. Release and let your whole body go limp.
2. Take a deep breath and hold it for a count of ten. Let it all out at once, letting your body go completely loose and limp.
3. Breathing normally, let your muscles relax more and more as you let out each breath.
4. Let your head hang down so your chin almost touches your chest. *Slowly* rotate your head in a circle, one way and then the other. Do this two or three times.
5. Imagine yourself on a warm beach, in a hot bath, or anywhere that seems relaxing to you. Breathe slowly and deeply.

Not all relaxation techniques (or mental preparation techniques) work for everyone. Experiment. Try to find the methods that make you the best performer you can be.

TELLING A STORY

Whether you realize it or not, you are a storyteller. You tell stories every day. For example, when you tell your best friend about an argument you had with another friend, when you tell your brother about a movie you saw, or when you tell your parents about your day at school, you are telling a story. **Storytelling** is the art of reciting to an audience. Storytelling is different from oral interpretation because you do not use a script. Instead, you rely on your memory to get all of the events in the right order. Composer Janet L. Hudnut tells this story:

> I remember one of my first lessons in anger. I was playing the piano one day at about age ten. I had just started practicing for a "gig" as we call it, which means playing for pay. Evidently the piano wasn't doing what I thought it should, so I started banging on it. My father reprimanded me, whereupon I said to him, "I am an artist, and artists do this all the time." He said, "Honey, the rest of us in this house are not 'artists,' so if you continue to need to do this, the piano will need to be removed."

When you were smaller you may have heard many stories told to you at home or in school. These may have been fairy tales, fables, or stories adults made up. By now you may have told such stories to younger children. You may have told and listened to stories while sitting around a campfire at a Halloween party or while hanging around with friends.

Why is storytelling important? As one child says, "Life would be boring without stories." In addition, some authors suggest that the stories you tell communicate a lot about you to other people—what you believe, what you think is important, funny, or sad, what you value. Storytelling helps to increase your vocabulary and improve your critical thinking, speaking, and listening skills as well as your imagination.

To become an effective storyteller, you need to practice storytelling techniques, including learning stories and developing your delivery skill.

INTERACT

Think about the events of the past week. What incident stands out in your mind? What makes it memorable? Tell the incident to a friend.

STORYTELLING TECHNIQUES

You may wish to tell an original story or a story written by someone else. When choosing a story to tell, look for one that has a simple plot, suspense, excitement, simple language, a limited number of characters, and a single theme. Most importantly, choose a story that you really want to tell. You might look at some of the selections at the end of chapter 16 to get ideas for storytelling.

Most beginning storytellers try to memorize the story word for word. Memorizing a story word for word is not a good idea, because you can't make the story your own. When you tell a story—such as an incident from your day—to a friend, you don't tell it as if it is a speech you've committed to memory. You have an image of the event in your mind and a sequence of what happened. You create the words as you tell the story. The same idea applies when telling a story you have read. Remember the sequence of events and images created in your mind. The only words you might want to memorize are a repeated phrase (such as "Little pig, little pig, let me come in"). To make the story your own, you have to use your own words.

Learning Stories

When you are learning to tell a written story, follow these steps:

1. Read the story over several times.
2. Close the book and try to imagine the sequence of the story in your mind.
3. Open the book and read the story again, this time for the words that will add color to your telling. These include descriptive, concrete words that describe shape, color, and design.
4. Repeat the same process of imagining the story in your mind.
5. Now write out, draw, or outline the story (whatever works best for you).
6. Retell the story in your own words, out loud, so you can hear how it sounds.
7. Tell the story to a friend or record it.
8. Retell the story until you are pleased with your performance.

Tips for Storytelling

Now that you have prepared your story, it's time to tell it to an audience. As you speak, keep the following tips in mind:

1. *Capture your audience with a well-baited hook.* Make them eager to hear the story before you begin the telling. This can be accomplished by creating an interesting introduction. Here are some introductions other students have used:

   If you have trouble sleeping at night, maybe you'd better stop listening to this story right now....

   In China, people do things differently....

Once, long ago, before yesterdays, before used-to-be's, back in the days when wishing did some good....

2. *Be selective.* Remember, your audience wants to hear what happened. Choose words, events, and characters carefully, and don't get bogged down in lengthy description. The good storyteller remembers to keep it simple.

3. *Rapport with your listeners is everything!* Eye contact is essential. Each listener should feel that the story is being told just for him or her.

4. *Create images.* As a storyteller you must create vivid images in your mind if you want listeners to see them too. Visualize the pictures and people you are describing. Encourage your audience to imagine with all five senses how things feel, look, smell, taste, and sound.

5. *Use vocal variety.* Be sure to vary your vocal tone, rhythm, pitch, volume, and intensity. Use silences or pauses that will give your listeners time to imagine.

6. *Tell it with zest.* Enthusiasm is contagious. If you enjoy your story, your audience will too.

7. *Make sure your audience knows when you are finished.* Your conclusion might be as simple as, "And that, my friends, is the story of 'The Boastful Bullfrog,' " or as complex as, "If the story was beautiful, the beauty belongs to all of us; if it was not, the fault is only mine who told it."
8. *Use props, if appropriate, to tell your stories.* Puppets, music sound effects, posters, or objects that are mentioned in the story may be used to great effect. Be creative.

Remember, the most important thing about storytelling is that it should be fun. If you are enjoying yourself, your listeners will too.

EVALUATING ORAL INTERPRETATION AND STORYTELLING

The introduction did not prepare us for the piece. I understood Liza and Professor Higgins. I did not understand who the Pickering character was supposed to be.

Your use of a quiet tone and pauses really helped create the magic feeling of Terabithia.

Just as you learned to evaluate group discussions, public speaking, and debate, you need to be able to evaluate oral interpretation and storytelling performances. As a critic you need to look at how effectively the performer communicates the meaning of a piece of literature. The purpose of a *critique* is to provide feedback to help the interpreter improve the next performance. The feedback you give and receive will help you improve your performance. Review the guidelines in Chapter 13 to help you critique effectively.

CRITIQUE FORMS

Different forms are used to evaluate the performance of various types of literature. You may find it interesting to experiment with creating your own critique forms. The sample critique form can be used for evaluation of an oral interpretation or storytelling performance.

PERFORMANCE CRITIQUE FORM

Name _____

Title of Selection _____

Evaluate each point as **S**—Superior, **E**—Excellent, **G**—Good, or **F**—Fair.

_____ 1. **Choice of Selections** Is this selection appropriate to the speaker and occasion? Was the literature selected of high literary merit?

_____ 2. **Adequacy of Introduction** Did it give enough information about the author, time, place, characters, and action to arouse attention and interest? Was it compatible with the selection?

_____ 3. **Understanding** Did the interpreter appear to understand the feelings, thoughts, and attitudes of the dramatic speaker?

_____ 4. **Analysis** Did the interpreter appear to understand the theme, conflict, and characters of the piece?

_____ 5. **Bodily Action** Did the interpreter's gestures, posture, and facial expressions contribute to an understanding of the literature? Did any of the bodily actions distract from the meaning of the piece?

_____ 6. **Vocal Work** Did the interpreter's voice contribute to an understanding of the literature? Were words pronounced clearly and correctly?

_____ 7. **Communication** Did the interpreter communicate the thoughts, emotions, attitudes, and intentions of the dramatic speaker? Did he or she *share with* rather than *read to* the audience? Was there sufficient eye contact with listeners?

_____ 8. **Additional Comments** _____

_____

_____

_____

SUMMARY

This chapter focuses on the performance of oral interpretation and storytelling. When preparing performance materials, interpreters cut the literature selections and create introductions for them. Performers must use sense recall, voice, and body to bring literature to life. Oral interpreters arrange their pieces, mark their materials, and create scripts for performance use. Rehearsal includes practicing to ensure both a total understanding of the material and a polished delivery. Storytellers try to create visual images in their listeners' minds. They select stories they wish to tell and learn them without actually memorizing. They work to engage the audience through their energy, language, and special techniques. Giving and receiving feedback helps improve both oral interpretation and storytelling performances.

CHAPTER REVIEW

THINK ABOUT IT

1. When cutting a piece of literature for oral interpretation, what are some things you might delete?
2. List the steps for preparing a script for oral interpretation.
3. What are the characteristics of a good introduction?
4. What are the steps necessary to order the selection in your mind?
5. What are some of the tips for storytelling?
6. What is the purpose of an oral interpretation or storytelling evaluation?

TRY IT OUT

1. Recite the alphabet, creating a happy mood by using only your voice. Recite it again, creating a sad or angry mood with your voice.
2. Use only facial expressions to create three different moods. Next use only posture to create the same three moods. Have class members identify the moods you are creating.
3. Choose a piece of literature you would like to interpret. Then cut the piece as necessary, write an introduction, and mark the script. Present the piece you prepared to the class. Use your body, gestures, voice, facial expressions, and eye focus to help you interpret the literature.
4. Work with a partner to discover many ways to present the same piece of literature. Each person should prepare a sample introduction, mark one copy of the script, and make any necessary cuts. Perform your versions for each other. Then combine your efforts and create a new presentation based on the best parts of each of your works.

PUT IT IN WRITING

1. Make journal entries listing suggestions and compliments you have received on the oral interpretations you have presented in class. At the end of the unit on oral interpretation, write a short paper that analyzes how you improved in your performance abilities.
2. In your journal, keep a record of your rehearsal techniques. Write a short paper in which you discuss which rehearsed techniques worked most effectively for you and which techniques did not help you. Make note in your journal of those techniques that worked best for you.

SPEAK ABOUT IT

1. Listen to an oral interpretation performance outside the classroom, such as a child's story record, a religious reading, or a professional performance. Describe and evaluate the effectiveness of the performance for your class.
2. Present an oral critique of a classmate's oral interpretation.
3. In groups of four perform pieces you prepared previously for a partner. Take turns being listeners and performers. The listeners should use an evaluation form to rate each performance and give constructive criticism to the performer.

CHAPTER 18

GROUP INTERPRETATION

KEY WORDS

choral speaking

offstage focus

reader's theatre

script patterns

suggestion

After completing this chapter, you should be able to

- define *group interpretation*, *choral speaking*, and *reader's theatre*.
- list standards for selecting material for choral speaking and reader's theatre.
- describe a variety of performance techniques for choral speaking and reader's theatre.
- prepare and perform a choral speaking presentation.
- prepare and perform a reader's theatre presentation.
- evaluate group interpretation performances.

The Adventures of Isabel

Group 1 { Isabel met an enormous bear
Isabel, Isabel, didn't care.

Group 2 { The bear was hungry, the bear was ravenous,
The bear's big mouth was cruel and cavernous.
The bear said, Isabel, glad to meet you,
How do, Isabel, now I'll eat you!

Group 1 { Isabel, Isabel, didn't worry
Isabel didn't scream or scurry.
She washed her hands and she straightened her hair up,

All   Then Isabel quietly ate the bear up.

—Ogden Nash

For centuries, human voices have been raised in choruses of song and speech. Group singing is more common than group speaking. You may not have spoken in groups, but probably you have sung in groups since you were a small child. Many pieces of literature can best be brought to life through group interpretation.

This chapter introduces two types of group interpretation, choral speaking and reader's theatre. You will be able to use your preparation and performance skills to work creatively in a group.

CHORAL SPEAKING

Choral speaking is speaking in unison. Speakers blend and combine their individual voices to create a group voice. Good choral speaking involves more than saying the correct words at the same time. Choral speakers create a special type of performance to help listeners experience a piece of literature. Choral speaking works well with literature that has a strong rhythm. For this reason, choral speaking groups frequently perform poetry.

Like the voices in a singing group, voices in a choral speaking group have different ranges. In a school choir, there may be soprano, alto, tenor, and bass voices. In a choral speaking group, the voices may be clustered into high, medium, and low; male and female; or some other way. When choral speakers perform, they hold their scripts much like choir members hold their musical arrangements. When performing, the speakers stand, or sit on stools facing an audience.

Choral speaking has many benefits. It allows you to improve your oral interpretation skills within a group and increase your self-confidence as a performer. Also, it is an enjoyable way to learn more about literature and interpretation. To become a choral speaker, you need to understand how to create script patterns, select the material, use performance techniques, and critique choral speaking.

CREATING SCRIPT PATTERNS

Script patterns are the ways in which the speakers' parts are divided. Imagine that you are planning a performance by a group of five speakers. They will do an interpretation of the following lines taken from Ecclesiastes 1:1–8, a well-known piece of biblical literature:

1 To everything there is a season,
and a time to every purpose under
the heaven.

2 A time to be born, and a time
to die;

3 A time to plant, and a time
to pluck that which is planted;

4 A time to kill, and a time to heal;

5 A time to break down, and a time
to build up;

6 A time to weep, and a time to
laugh;

7 A time to mourn, and a time to
dance;

8 A time to cast away stones, and a
time to gather stones together;

9 A time to embrace, and a time to
refrain from embracing;

10 A time to get, and a time to lose;

11 A time to keep, and a time to cast
away;

12 A time to rend, and a time to sew;

13 A time to keep silent, and a time to
speak;

14 A time to love, and a time to hate;

15 A time of war, and a time of peace;

16 To everything there is a season,
and a time to every purpose under the heaven.

How would you divide the work of the speakers? Would you have all five voices say everything or would you let the speakers take turns? Depending on your script pattern, there are several ways to divide these lines. Here are some of the possibilities:

1. *Everyone speaks in unison.* All voices move through a piece together.

2. *Each person in the group reads one line.* If the piece is long, the first speaker starts the pattern again. For example, if there are five readers for Ecclesiastes, person 1 reads lines 1, 6, and 11, plus the last line. Person 2 reads lines 2, 7, and 12, plus the last line. And so on. Everyone reads the last line.

3. *One person reads the first line or section; a second person reads the second line or section with the first person; and so on until everyone is reading in unison.* For example, since the full Ecclesiastes piece has sixteen lines, person 1 speaks the opening three lines, persons 1 and 2 the next three lines, and so on. The closing line is recited by the entire group.

4. *One person or group reads a line or section.* Another person or group responds. For example, in the Ecclesiastes piece, two groups respond to each other dividing each line. Group 1 says, "A time to be born." Group 2 responds, "A time to die."

5. *Several persons have solos and then are joined by the group.* Individuals speak, and then the whole group speaks. If the piece is long, this can be repeated several times. In the Ecclesiastes example, individual speakers might perform the first half of each line and the group could speak the rest in unison.

As you can see, there are many different ways to create a group script. Usually the entire group speaks together at some time during the performance.

Look at the following examples of speaking scripts for a chorus of voices:

A Goblin Lives in Our House

Solo 1: A goblin lives in our house
High voices: in our house,
Low voices: in our house,
Unison: A goblin lives in our house all the year round.
Solo 2: He bumps
Solo 3: And he jumps
Solo 4: And he thumps
Solo 5: And he stumps
Solo 6: He knocks
Solo 7: And he rocks
Solo 8: And he rattles at the locks.
Solo 1: A goblin lives in our house.
Low voices: in our house,
High voices: in our house,
Unison: A goblin lives in our house all the year round.

—From the French,
adapted by Louise Abney

Battle Won Is Lost

Unison: They said, "You are no longer a lad."
Solo 1: I nodded.
Unison: They said, "Enter the council lodge."
Solo 2: I sat.
Unison: They said, "Our lands are at stake."
Solo 3: I scowled.
Unison: They said, "We are at war."
Solo 4: I hated.
Unison: They said, "Prepare red war symbols."
Solo 5: I painted.
Unison: They said, "Count coups."
Solo 6: I scalped.
Unison: They said, "You'll see friends die."
Solo 7: I cringed.
Unison: They said, "Desperate warriors fight best."
Solo 8: I charged.
Unison: They said, "Some will be wounded."
Solo 1: I bled.
Unison: They said, "To die is glorious."
Solo 2: They lied.

—Phil George

INTERACT

With four or five classmates, select a piece of your choice and plot out a speaker script. Then do a reading for the class and explain the reasons for plotting out your script the way you did.

SELECTING MATERIAL

Some literature demands to be read by a group in unison rather than by a lone voice. The group reading will make the meaning more easily understood. To select and analyze literature for choral speaking, follow the same guidelines as you did for oral interpretation in Chapter 16. In addition, literature for choral speaking must have these three qualities: strong rhythm, variety of moods, and a strong theme.

Rhythm

In choral speaking the strong rhythm of the literature is extremely important. The rhythm helps keep the group members speaking together whenever necessary. The poem "Miss Bitter" contains strong rhythm and should be spoken at a quick pace, conveying humor.

Miss Bitter

Sister Bitter
(baby-sitter
Violet Amanda Bitter)
loved to sit,
but, rather sadly,
though the babies
loved her madly,
though they loved her
every bit,
never got
a chance to sit
since they found her
with her knitting
since the day
they found her, sitting
knitting on the baby's knee,
having buttered toast and tea.
When they cried:
"AMANDA BITTER"
Most outrageous baby-sitter
"BITTER! You get off that knee!"
She inquired:
"Want some tea?"

—N. M. Bodecker

Variety of Moods

The changes in mood in a piece of literature can be shown by the use of different types of voices. For example, a serious part may be spoken by low voices, while a playful part may be performed by high voices. Not all poems have strong mood changes, but some variety within a poem is necessary for good choral speaking.

Theme

When a group performs, the audience is watching and listening to a number of people at work. Therefore, the message must not be too complex or difficult to find. In some literature the theme is hidden, and the reader must search for the author's clues to bring it out. Sometimes an individual interpreter may be able to share such a theme with listeners, but in group performance, a hidden theme could be totally lost. Unless material is direct, the listeners will become confused.

Read the following poem and try to identify its theme. How would you emphasize the theme in choral speaking?

Jigsaw Puzzle

My beautiful picture of pirates and treasure
Is spoiled, and almost I don't want to start
To put it together; I've lost all the pleasure
I used to find in it: there's one missing part.

I know there's one missing—they lost it, the others,
The last time they played with my puzzle—and maybe
There's more than one missing: along with the brothers
And sisters who borrow my toys there's the baby.

There's a hole in the ship or the sea that it sails on,
And I said to my father, "Well, what shall I do?
It isn't the same now that some of it's gone."
He said, "Put it together; the world's like that too."

—Russell Hoban

INTERACT

Work with a partner to create a choral speaking script. From an anthology of poetry, select three pieces you think would work well for choral speaking. Create a script pattern for one of the poems.

TECHNIQUES FOR CHORAL SPEAKING

As a choral speaker, you will use many of the performance techniques you learned in Chapter 17. To be an effective choral speaker, you must also know how to perform well as a group and how to speak precisely, use scripts, and use space.

Speaking Precisely

Choral speaking requires teamwork. Like members of a basketball team, marching band, or cheerleading squad, the members of a choral speaking group must cooperate if the group is to meet its goal. Choral speaking takes team effort. When people speak together, they have to start and stop at the same time, pronounce words in the same way, and speak clearly. They also have to learn to speak with the same rhythms and speech patterns, all of which takes a great deal of practice.

Using Scripts

In your mind, picture four performers standing in a row. Person 1 is reading from his notebook. Person 2 is reading from her poetry book. Person 3 is holding a crumpled piece of paper but never looks at it. Person 4 reads from three note cards. What picture does this present to an audience?

To present a group image, all performers must handle their scripts in the same way. Most choral speaking groups back their scripts with construction paper or place them in large folders. Usually each speaker knows the piece well and only needs to glance at the script rather than read it. When scripts are used they should be raised and lowered, and opened and closed, by all members of the group at the same time. Sometimes a group memorizes the literature it will perform and

appears without scripts. This allows the group to move more easily.

Using Space

Each member of a performing group needs to be aware of where individuals are placed and how they move. Sometimes the group sits or stands in a line in front of the audience, and often speakers with similar voices are placed together. In a large group, the stronger voices may be placed in the back and the softest voices in the front. The individuals who do solo speaking may step out in front of the group when performing.

The performance starts as the group enters the performance space. For this reason, members should plan an organized entrance and exit.

Usually the group members remain standing or sitting next to each other. If the literature contains action, the group may sway, point, wave their arms, or perform other movements to get a message across. Often groups who perform for children will use movement to help keep the children's attention. Think about how a group of six might move to each of the following sets of lines.

Set A
And he huffed,
and he puffed,
and he blew the house down.

Set B
Double Dutch
Double Dutch
Ropes beat sidewalks clean.
Feet are jumping
Arms are pumping
One minute!
That's my dream.

CRITIQUING CHORAL SPEAKING

Your voice was so loud it kept distracting me.

Be sure to keep your scripts at about the same level. I could not see Carol's face, and Nathan's script was moving up and down.

As a critic or listener, you may be called upon to give feedback on choral speaking performances. The techniques you learned in Chapter 17 for critiquing interpretation apply to choral speaking. In addition, you will want to consider criteria that relate specifically to group work. You might find the sample group critique form useful in providing helpful feedback to performers.

GROUP CRITIQUE FORM

	Always	Sometimes	Never
Voice			
Members' voices blended in unison.			
Members started and stopped together.			
Members pronounced words in the same way.			
Members varied vocal tone to show meaning.			
Body			
Members adapted facial expressions to the material.			
Members moved in unison.			
Members looked at listeners regularly.			
Members entered and exited in unison.			
Scripts (if used)			
Members held scripts in similar ways.			
Members' faces could be seen over their scripts.			
Material/Script Patterns			
Material was appropriate to the audience.			
Choice of script pattern helped communicate the meaning.			

READER'S THEATRE

Reader's theatre is a type of group interpretation in which speakers present literature in a dramatic form. But instead of acting out the literature as in a play, the speakers suggest the characters by using their voices, facial expressions, and some gestures. Reader's theatre may be performed using many kinds of literature, including short stories, plays, poetry, parts of novels, or material from newspapers or magazines. Reader's theatre brings many kinds of literature alive in creative ways. Although there are guidelines for performing reader's theatre, performers are encouraged to experiment with different ways to reach the audience.

The following short example shows how a piece of prose fiction might be scripted for a reader's theatre production. You can see how a speaker provides the narration; others provide the dialogue.

Narrator: Amanda shuffled to the front of the room avoiding the glances and snickers from those around her. She stared stone-faced at her unlaced shoes.

Speaker 2: Amanda.

Narrator: Ms. Parsons said, wagging her finger.

Speaker 2: How many times must I remind you fighting will not be tolerated in this class?

Narrator: Keith, hiding behind his history book, snickered.

Speaker 3: Here we go again. This girl is on her way out. We did it.

Narrator: Amanda looked at her shoes as if tying them with her eyes.

Speaker 2: Young lady. Have you nothing to say for yourself?

Narrator: Continued a frustrated Ms. Parsons. Amanda sniffled. A large tear, brimmed on her lower eyelid, spilled onto her cheek.

Speaker 4: No, ma'am.

Narrator: She whispered. Keith fell out of his chair laughing. At this, Ms. Parsons turned to him.

As you can tell, in this example each person speaks one character's part of the dialogue. The narrator provides additional information to help the audience understand exactly what is happening.

To perform and appreciate reader's theatre, you need to understand the use of suggestion, performance techniques, selection of material, and ways to evaluate reader's theatre performances.

SUGGESTION

Reader's theatre is sometimes called "theatre of the mind," because the action and scenery are created in the audience's mind, not on the stage. The key to this creation process is called suggestion. **Suggestion** is the way speakers create most of the action, props, and scenery in the audience's imagination through their performance skills. Imagine the scene with Amanda in the classroom. The reader who plays Amanda will not actually walk forward to show the meaning of the dialogue. She will remain in her place within the group of readers and look down. The reader who plays Keith may hold his script in front of his face to represent the history book.

Action in a play would be different. In a play, the actor playing Amanda would actually shuffle to the front of the room, and the actor playing Keith would hold a real history book. The use of suggestion in reader's theatre forces the audience members to use their imaginations. They may have to imagine a car chase or a funeral or a farmhouse in a tornado. The performers will suggest these scenes but will not play them out as they would in a theatre production. Reader's theatre performers do not *become* the characters; they only *suggest* the characters.

TECHNIQUES FOR READER'S THEATRE

The performance techniques of reader's theatre help performers to create this suggestion for the audience. These techniques include scripting, staging, eye focus, movement, and technical support.

Scripting

Usually one or two people act as narrators for reader's theatre. They also may read the parts of minor characters if there are not enough other performers. Although one speaker usually speaks for the same character, there may be times when all the performers become a crowd or perform the same motion, even if not all the characters are involved. For example, when performing the sentence, "Adam stepped back as the track team raced by," the person playing Adam may sit back on his stool while the rest of the cast may pump their arms to pantomime running by.

Staging

The most common way of staging reader's theatre is to have the characters sit on stools in a line or semicircle facing the audience. Sometimes the stools may be arranged on platforms in various positions. The staging is always simple. Usually the performers use scripts, although sometimes they perform from memory. All characters remain onstage during the performance. If an important character leaves or dies, that speaker could hang his or her head down or turn his or her back to the audience. If the character reenters, he or she can look up or turn toward the audience. In most productions, the cast members do not enter or exit.

Eye Focus

During most reader's theatre performances, the cast members look toward the audience. The readers may look somewhere over the heads of the audience, perhaps at a spot on the back wall.

Another technique is called **offstage focus.** When using offstage focus, the speakers pretend there is a mirror behind the audience and that they are all reflected in it. When characters speak to each other, they speak to the imagined reflection. For example, when the second speaker, Ms. Parsons, talks to speaker 4, Amanda, she will look at the imagined reflection of Amanda on the back wall.

Even during a dialogue, the speakers usually look out over the audience. On occasion, characters will look at each other. During an important romantic scene or argument, two characters may talk directly to each other.

Movement

Usually reader's theatre involves little movement. The audience is to picture the movement in their minds. The speakers might suggest or pantomime some movement using changes in facial expressions, gestures, and posture. In our classroom scene, the speaker playing Keith will not try to fall out of the chair but will lean to one side. Mrs. Parsons will waggle her finger.

If important movement involves two characters, you can see them react to each other. If the script says, "Keith pulled Amanda's braid," Keith will pantomime a yanking action, and Amanda will grasp her head and gasp.

Offstage Focus

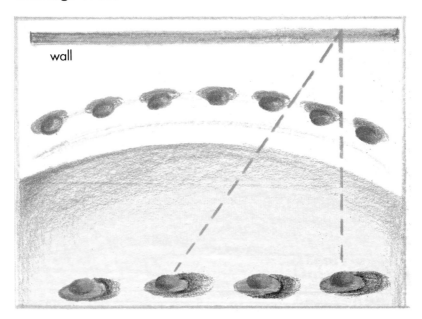

wall

Technical Support

Reader's theatre can be performed with very little technical support. Cast members rely on simple costumes, a few well-chosen props, lighting, or music to help create the suggestion. Scenery is rarely used. The cast usually performs in front of a curtain or solid-colored wall.

Cast members often wear well-coordinated everyday clothes, such as white shirts and dark pants. Special touches can be added. For example, a farmer may wear a straw hat, or a basketball player may wear a team jersey. Props are seldom used, but if the piece being performed calls for a particular prop, such as a book or an umbrella, it may be used.

Lighting and music also help create the suggestion for the audience. Turning lights on and off can mark the beginning and end of a scene. In stage productions, spotlights might move from one speaker to another for dramatic effect. Sometimes a slide projector is used to create pictures behind the performers. Music and sound effects may be added. However, reader's theatre performances should not rely too much on technical support. Such support must never limit the audience's imagination.

INTERACT

Find a copy of the book *The Little Prince,* by Antoine de Saint-Exupéry, from the library. In groups of four, discuss how you might stage a production of thirty to forty lines of this literature with five performers. In your plan, pay careful attention to who will speak, how your cast members will be arranged, the important character movement, and eye focus. You need not worry about technical support.

SELECTING LITERATURE

When performing reader's theatre, you may use one long piece of literature or several short pieces. When selecting literature for reader's theatre, you need to look for strong characters, a strong theme, picturesque language, and clear conflict.

Characters

Characters must stand out in reader's theatre. The audience must create these people in their minds. Therefore, characters must be easily pictured and remembered. Whether it's because of her language or because of her spunk, Anne of Green Gables stands out as a strong character. Look for pieces with dialogue. This will make the material more interesting for the audience.

Look at the strong characters in the following scene from the play *Step On a Crack.*

Ellie: *(Tentatively.)* Hey Pop. tell me about my real mother.

Max: How come you want to hear about her all the time these days?

(Ellie sits at his feet and rests against his knees.)

Ellie: I just do. Hey do you remember the time it was my birthday and you brought Mom home from the hospital, and I didn't know she was coming that time? I remember I was already in bed and you guys wanted to surprise me. She just came into my room, kissed me goodnight and tucked me in, just like it was any other night.

Max: *(Moved)* How could you remember that? You were just four years old.

Ellie: I just remember.

Max: Your mother was a wonderful person and I loved her very much.

Ellie: As much as you...like Lucille?

Max: Ellie.

Ellie: Was she pretty?

Max: She was beautiful.

Ellie: Do I look like her?

Max: Naw, you look more like me, you mug.

Ellie: *(Suddenly angry)* Why does everything have to change?

Max: Hey.

Ellie: How come Lucille is always so neat and everything? I bet she never even burps.

Max: She does.

Ellie: HUH!

Max: I heard her once.

Ellie: Do you think I'd look cute with makeup on?

Max: You? You're just a kid.

Ellie: But Lucille wears makeup. Lots of it.

Max: Well, she's grown up.

Ellie: Hey, do you know how old she is?

Max: Sure. Thirty-five.

Ellie: How come you married such an old one?

Max: That's not old.

Ellie: Huh!

Max: Why, I am older than that myself.

Ellie: You are?

Max: Ellie, you know how you get to go to camp in the summer. You get to go away all by yourself.

Ellie: Yeah, but I'm not going anymore.

Max: You're not?

Ellie: Nope, look what happened the last time I went. You and Lucille got to be good friends, then as soon as I got back, you got married. Who knows, if I go away again I might get back and find out you moved to Alaska.

Max: We wouldn't do that.

Ellie: You might.

Max: Ellie, kids can't always go where parents go. Sometimes parents go away all by themselves.

Ellie: How come ever since you got married I am such a kid. You never used to say I was a kid. We did everything together. Now all I hear is, "Kids can't do this." "Kids can't do that." "Kids have to go to bed at eight-thirty." "Kids have to clean up their rooms." Why does everything have to change?

Max: Nothing's changed. I still love you the same. Now there's just two of us who love you.

Ellie: HUH!

Max: I just wish you'd try a little harder to...

Ellie: To like Lucille? Why should I? She doesn't like me. She likes cute little girls who play with dollies.

Max: Well she got herself a messy little mug that likes junk.

          (Ellie pulls away.)

Max: I'm just kidding. She likes you fine the way you are.

Ellie: Oh yeah, well I don't like her.

Max: Why not?

          (Lucille enters and overhears the following.)

Ellie: 'Cause...'Cause...'Cause she's a wicked stepmother....*(Ellie giggles in spite of herself.)*

Theme

In order to hold an audience's interest, your literature must have a strong theme. Listeners should be able to identify the theme easily and follow it throughout the piece. If the theme is hidden, it will be difficult to bring it to the audience through reader's theatre.

Language

Performers of reader's theatre rely on picturesque language to help create their suggestion. The language must be descriptive and exciting to hold the audience's interest. It must create mental pictures for the listener.

Conflict

The best scenes for reader's theatre show conflict. It may be conflict within a person, between people, or between a person and the environment. The conflict holds the audience's attention. It makes people listen to find out how the conflict is resolved.

You can see a good example of person-to-person conflict in the story *The Field*.

The Field

Once there was a great field. At one edge of the field, there were trees and bushes and on the other a thin country road that curved about untraveled for many miles.

In the field were rocks, high gray piles of stone, good for the climbing, hiding, and exploring games of children.

In the middle of the field there was a tree, a single tree that had been growing for more than a hundred years. It was gnarled and its branches spread in many directions. The children from the neighboring villages would use the tree for home base in their games of tag and hide-and-go-seek.

The field lay just between the Kingdoms of Aura and Ghent. Both kings claimed the field even though it was bare except for the rocks and the tree and the children who played in it.

"Mine," said the King of Aura, politely.

"Mine," answered the King of Ghent in a louder voice.

Then the people of both countries began to say ugly things about each other.

And soon two armies gathered—one on each side of the field.

The battle began. The Aurians were camped by the bushes and the trees, and the Ghentians were over on the other side of the road.

In the tree in the middle of the field a robin had built her nest of twigs and grass. She had woven it together and now the nest hidden by the summer leaves held three blue eggs. Carefully, the mother sat on her eggs even though the arrows whizzed past the tree and the shotguns made sounds of thunder and there was the sound of screaming when soldiers were hurt or frightened. The bird stayed on her nest although there was crying and singing and shouting as the men moved up to the foot of the tree and then retreated.

One morning when the soldiers were starting to shoot at each other again, the robin flew down to the grass and unearthed a worm. As she pulled it from the soil, the guns pounded the ground and the soldiers moved up and down, hiding and crawling in the thick grass, and there was smoke in the air and blood on the rocks where the children had played.

As the robin was flying back to her nest an arrow with a sharp tip flew past the crouching soldiers and pierced the throat of the bird. Her wings fluttered for a moment and then she fell like a heavy stone. Only one soldier saw her fall.

Then a shell from the king's prize cannon boomed across the field and landed not far from the tree.

The earth shook and the tree trembled and the branches wavered and the nest with the three small eggs fell down to the ground.

The young soldier watched the nest fall. He crawled over the rocks and the twigs and found the three small eggs unbroken. Not even a crack was on the shells.

The soldier put his shotgun down on the ground. He took off his iron gray helmet, and turning it over, he filled it with grass and a dandelion and some clover. He carefully placed the nest in the matted grass and cradled the helmet in his arms. He sat for a while watching the eggs in his helmet.

The commanding officer came by and saw one of his soldiers sitting down.

"Come on soldier, let's go...put your helmet on."

The young man, carrying his helmet, reached for his gun and started forward.

"Put your helmet on," the officer shouted.

There was a pause as the soldier looked down at the eggs.

"I can't, sir," he said.

"There's no such thing as can't in this man's army," yelled the officer. "Put your helmet on your head."

The soldier put down his gun.

"I think," he said in a very quiet voice, "I think I'm going home now, sir."

The commanding officer turned red in the face but the young man, carefully holding his helmet under his arm, turned around and walked off the field, past the bushes and trees.

On his way home the three eggs broke open and three small wet birds opened their tiny beaks for food. The soldier stopped. He gathered some berries from a nearby bush and offered them gently to each bird in turn. The soldier smiled. Then the birds settled down, resting on one another, and fell asleep.

—Anne Roiphe

INTERACT

Prepare the story "The Field" for a reader's theatre performance for four to six speakers. Present it for the class.

CRITIQUING READER'S THEATRE

The commanding officer and the young soldier were talking at the same time.

There needs to be more use of facial expression to show emotions.

As a critic or listener, you may be called upon to give feedback after a reader's theatre performance. As with public speaking, effective feedback can help performers improve their skills. You may find the reader's theatre critique form useful in your evaluations.

READER'S THEATRE CRITIQUE FORM

Group members _____

_____

_____

Title of selection _____

	Always	Sometimes	Never

Voice

Members blended in unison when appropriate _____ _____ _____

Voices could be distinguished from each other easily _____ _____ _____

Character voices remained the same thoughout the performance _____ _____ _____

Effective use of stress, pause, inflection, pitch, and volume _____ _____ _____

Body

Members adapted facial expressions to the material _____ _____ _____

Members moved in unison when appropriate _____ _____ _____

Members looked at listeners regularly _____ _____ _____

Members entered and exited in unison _____ _____ _____

Scripts (if used)

Members held scripts in similar ways _____ _____ _____

Members' faces could be seen over scripts _____ _____ _____

Material

Material was suitable to the audience _____ _____ _____

Material was well scripted to show meaning _____ _____ _____

Material was suited to reader's theatre _____ _____ _____

Theme was communicated clearly _____ _____ _____

Staging

Costumes, props, and lights supported theme _____ _____ _____
Characters were consistently placed on wall by
speakers _____ _____ _____

Movement held the interest of the audience _____ _____ _____

SUMMARY

This chapter introduces group interpretation by discussing choral speaking and reader's theatre. To create a choral speaking performance, you need to be able to create script patterns using voices in different ways, and to select material that works well in group reading. As a performer you need to know how to speak precisely, use the scripts, and use space. Finally you need to be able to critique choral speaking. To create a reader's theatre performance, you need to understand the use of suggestion. You also need to know the performance techniques of scripting, staging, eye focus, movement, and technical support. You must select your material carefully and know how to critique reader's theatre. Group interpretation will help you develop self-confidence, performance and analysis skills, and literary knowledge. It is an exciting way to approach literature.

CHAPTER REVIEW

THINK ABOUT IT

1. Define *choral speaking* and *reader's theatre.*
2. What three criteria should you use for choosing a choral speaking selection?
3. List three criteria for selecting literature for a reader's theatre performance.
4. Why is reader's theatre called "the theater of the mind"?
5. Describe three performance techniques used in choral speaking and three used in reader's theatre.

TRY IT OUT

1. With a small group of classmates, choose several pieces of literature appropriate for a group of elementary school children. You might use a book by Dr. Seuss or a group of poems by Shel Silverstein. Discuss why the literature is appropriate for choral speaking. Use the selection criteria discussed in this chapter.
2. In small groups brainstorm themes for a reader's theatre presentation. Possible ideas might include world peace and growing up. Also brainstorm pieces of literature that could be used with each theme.
3. Cut and adapt a short story or a one-act play for reader's theatre. Rehearse and present the piece in class.

PUT IT IN WRITING

1. Choose a piece of literature for choral speaking or for reader's theatre. Analyze the literature according to the appropriate criteria discussed in the text. Explain why you believe the piece of literature would work well for reader's theatre or choral speaking. Also, describe what performance techniques you would use in presenting it. For example, would you use technical support? Include your analysis in your journal.
2. After performing a group interpretation, write a paper in which you discuss the performance techniques you used and how well they worked. For example, how did your group use space? How might the techniques change if you were to do the performance again?

SPEAK ABOUT IT

1. Critique a choral speaking or reader's theatre performance given by your classmates. Use one of the forms in this chapter or create one of your own. Share your critique orally with the performers. Be sure to follow the guidelines discussed in this unit.
2. Choose one of the script patterns discussed in this chapter and use it for a piece of literature you chose from number 1 of the Try It Out. Rehearse the choral speaking script with your group, and present it to an elementary classroom. Explain choral speaking to your audience.

GLOSSARY

acquaintances: persons whom one knows but who are not close friends.

adjournment: closing of a meeting.

affirmative: in debate, the side that argues in favor of an issue or change.

agenda: list of subjects to be discussed at a meeting.

amendment: proposed change in a parliamentary motion.

argument: conversation in which two or more people express different points of view on a topic.

articulators: tongue, teeth, jaw, hard and soft palate, and lips, which form sound into words.

audience analysis: information about the audience that helps the speaker communicate with the members. It includes basic data, beliefs, and attitudes.

audience goal: speaker's description of what the listeners should be able to do after the speech is completed.

audiovisual aids: nonverbal supporting materials, such as graphs and diagrams, that help the speaker make his or her points more clearly and interest the audience.

bandwagon appeal: type of faulty reasoning that suggests a person should do something because everyone else is doing it.

brainstorming: group discussion technique in which as many ideas as possible are listed aloud before group members give feedback to the ideas.

brief: outline of a debate case, containing arguments and evidence.

buzz group: small groups of audience members that discuss problems and report solutions to the larger group.

by-laws rules that govern the procedures to be followed by a group.

call previous question: move to an immediate vote within parliamentary procedure.

card stacking: type of faulty reasoning that involves the piling up of information with very little support in favor of an idea.

case: all the arguments that will be made to support the affirmative or negative position.

cause-effect reasoning: suggests that one event produces a second event.

chairperson: name for the person who leads a meeting.

channel: means by which a message is transmitted.

choral speaking: type of group interpretation in which speakers blend and combine their voices to create a group voice.

clarity: clearness of a speaker's words.

clique: subgroup whose members tend to "stick" together and avoid other people.

committee: subgroup of a larger group, formed to carry out a specific task.

communication: process of sending and receiving messages to share meaning.

487

communication acts: major reasons for communicating. They are: to share information, discuss feelings, manage persuasion, follow social rituals, and use imagination.

communication strategies: verbal and nonverbal messages created to reach a specific goal.

competency steps: course of action that competent communicators follow. They are: thinking of strategies, selecting a strategy, acting on the strategy, and evaluating the strategy's effect.

competent communicator: person who develops a number of strategies for dealing with communication situations and follows the competencey steps to become more effective.

conclusion: final part of a speech that summarizes the main points, reminds the audience of the goal, and provides a clear ending.

conflict: a person's struggle with other individuals, nature, a hostile environment, or the self.

connected information: new information that is related to information the audience already knows.

connotative meaning: emotional or personal response to a word.

constitution: document that describes the nature and purpose of a group.

constructive criticism: feedback that tells a speaker what worked well, what could be improved, and how to improve.

context: setting and people that surround a message.

creative listening: type of listening in which one uses active imagination to interpret a message.

criteria: standards that a solution has to meet in order to be acceptable.

critic: person who judges or evaluates.

critical listening: type of listening in which one examines a persuasive message and makes decisions about the findings.

critique: formal feedback given by a critic to a performer.

cutting the literature: shortening material for oral interpretation without drastically changing its meaning.

debate: speech competition of spoken arguments between individuals or teams with rules, time limits, and a winner and loser.

deductive reasoning: using a general idea to reach conclusions about very specific instances.

delivery: way in which a speaker uses voice and body to present a speech. It includes speaker confidence, methods of delivery, personal delivery, rehearsing the speech, and use of audiovisual aids.

denotative meaning: dictionary meaning of a word.

diaphragm: muscle that separates the chest from the abdominal cavity.

dramatic speaker: voice that is heard telling the story or poem during a reading. Often, the dramatic speaker is one of the main characters in the literary material.

empathic listening: type of listening that involves listening to another's feelings

empathy: ability to put oneself in another person's place to understand what that person is feeling.

ethical decisions: choices that have to do with questions of right and wrong.

evaluating: third step in the listening process in which a listener examines the message and makes a judgment.

extemporaneous method: delivery in which the speaker uses a prepared outline but does not plan each word or sentence.

external barriers: situations in the environment that keep listeners from paying attention to the speaker.

eye focus: where a performer looks while interpreting a piece of literature.

fact: information based on evidence that can be proved or disproved.

faulty reasoning: incorrect or false reasoning.

feedback: other people's responses to a message that let the speaker know how he or she is doing.

first meetings: beginning stages of developing a relationship.

floor: name for the "right to speak" in parliamentary procedure.

flow sheet: in debate, a diagram of the arguments, listed in parallel columns across a page.

formal feedback: planned comments (written or oral) intended to affect the speaker's next speech.

forum: discussion in which the audience participates.

gestures: movements of the head, shoulders, hands, or arms that speakers use to describe or emphasize a point.

glittering generalities: type of faulty reasoning that is not supported with specific information and is not linked to the main point.

group: small number of people who share a common purpose or interest, communicate easily and regularly among themselves, participate in planning and decision making, and feel connected to the other members.

group communication: type of communication that occurs when people participate in a group for social or work purposes.

group norms: ways in which people are expected to act as group members.

group problem solving: method group members use to solve problems. It involves the following steps: (1) identify the problem, (2) analyze the problem, (3) set criteria for a solution, (4) develop solutions, and (5) select a solution.

group purpose: group's reason for existing.

hearing: act of receiving sound.

hyperbole: figure of speech that consists of an intentional exaggeration.

impromptu method: delivery in which the speaker talks without notes and without much preparation.

inductive reasoning: using many specific pieces of information to reach a general conclusion.

informal feedback: verbal and nonverbal messages given spontaneously to the speaker.

informative listening: type of listening to gain information, directions, or news.

informative speech: speech that presents or describes information.

intellectual side of self: how a person handles ideas, values and beliefs.

interpersonal communication: type of communication in which people (usually two persons) share meanings in order to build and maintain long lasting and important relationships.

interpreting: second step in the listening process, in which a listener uses his or her own experience to give meaning to the message.

interpretive communication: type of communication in which a speaker brings literature to life for an audience.

interview: conversation with the purpose of obtaining information.

introduction: beginning of a presentation that gains attention, presents the topic, and connects the speaker to the audience.

Johari window: a four-part box diagram representing the awareness people have of themselves and others.

larynx: voice box that contains the vocal cords.

Lincoln-Douglas debate: type of debate in which one person on each side debates a proposition of value.

listening: process of receiving, interpreting, evaluating, and responding to messages.

majority: more than one-half of those people voting.

manuscript method: delivery in which a speaker writes out the entire speech and delivers it from this paper.

marking the script: writing symbols on the oral interpretation script to help a speaker remember how to read it.

memorized method: delivery in which a speaker memorizes the speech and delivers it word for word.

metaphor: figure of speech that compares two things that are *not* alike. Metaphors do not use the words *like* and *as.*

minority: less than one-half of those people voting.

minutes: written report of what happens at a meeting.

motion: proposed action for a group to consider for parliamentary action.

moderator: person who keeps a panel or symposium discussion moving and makes sure everyone's ideas are heard.

mood: the emotional content of a piece of literature.

name calling: type of faulty reasoning that attacks the person rather than the person's ideas by using unpopular names or labels.

negative: in debate, the side that argues against an issue or change.

noise: anything that interferes with a listener's ability to receive a message.

nonverbal messages: communication expressed without words; it includes appearance, facial expression, eye contact, posture, gestures, voice and space or time.

offstage focus: focusing one's eyes on the imagined reflection of other performers.

onomatopoeia: figure of speech in which a word sounds like its meaning.

opinion: judgment based on beliefs or feelings.

oral history: story that is told over and over and passed down through generations without being written.

oral interpretation: reading literature aloud to communicate meaning to an audience.

order of business: sequence in which a group will discuss topics.

panel discussion: discussion during which a subject is explored by the group members in front of an audience.

parliamentarian: person responsible for making sure parliamentary procedure is followed.

parliamentary procedure: set of rules based on *Robert's Rules of Order Newly Revised* for running large group meetings.

perception: process of giving meaning to information learned through the five senses.

personification: figure of speech that gives human characteristics to nonhuman things.

persuasion: process of changing a listener's beliefs or moving a listener to action.

persuasive speaking: type of speech in which a speaker attempts to convince an audience of certain beliefs or the need for certain actions.

pharynx: muscular sac between mouth and esophagus.

physical side of self: how a person looks and uses his or her body for physical activities.

pitch: highness or lowness of a speaker's voice.

plot: storyline of a piece of literature.

policy debate: debate in which the affirmative and negative teams debate a proposition of policy.

problem-solution order: method of organizing the points of a speech based on two major areas: the problem and the solution.

process order: method of organizing the points of a speech based on the way something works.

proposition: statement of a problem, worded so there are clearly two sides

to the argument.

proposition of fact: statement that says something is or is not true.

proposition of policy: statement that says something should or should not be done.

proposition of value: statement that says something is good or bad, right or wrong, useful or useless.

public communication: type of communication in which an individual communicates before a large audience. This includes public speaking.

public speaking: type of speaking in which one person addresses a group for a specific purpose.

purpose statement: sentence that summarizes the main idea or purpose of the speech.

quorum: number of members who must be at a meeting in order to conduct the meeting and make binding decisions.

rate: speed at which the speaker speaks.

reader's theatre: type of group interpretation in which speakers present literature in a dramatic form.

rebuttal: in debate, the process of rebuilding one's case after it has been attacked by the other team.

receiving: first step in the listening process, which involves hearing and seeing messages.

recess: to take a break from a meeting for a set period of time.

refutation: process of attacking the opposing side's argument in a debate.

research: everyday process of investigation.

resonators: hollow chambers, such as the mouth, pharynx, and nasal cavities, that increase sound.

responding: fourth step in the listening process, which involves giving verbal or nonverbal feedback to the speaker.

rhyme: words that sound alike.

rituals: informal rules or patterns for interaction.

role: personal pattern of communication that characterizes one's place in a group.

script patterns: ways in which the speakers' parts are divided in group interpretation.

second a motion: show support for a parliamentary motion.

secret ballot: written vote used for nominations and controversial topics.

self-barriers: personal attitudes or behaviors that interfere with listening.

self-concept: one's picture of oneself formed from personal beliefs and attitudes.

self-esteem: one's opinion of oneself based on personal self-concept.

sense recall: remembering experiences a performer has had that will help him or her suggest images to the audience.

setting: time and place in which a piece of literature is set.

simile: figure of speech that compares two things that are *not* alike, using words such as *like* or *as.*

slang: informal language that is unique to a particular group.

social ritual speech: short, informative speech that follows the same pattern every time it occurs.

social side of self: how a person relates to other people.

space order: method of organizing the points of a speech based on the physical relationship of people, places, or objects.

speaker barriers: characteristics of the speaker that interfere with the audience's listening.

speech to inform: speech in which the speaker's purpose is to increase the knowledge of the listeners.

speech to persuade: speech in which the speaker's purpose is to convince the listeners to hold a certain belief or to act in a certain way.

stage fright: nervousness when addressing an audience.

stereotyping: labeling people as part of a group and treating them as if they possessed only the characteristics of that group.

storytelling: the art of reciting to an audience.

style: way that a piece of literature is written.

subgroup: smaller group within a group.

suggestion: way in which speakers create most of the action, props, and scenery in the audience's imagination through their reader's theatre performance skills.

support: messages that make people feel good about themselves.

supporting material: material that develops the main points of the speech.

survey: method of gathering information and opinions from a large number of people.

symposium: group discussion during which members give short speeches to an audience.

table a motion: in parliamentary procedure, to put a motion aside to be discussed at another time.

testimonials: using expert opinion or statements to create positive feelings for a person, thing, idea, or event.

theme: main idea of a piece of literature.

time order: method of organizing the points of a speech by placing them in a chronological pattern.

topical order: method of organizing the points of a speech by breaking a whole topic into its natural parts.

trachea: windpipe through which air passes in and out of lungs.

transition: words or phrases that form links between ideas.

unrelated testimonials: type of faulty reasoning that involves using a person who is not an expert to create positive feelings for a person, thing, idea, or event.

verbal messages: words one uses when communicating.

visualize: process of imagining every move in one's mind before actually performing the act.

vocal cords: two elastic folds of membrane, with a slit between them, that produce sound when they vibrate.

vocal quality: sound or tone of a speaker's voice.

volume: loudness or softness of a speaker's voice.

INDEX

Credits

Grateful acknowledgment is given authors, publishers, photographers, and agents for permission to reprint or reproduce the following copyrighted material.

Literary Credits

Chapter 3

63, Martin Luther King, Jr., excerpt from "I Have a Dream." Reprinted by arrangement with the Heirs of the Estate of Martin Luther King, Jr., c/o Joan Daves Agency as agent for the proprietor. Copyright 1963 by Martin Luther King, Jr., copyright renewed 1991 by Coretta Scott King.

Chapter 4

90, *How to Say No and Keep Your Friends: Peer Pressure Reversal for Teens and Preteens*, written by Sharon Scott, copyright 1986. Reprinted by permission of HRD Press, Inc.

Chapter 5

113, Johari window, from *Group Processes: An Introduction to Group Dynamics* by Joseph Luft, reprinted by permission of Mayfield Publishing Company. Copyright © 1984, 1970, and 1963 by Joseph Luft.

Chapter 10

240, *Readers' Guide to Periodical Literature*, copyright © 1986 by the H.W. Wilson Company. Material reproduced by permission of the publisher.

245, Edward O. Wilson, excerpt from "The High Frontier of the Rain Forest Canopy," *National Geographic* 180, no. 6 (December 1991): 102ff. Reprinted by permission of the National Geographic Society.

248, Jerry Thornton, "CHA Kids Follow a Path of Safety," © Copyrighted Chicago Tribune Company, all rights reserved, used with permission. March 27, 1992.

Chapter 13
333, "533-12 Freeze," by permission of Matthew N. Wilkinson.

Chapter 14
358, Kenyatta Wilson, "I Think the Best—I Expect the Best."

363, "Meeting America's Challenge," by permission of Aliya Esmail.

Chapter 16
397, Kathleen (George) Kearney, "Whatcha Gonna Do?"

399, Edwin A. Hoey, "Foul Shot," reprinted by permission of *Read* magazine, published by Field Publications. Copyright © 1962.

400, Jack Prelutsky, "Mean Maxine," from *The New Kid on the Block*, copyright © 1984 by Jack Prelutsky. By permission of Greenwillow Books, a division of William Morrow & Co., Inc.

400, Ted Hughes, excerpt from *Poetry Is*, Doubleday & Co., Inc., 1970, p. 12.

401, Carol Watkiss, "Forget-Me-Not," published in *Edda Literary Magazine*, Homewood-Flossmoor H.S., Chicago, 1984, pp. 31-32.

406, Cynthia Voigt, excerpt from *Dicey's Song*, reprinted with the permission of Atheneum Publishers, an imprint of Macmillan Publishing Company. Copyright © 1982 Cynthia Voigt.

406, Beverly Cleary, a passage (pp. 14-15) from *Dear Mr. Henshaw*, copyright 1983 by Beverly Cleary. By permission of Morrow Junior Books, a division of William Morrow & Co., Inc.

407, Anne Frank excerpt from Anne Frank, *The Diary of a Young Girl*, Doubleday & Company, Inc., 1967, p. 129.

408, "Mending," reprinted with permission of Atheneum Publishers, an imprint of Macmillan Publishing Company, from *If I Were in Charge of the World and Other Worries* by Judith Viorst. Copyright © 1981 by Judith Viorst.

410, L.M. Montgomery, excerpts from *Anne of Green Gables*. Copyright © 1980, copyright renewed 1935 by L.C. Page & Company, now a division of Farrar, Straus and Giroux, Inc.

412, Gerda Klein, excerpt reprinted from *The Blue Rose*, by permission of Lawrence Hill & Co. Copyright 1974.

Chapter 3
53, © Jill Salyards 1993.
63, © 1989, Peter Gould, FPG International Corp.

Chapter 4
79, R. Frerck/Odyssey Productions/Chicago (teens greet), and M. Finefrock/Unicorn Stock Photos (handshake).

Chapter 8
191, Art Shay.
193, A. Vohra, Unicorn Stock Photos.

Chapter 9
226, W. Spunbarg/PhotoEdit.

Chapter 10
256, © David Madison 1993.

Chapter 11
273, © 1988, D. Cody, FPG International Corp.
275, T. Wagner/Odyssey Productions/Chicago.

Chapter 12
287, © 1989, Jim Pickerell, FPG International Corp.
290, © 1992, John Terence Turner, FPG International Corp.

Chapter 13
311, © 1992, Mark Reinstein, FPG International Corp.
316, R. Frerck/Odyssey Productions/Chicago.
323, Art Shay.

Chapter 14
344, M. Morris, Unicorn Stock Photos.
352, Agence France-Presse.

Chapter 15
374, © 1992, Stephen Agricola.

Chapter 16
393, North East Independent School District, San Antonio, Texas.
398, NASA (National Aeronautics and Space Administration).

Chapter 17

431, North East Independent School District, San Antonio, Texas.

450, © Jill Salyards 1993.

Chapter 18

481, North East Independent School District, San Antonio, Texas.

All other photography by Jeff Ellis.

Graphic design and illustrations by Ophelia Chambliss.

Thanks to the administration and students at the following schools for allowing photographs to be taken: Evanston Township High School, Evanston, Illinois; Carmel High School, Mundelein, Illinois; Maine Township High School West, Des Plaines, Illinois; and Niles Township High School West, Skokie, Illinois.

NTC ENGLISH AND COMMUNICATION ARTS BOOKS

Business Communication
Business Communication Today! *Thomas & Fryar*
Handbook for Business Writing, *Baugh, Fryar, & Thomas*
Meetings: Rules & Procedures, *Pohl*

Dictionaries
British/American Language Dictionary, *Moss*
NTC's Classical Dictionary, *Room*
NTC's Dictionary of Changes in Meaning, *Room*
NTC's Dictionary of Debate, *Hanson*
NTC's Dictionary of Literary Terms, *Morner & Rausch*
NTC's Dictionary of Theatre and Drama Terms, *Mobley*
NTC's Dictionary of Word Origins, *Room*
NTC's Spell It Right Dictionary, *Downing*
Robin Hyman's Dictionary of Quotations

Essential Skills
Building Real Life English Skills, *Starkey & Penn*
English Survival Series, *Maggs*
Essential Life Skills, *Starkey & Penn*
Essentials of English Grammar, *Baugh*
Essentials of Reading and Writing English Series
Grammar for Use, *Hall*
Grammar Step-by-Step, *Pratt*
Guide to Better English Spelling, *Furness*
How to be a Rapid Reader, *Redway*
How to Improve Your Study Skills, *Coman & Heavers*
NTC Skill Builders
Reading by Doing, *Simmons & Palmer*
Developing Creative & Critical Thinking, *Boostrom*
303 Dumb Spelling Mistakes, *Downing*
TIME: We the People, *ed. Schinke-Llano*
Vocabulary by Doing, *Beckert*

Genre Literature
The Detective Story, *Schwartz*
The Short Story & You, *Simmons & Stern*
Sports in Literature, *Emra*
You and Science Fiction, *Hollister*

Journalism
Getting Started in Journalism, *Harkrider*
Journalism Today! *Ferguson & Patten*
Publishing the Literary Magazine, *Klaiman*
UPI Stylebook, *United Press International*

Language, Literature, and Composition
An Anthology for Young Writers, *Meredith*
The Art of Composition, *Meredith*
Creative Writing, *Mueller & Reynolds*

Handbook for Practical Letter Writing, *Baugh*
How to Write Term Papers and Reports, *Baugh*
Literature by Doing, *Tchudi & Yesner*
Lively Writing, *Schrank*
Look, Think & Write, *Leavitt & Sohn*
Poetry by Doing, *Osborn*
World Literature, *Rosenberg*
Write to the Point! *Morgan*
The Writer's Handbook, *Karls & Szymanski*
Writing by Doing, *Sohn & Enger*
Writing in Action, *Meredith*

Media Communication
Getting Started in Mass Media, *Beckert*
Photography in Focus, *Jacobs & Kokrda*
Television Production Today! *Kirkham*
Understanding Mass Media, *Schrank*
Understanding the Film, *Bone & Johnson*

Mythology
The Ancient World, *Sawyer & Townsend*
Mythology and You, *Rosenberg & Baker*
Welcome to Ancient Greece, *Millard*
Welcome to Ancient Rome, *Millard*
World Mythology, *Rosenberg*

Speech
Activities for Effective Communication, *LiSacchi*
The Basics of Speech, *Galvin, Cooper, & Gordon*
Contemporary Speech, *HopKins & Whitaker*
Dynamics of Speech, *Myers & Herndon*
Getting Started in Public Speaking, *Prentice & Payne*
Listening by Doing, *Galvin*
Literature Alive! *Gamble & Gamble*
Person to Person, *Galvin & Book*
Public Speaking Today! *Prentice & Payne*
Speaking by Doing, *Buys, Sill, & Beck*

Theatre
Acting & Directing, *Grandstaff*
The Book of Cuttings for Acting & Directing, *Cassady*
The Book of Scenes for Acting Practice, *Cassady*
The Dynamics of Acting, *Snyder & Drumsta*
An Introduction to Modern One-Act Plays, *Cassady*
An Introduction to Theatre and Drama, *Cassady & Cassa*
Play Production Today! *Beck et al.*
Stagecraft, *Beck*

For a current catalog and information about our complete line
of language arts books, write:
National Textbook Company
a division of NTC Publishing Group
4255 West Touhy Avenue
Lincolnwood (Chicago), Illinois 60646-1975 U.S.A.